I0889867

ONE CONTINUOUS LINE

Vikramaditya
Prakash

ONECONTINUOUSLINE

Art, Architecture
and Urbanism of
Aditya Prakash

MAPIN
PUBLISHING

First published in India in 2020 by
Mapin Publishing Pvt. Ltd
706 Kaivanna, Panchvati, Ellisbridge
Ahmedabad 380006 INDIA
T: +91 79 40 228 228 • F: +91 79 40 228 201
E: mapin@mapinpub.com • www.mapinpub.com

Text © Vikramaditya Prakash
Illustrations © Aditya Prakash Foundation, unless otherwise noted.

All rights reserved under international copyright conventions. No part of this book may be reproduced or transmitted in any form or by any means, electronic or mechanical, including photocopy, recording or any other information storage and retrieval system, without prior permission in writing from the publisher.

The moral rights of Vikramaditya Prakash as author of this work are asserted.

ISBN: 978-81-89995-68-3

Copyediting: Vineetha Mokkil / Mapin Editorial
Proofreading: Mithila Rangarajan / Mapin Editorial
Editorial Supervision: Neha Manke / Mapin Editorial
Design: Ishan Khosla Design LLP, New Delhi, India
Production: Gopal Limbad / Mapin Design Studio
Printed in Chaina

Front cover
Portico of Chandigarh College of Architecture before it was painted, c.1969. APF.

Page 6
Half-painted portico mural of Chandigarh College of Architecture, APF

Page 10
Collage of Boys' Hostel, Agricultural University Ludhiana, and one of Prakash's bird drawings, Collage by Thorey Munro

Enjoy slideshows, audios and videos from this book on your smartphone using the free **BooksPlus: Augmented Reality** app.

1. Scan this QR code to download the **BooksPlus** app or visit www.booksplusapp.com.

2. Launch the app.

3. Point your smartphone at an image in this book with the symbol.

4. Enjoy the videos, audios and slideshows on pages 27, 56, 73 (right), 77, 82 (below right), 89, 93 (top left), 141, 166-167, 171, 201 (right), 211, 214 (left), 222, 234 (left), 243, 266, 270, 285.

The slideshows present the art of Aditya Prakash from his vast oeuvre of paintings and drawings.

In these audios, Aditya Prakash talks about:

- his work and experiences in the building of city of Chandigarh and shares his views about an architecture based on climate, sustainability and planning for the people
- his experiences and learnings while working as part of the Chandigarh Project team led by Le Corbusier
- the differences between Indian and Western ideas of space and therefore the need for localized architectural solutions
- the need for people-oriented, all-inclusive, sustainable urban planning

In these videos, watch author Vikramaditya Prakash in conversation with Ayad Rahmani, Assoc. Professor of Architecture, Washington State University, discuss:

- the title, the timing and purpose of the book
- Aditya Prakash's support and critique of the modernist project
- Aditya Prakash's decision to stay in or out of politics
- Aditya Prakash's take on the Indian market and question of the brick
- "Translation" as form of "corruption"
- his choice of rhetoric and how to use the book
- a special memory of his father

BooksPlus®: Augmented Reality powered by ignitesol.com. For further support, write to us at support@booksplusapp.com

For *Saher*, *Renzo*, and *Saumya*

This book is as much about your
future as it is about your past

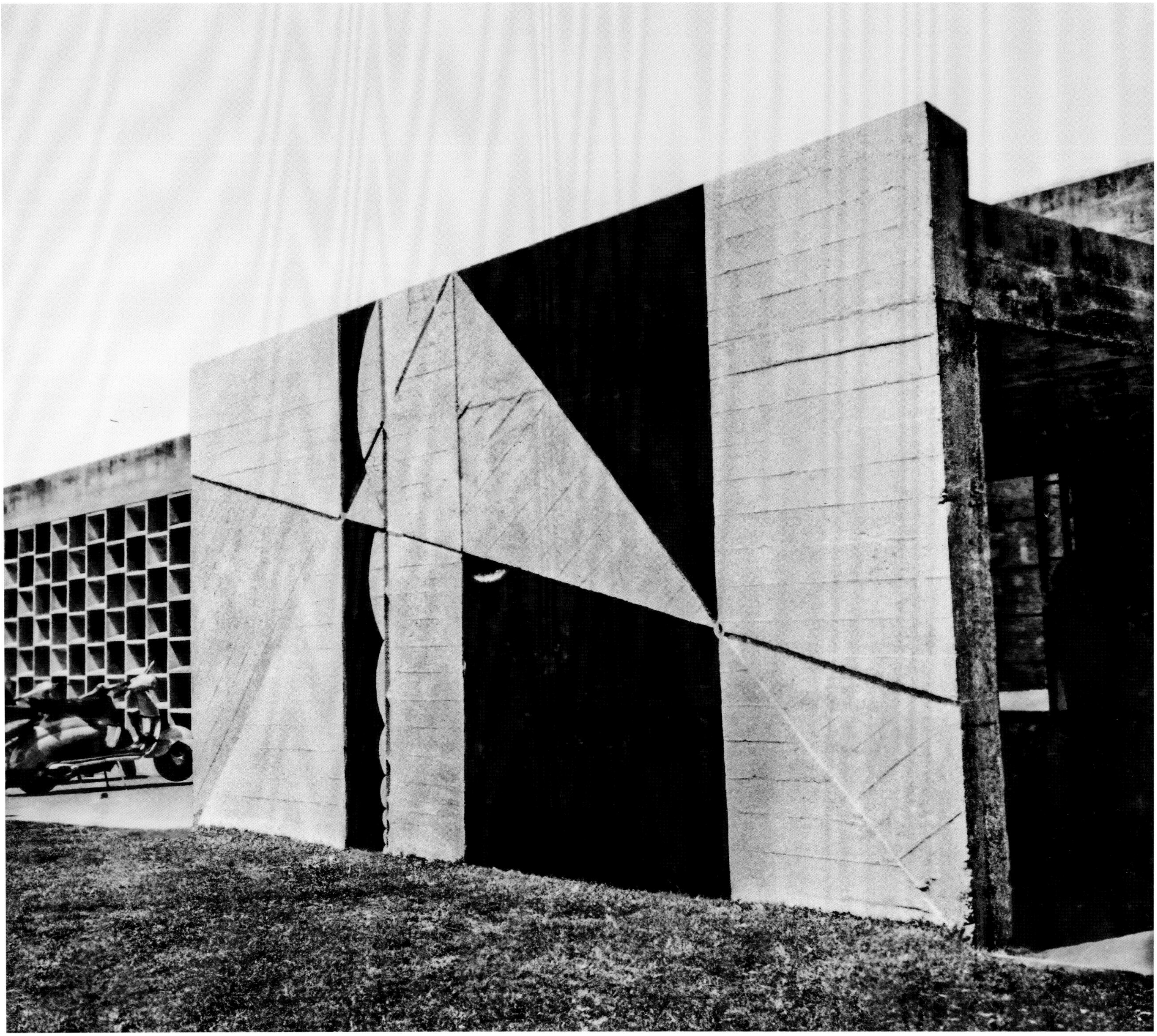

CONTENTS

Acknowledgements 11
Foreword by Maristella Casciato 15
Chronology 18
Timeline 19

INTRODUCTION 24

FROM MUZAFFARNAGAR TO LONDON 32

The Franconia 40
London 41
Return to India 46

THE CHANDIGARH CAPITAL PROJECT TEAM 52

Interrogating the 'Modern Style' 66
Learning from the 'Master' 72
Frame Control and the Indian Modulor 76
Tagore Theatre 86
Structure and its Expression 94
Furniture 98

DESIGNING THE AGRICULTURAL REVOLUTION 106

Campus Planning and Design 111
Argus and Rolleiflex 118
The Urge to Sculpture 132
Beginning to Paint 138

PRINCIPAL, CHANDIGARH COLLEGE OF ARCHITECTURE 148

Research Cells 154

Energy Crisis: The Self-Sustaining Linear City Vision 164

The Animal 172

Writing in Free Verse 185

Abhinet and Tagore-iterates 188

The Painting Studio 201

The Undoing of Postmodernism 214

ON HIS OWN 222

Arcon Architects 226

The Animal, Again 232

Indic Motifs 240

The Female Form, and the Lingam 250

The New Millenium 259

Our Get-Together 264

Zindagi Retire Nahin Hoti 265

CONCLUSION: GLOBAL MODERNISM 270

Nehruvian Global Modernist 273

Diffractive Modernism 277

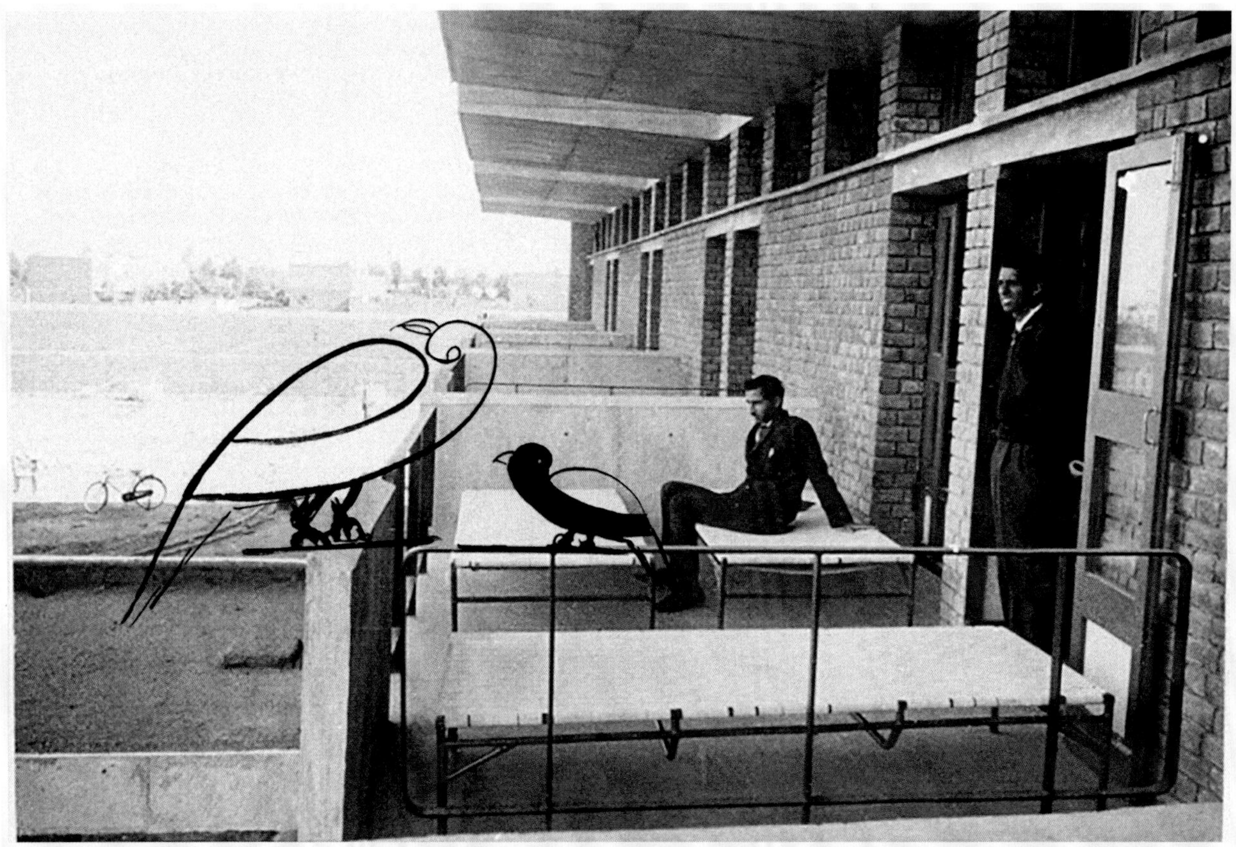

ACKNOWLEDGEMENTS

This book began on a typical June afternoon, 45°C, sweat dripping down my neck. I was in Chandigarh to organize the papers and drawings of the Aditya Prakash Foundation and before I had the sense to install air-conditioners, I started to type to distract myself from the blazing heat.

Magically, the writing just flowed. Lakshmi Krishnaswamy, who had already worked on a Master's thesis on Prakash, Eashan Chaufla, a recent graduate of RISD who was in Chandigarh wondering what to do next, and Vishal Khandelwal, a Michigan doctoral student, joined me, and together we started to organize the archives, document the work, and mock up the book. Without them, nothing would have been achieved.

My old school friend Jyoti (Sangari) and her husband Sunil Chaufla not only had the air-conditioners installed, they provided all the critical infrastructural support that enabled us to survive. But it was Leela, my mother's maidservant, who kept us fed, comfortable, and accounted for. Ariadna Alvarez Garreta managed the affairs of the Aditya Prakash Foundation in my stead.

Bipin Shah, the fabulous publisher of Mapin, a long-time believer in this project, made the trek from Ahmedabad several times to see the work and vet our conception of the book. It was Bipin making the case for not compromising on the visual quality of the book that really made us believe that we might have something good on our hands. On artist Bheem Malhotra's recommendation, we hired Surinder Mohan Dhami, the fabulous photographer who, with the help of his daughter Amrita, worked hard for days documenting all the art. Amit Ittyerah came down from Delhi to help for a couple of days, as did Sandeep Virmani, who was happy to recall for us his times in Chandigarh working with Prakash. Many of the drawings published in this book are Sandeep's. Anand Bhatt, the tireless editor of Architexturez.asia, camped out for a week in Chandigarh, and helped me think about Prakash's work from a broader perspective.

Once back in the United States, Maristella Casciato and Mark Jarzombek were the first to read the manuscript and provide me with critical feedback. Maristella, thank you also for your thoughtful Foreword, as also for putting me in touch with the Canadian Centre for Architecture. Warren Etheredge responded to his reading of the manuscript by taking on the voice of a critical son on my podcast 'ArchitectureTalk'. Thorey Munro was the final reader of the manuscript.

Martien de Vletter of the Canadian Centre for Architecture, Montreal, made a trip all the way to Chandigarh to evaluate the Aditya Prakash Archives; as did Linda Vlassenrood of the International New Town Institute, Rotterdam. Robert Desaulnier and I developed a warm friendship during the three days he spent in Seattle sorting through and appraising the Aditya Prakash Archive.

This book has been fabulously designed by Ishan Khosla and his team in New Delhi. I am deeply grateful to Ishan for taking on the job of design as a dedicated intellectual challenge beyond the matter of layout. It shows. In Ahmedabad, Neha Manke, Gopal Limbad and the rest of the staff of Mapin Publishing provided critical support in a timely and very professional manner. To them all my humble thanks.

Tom Avermaete and Janina Gosseye had the foresight to conceive the Modern Architecture's Shadow Canon series. I am so thankful that they considered this book for it and recommended it to James Thompson at Bloomsbury.

I owe an eternal and ongoing debt to the faculty and staff of Chandigarh College of Architecture who have helped and supported me through the years in invaluable ways, as also to the offices of the Chief Architect and of the Advisor of Chandigarh Administration. There are too many invaluable people on that list to be individually named; you know who you are. I would like to express special gratitude to Mr. Shivdatt Sharma, and his family, for their steadfast support and encouragement, as also I must thank the legions of students of Aditya Prakash who have contributed to this book in innumerable small ways. Important references were provided by Janice Reed, after consulting with her parents, Donald and Heather Edwards, old friends of Aditya Prakash. Dr. Virendra Mehndiratta, Harish Bhatia, S. S. Bhatti, P. L. Luthra, Tarun Mathur, R. R. Handa, M.N. Sharma, Pradeep Bhagat, and Kiran Joshi helped smooth the way in various ways.

The great history theory faculty of the Department of Architecture, University of Washington provided useful feedback at various stages, and in particular during a "Long Table Conversation" where I fielded some of the early ideas presented in the last chapter. I would never have been able to complete the manuscript without the highly organized and razor-sharp mind of my student, Deepthi Bathala.

I am grateful to the Office of the Dean, College of Built Environments for the sabbatical leave that facilitated the research for this book, as also to the Graham Foundation for Advanced Studies in the Fine Arts , Chicago and the A3 Foundation, Panchkula, which supported this book with a grant.

For their long-term support of the Chandigarh project in general I would like to thank my global friends Franz Ziegler, Frits Palmboom, and Kunle Adeyemi, all from the Netherlands, my home in Europe, as also my very good American friends Sanjay Advani, Mark Jarzombek, Nicole Huber, Jorge Otero-Pailos, Anthony Vidler, Satish Kolluri, and David Turnbull. To Glen Barfield I owe special thanks, for assiduously documenting and putting up the first exhibit on Prakash, in the corridor of Chandigarh College of Architecture, in March 2009.

My sisters Vandana Kumar and Chetna Purnami helped me with critical parts of the narrative, but it was my mother, Savitri Prakash, who was always ready to listen to what I was trying to say, to correct it, and provide invaluable insights and information. Rahul and Nandini Gupta provided logistical support at critical moments. To my wife, Leah, thanks just for putting up with me.

FOREWORD

Maristella Casciato

In the summer of 1951, Le Corbusier joined CIAM 8, which was held about 20 miles north of London in the suburban village of Hoddesdon. The conference was just the third to follow the close of WWII, after CIAM 6 in Bridgwater, England in 1947, and CIAM 7 in Bergamo, Italy in 1949. The climate in England in 1951 was undoubtedly more optimistic than elsewhere in Europe: while the gloomy atmosphere of war still loomed over bombed-out city centres on the continent, the Festival of Britain, which opened two months before CIAM 8, enthusiastically celebrated the promise of recovery, progress, and faith in the future.

It was in this context that Aditya Prakash (born in 1924 in Muzaffarnagar, Uttar Pradesh) made his life in London, where he had moved in early August 1947. Unlike his architect colleagues from South Asia who had been present at CIAM meetings—Sinhalese architect Minnette de Silva had attended CIAM 6 in Bridgwater, while Indian designer Balkrishna Doshi took part in CIAM 8 in Hoddesdon—Prakash never joined the conference. Nevertheless, he had become acutely aware of the discourse on planning the modern city advocated in the Athens Charter through his acquaintance Maxwell Fry, who had been a founding member of the MARS group (the British chapter of CIAM) known for its innovative master plan for London.

The Hoddesdon conference marked the apex of CIAM's research into community urbanism and functional planning that was to revitalize war-torn city centres. It saw the attendance of delegates from twenty-two official groups, a few individual members representing chapters under reorganization or still in formation, and an unknown number of students. The resulting publication, *CIAM 8 The Heart of the City: Towards the Humanization of Urban Life*, edited by J. Tyrwhitt, J.L. Sert, and E. N. Rogers, represented the architects' and planners' effort to enhance the dignity of human life and to integrate diverse facets of human experience into the design of cities. The book came out in record time, just one year after the congress, and was one of the finest produced by CIAM, giving evidence of the maturity of thought that had been developed over the preceding decades of activity. It was within this fecund intellectual context that Prakash developed his architectural and urbanistic point of view. The robust network of modern architects forged through CIAM had established a fertile ground for rethinking the city, one which was best revealed in *CIAM 8 The Heart of the City*, and one which would prove deeply influential for the young Prakash.

Le Corbusier's work in Chandigarh figures centrally in *CIAM 8 The Heart of the City*. Since early 1951 news of Le Corbusier's appointment as architectural adviser to the government of Punjab had spread rapidly. In this role, Le Corbusier was tasked with designing the master plan for the new capital of the state, to be named Chandigarh. The commission would evolve in scale and scope over the next decade, resulting in multifarious achievements marking the last fifteen years of the Swiss-French architect's illustrious career. The Chandigarh project was not Le Corbusier's alone, however. It was instead the result of the work of collaborative teams that oversaw construction on site and of the Architects' Office that was created to follow up on all building operations. While Le Corbusier was assigned the role of Architectural Adviser, his three partners—his cousin Pierre Jeanneret and the British couple Maxwell Fry and Jane Drew—were engaged as Senior Architects. This overlapping of responsibilities was further complicated by Prime Minister Nehru's plan to shape Chandigarh as a training and learning laboratory for young Indian professionals.

Le Corbusier conjured up an indispensable role for himself within this collaboration—that of the *berger amical* (the friendly shepherd). "The Indian youth," he wrote to the secretary of Indian Embassy in Paris, "must have a fundamental part in this endeavour; it is they who will be realizing it in the course of the years... in a way what they need is a friendly shepherd..." And as a matter of fact, a group of Indian architects and engineers became engaged in the Architects' Office under the direct leadership of the senior architects. Among these was Aditya Prakash.

When Fry returned to London in 1952, after a year spent in Chandigarh, he recalled young Aditya's maturing passion for architecture. Fry interviewed Prakash and immediately hired him to join the Architects' Office. Aditya would stay on in this role for almost a decade, before moving to Ludhiana where he would be charged with the design of the city's agricultural campuses. On the Chandigarh project, he initially assisted Jane Drew. When the couple left the project in 1954 Prakash began working directly with Pierre Jeanneret, and the professional relationship between the two architects soon flourished. Prakash also started working closely with Le Corbusier during his regular visits to Chandigarh. In these years, the young architect gained confidence in his intellectual growth and design talents: he was open to receive the symbolic message represented in the Corbusian Open Hand.

CIAM 8 The Heart of the City arrived too early to survey the outstanding results achieved at Chandigarh by the architectural team who stood by Le Corbusier. Still, it sketched out the future city's promise: in its first part, the book includes essays by Le Corbusier and Maxwell Fry; in its second part, the book gives a detailed description of the Chandigarh plan. In their respective essays, both Le Corbusier and Fry deal with the idea of the urban "Core" and make key references to the new Punjabi capital as a prime example illustrating that the "Core is a place for the expression of human life." Le Corbusier concludes his essay with a paragraph titled *The Many Cores of a Town: Chandigarh*, where he explains the plan of the city through the presence of many different centres linked by a "civic valley." The book is a celebration of Chandigarh before Chandigarh—a confirmation of the high esteem the book's editors held for the project.

At this stage of its conception Chandigarh is a city of principles, of decisive innovations, and of communities who share millenary histories and venerable religions; it is the miracle of the architect who can construct because he knows how to create meeting places celebrating human life.

"I have tried to show," writes Le Corbusier in his last sentence, "that LIFE forges the tools." No words can be more evocative of his thinking than the sketch of *la "boite à miracle,"* a challenge to the self, and a promise to his team and to the Indian assistants. It is this idea, this challenge, that Aditya Prakash takes up in his work over the following decades.

CHANDIGARH CAPITAL PROJECT TEAM

SENIOR ARCHITECT, AGRICULTURAL UNIVERSITY CAMPUSES, LUDHIANA

1957

First volume of *Ekistics* published

Petrol pumps, Chandigarh

al Crafts
m founded

ury building

l Complex
lan

1958

Military Guest House, Sector 22

Indo-Swiss Training Centre

Chandigarh College of Art with Le Corbusier

1959

Seminar on Architecture, Lalit Kala Akademi, New Delhi

MoMA's 'Design Today in America and Europe' travelling exhibit in India

1960

Developed Frame Control

1961

Master plan of Islamabad, Pakistan

National Institute of Design founded in Ahmedabad

Chandigarh College of Architecture

Doxiadis's "Ecumenopolis"

Tagore Theatre

1963

Bus terminus

Developed Staggering Balcony theory

Hindustan Machine Tools campus, Hyderabad

1964

First paintings

Jagat theatre opens

1965

Indo-Pak war

Plan for Gandhinagar, Gujarat

1966

Chandigarh becomes Union Territory

Punjab Agricultural University, Ludhiana, Hissar and Palampur

Superstudio founded

1967

Arte Povera movement begins in Italy

1968

Indian Modulor

DELHI POLYTECHNIC

LONDON POLYTECHNIC & GLASGOW SCHOOL OF ART

1924

Aditya Prakash born on March 10 in Muzaffarnagar

1945

Second World War ends

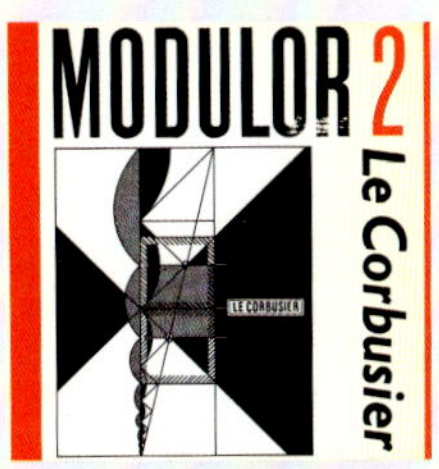

Le Corbusier invents the Modulor

1946

Abstract Expressionism

Marg magazine founded

1947

India gains independence

Partition of India

1948

Koenigsberger's plan for Bhubaneshwar, Orissa

1949

Albert Meyer's plan for Chandigarh

1950

Pop Art

Ahmedabad Mill Owners' Association Building

1951

Le Corbusier's first India visit

Sixty paintings for 1951 Festival of Britain exhibition

1952

Modern Architects' Group

Work in Glasgow

1953

Type 6 Housing

Maternity Hospital, Sector 16

Opening of Chandigarh city

The Independent Group

1954

District Courts, Sector 17

1955

Reyner Banham's 'The New Brutalism'

Jagat & Neelam theatres

1956

Natio
Museu

Treas

Capito
final p

TIMELINE: LIFE & WORK OF ADITYA PRAKASH

1934–1947	**Schooldays and college in colonial north India,** MUZAFFARNAGAR, NEW DELHI
1947–1952	**In the UK, studying to become an architect,** LONDON, GLASGOW
1953–1963	**Part of the Chandigarh Capital Project Team,** CHANDIGARH
1963–1967	**Senior Architect of the Agricultural University campuses,** LUDHIANA
1968–1982	**Principal, Chandigarh College of Architecture,** CHANDIGARH
1982–2008	**Independent architect, painter, dramatist,** CHANDIGARH

INDEPENDENT ARCHITECT AND PAINTER IN CHANDIGARH

1990

1992

First solo painting exhibition at the Taj Mahal Palace hotel, Bombay (Mumbai)

1993

1994

Exhibition at Kamalnayan Bajaj Art Gallery, Bombay

Exhibition at Punjab Lalit Kala Akademi, Chandigarh

1995

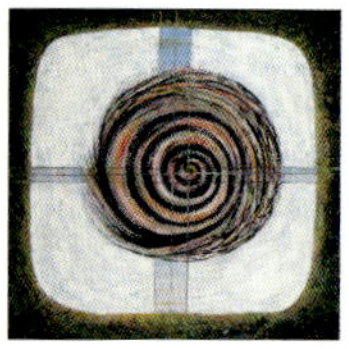

1996

Permanent stage for Sector 17

Lajpat Rai Elders Home, Jalandhar

1997

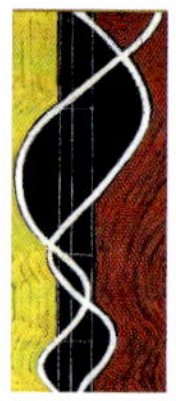

1998

Exhibition at Alliance Francaise, Chandigarh

2000

2001

2002

2003

2004

2005

2006

First performance of *Zindagi Retire Nahi Hoti*

2008

Prakash died on August 12 in Ratlam

■ WORKS OF ADITYA PRAKASH
■ EVENTS DURING ADITYA PRAKASH'S LIFETIME

PRINCIPAL, CHANDIGARH COLLEGE OF ARCHITECTURE

1969

1970

K.C. Theatre

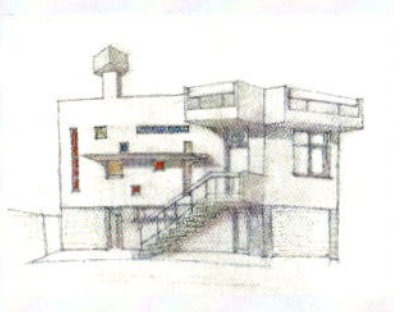

Prakash residence, Sector 8

J&K Academy for Art, Culture and Languages

1971

1972

Rehri studies

1974

1975

1976

Open-air theatre, Sector 23

Study on self-sustaining settlements for *Ekistics*

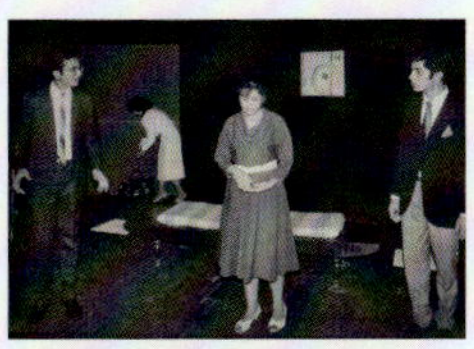

Founded Abhinet theatre group

Started 'Our Get Together'

1978

1979

1980

Published *Chandigarh: A Presentation in Free Verse*

1982

Yoga Kendra, Meerut

Milkfed plant, Jalandhar

Thapar Institute of Engineering & Technology, Patiala

1983

Published *Reflections on Chandigarh*

1984

Punjab State Cooperative Bank Ltd.

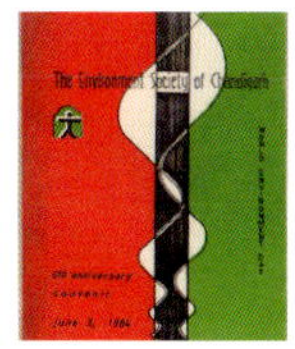

The Environment Society of Chandigarh

1985

RBI housing, Chandigarh

Dr. Bhimrao Ambedkar University, Lucknow

1987

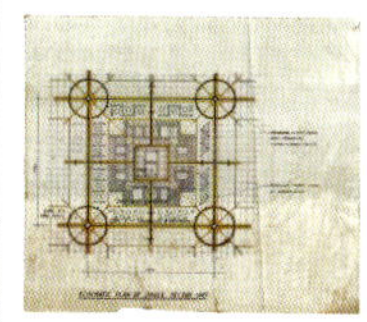

Linear City plan

1989

Brahma Kumaris, Sector 33

INTRODUCTION

Jawaharlal Nehru, the first Prime Minister of independent India, speaking at an event at the cricket stadium in Sector 16, Chandigarh
Photo credit: Fonds Pierre Jeanneret, Canadian Centre for Architecture, Montréal; Gift of Jacqueline Jeanneret

Aditya Prakash speaking at the Chandigarh College of Architecture, c. 1972, APF

Aditya Prakash belonged to the first generation of Indian modernists, the lodestar group of civil servants that took on the reins of responsibility in India under Prime Minister Jawaharlal Nehru immediately after Independence in 1947. He worked most of his life as a salaried employee of the Government of India, but his work and his life were not circumscribed by the hierarchy-bound limitations of government service. To be sure, he considered his status as a state employee to be a profound responsibility; the work of the government was believed to be by many of his generation to be the true work of and for the people of India. The free spirit of the Independence movement was still in play, and the connectivity between city, citizen, and nation seemed vivid and self-evident. The Government of India was the nation's hope, and the Nehruvian nation-state was the torchbearer to a newly-independent people's aspirations. Authorship, identity-building and ego-mongering were not the purpose of the salaried employee. Rather, the paramount aspiration for many young professionals was to be subsumed within and become an instrumental part of the rising waters of the nation-state.

At the same time, there can be no doubt that Aditya Prakash modelled his personal aspirations after the most colossal individualist working in Chandigarh at that time. Like Le Corbusier, Prakash did not consider anything beyond his reach. Ignoring disciplinary boundaries, he viewed all aspects of his work to be multiple dimensions of a single quest—how to understand the purpose of life, enjoy it, and keep the interests of the poorest at heart. This is the "one continuous line" that is referred to in the title of this book. In the modernist mould, the purpose of architecture (and a life lived in architecture) was to provide innovative solutions to the problems of living. "Just get on with it" was one of his life's mottos, and he never hesitated to set out his solutions to the smallest problem that he saw to the largest—from improvements to the design of the *rehri*s, the small mobile shops that still ply the roads of India, to reimagining a new form of urbanism for India in the form of an infinite, self-sustaining linear city.

The "one continuous line" also refers to Prakash's keen interest in exploring the possibilities of generating form using, literally, one continuous line. Repeatedly, Prakash would return to the one continuous, twisting and turning line to create art, explore geometric proportion, and even design furniture. Something about a line that could effortlessly thread difference appealed to his imagination, and induced a sense of satisfaction in having resolved a formal puzzle. "For me painting is an act of relaxation, of prayer, and of releasing me from the rigidity of the architectural profession," he once wrote, identifying the creative act as a process of mediating the anxieties of "real" life.[1]

With baggage from a troubled childhood marked by deprivation in colonial India, an adolescence cultivated in the institutions of post-war England, and a professional career propelled by the ambition to surpass the "masters"—even as he modelled himself on them—Prakash's life and work were produced by the contentions of postcolonial India, and reflected them.[2] Nehruvian India set itself the task of not only "catching up" with the West, but of outdoing it in substantial ways. Mahatma Gandhi's use of English law against the colonists, amplified by the moral high ground of his own home-spun political resistance strategies like non-violence and *satyagraha*, had set the precedent of how India could masterfully outwit its colonial masters. With that example, the Indian expectations for Independence were very high, even as the task at hand seemed formidable. The Le Corbusian way of working, by which every complex problem could be tackled with clinical surgery and grace, seemed tailor-made for both, a postcolonial India imbricated with great expectations as well as for a young Aditya Prakash who joined the Nehruvian project with high personal ambition.

At the same time, however, Prakash's journey and struggle to self-actualize was itself constructed as a critique of the Nehruvian-Le Corbusian world, reinterpreted/reshaped via his own understanding of life's imperatives. Starting out as a loyal soldier in the Nehruvian army and a devoted acolyte of Le Corbusier, Prakash came to define his beliefs and work via the models of Mahatma Gandhi, Pierre Jeanneret, and Buckminster Fuller, all of whom he imagined as being simultaneously more modest and visionary in their ideas. Pierre Jeanneret, himself in a complex Oedipal relationship with Le Corbusier, became an important mentor for Prakash early in his career. Prakash would often refer to Jeanneret as his "guru." Gandhi and Fuller served as more distant mentors, as did later, Constantinos Doxiadis, Jacqueline Trywhitt, Ernst F. Schumacher and Dr. V. N. Vasantharajan. Prakash lay great store in friends and friendships, particularly with fellow travellers of the Nehruvian aesthetic-intellectual world, such as the writer Mulk Raj Anand, actors Prithviraj Kapoor and Zul Vellani, and architects Charles Correa, Joseph Allen Stein, and Achyut P. Kanvinde.

Prakash arguably did some of his most important work in Ludhiana in the mid-sixties, but his life was dominated by the story of the start-up provincial capital city of Chandigarh from its uncertain beginnings in the 1950s, to its maturation in the 1960s and 1970s, and its "success" and expansion from the 1980s onwards. Prakash lived most of his life and raised his family

Scan image with the **BooksPlus** app

A continuous line "doodle" by Prakash, APF

in Chandigarh, and remained faithful to it to the very end. He credited his Chandigarh experiences with opening his doors of perception.[3] He constructed his life's work as a custodian of its legacy, not in the sense of a missionary intent on preserving the city's look and character, but as one faithful to its experimental praxis. He set up his living room as an open forum where he endlessly debated the Chandigarh experiment with the constant stream of architects, painters, and film makers passing through the city. One imagines that Chandigarh's 2016 induction into the UNESCO World Heritage list would not have passed muster with Prakash. For him, the legacy of the city could only be "protected" via critique, by thinking, designing, and planning beyond it.

No matter what the situation or question, Prakash's mind was at play, always willing—and not always successfully—to turn things upside down and evaluate them from another perspective. He became an architect initially to pay the bills, but then learnt to extract the inherent systems of built things, their DNA, to make purposeful, rigorously "form-follows-function" buildings that were both loved and dismissed by the public. He started to paint as a solitary shelter from life's challenges, but by the end it had become his daily passion. He became an urbanist because the Chandigarh experiment showed him that cities could be designed, which also convinced him that they could be drastically improved upon. He became a theatre enthusiast to compensate for a reserved personality, and that developed into a full-fledged love of the stage. He became an academic reluctantly, believing that research could yield new knowledge, but became more uncertain about the prowess to actually address big questions. He designed furniture and lamps because he needed them and he formed various intellectual study groups—the Modern Architects Club, Chandigarh Architects Forum and the long-lived, "Our Get-Together"—because he enjoyed sitting with like-minded people to have a good conversation and a great laugh.

This book is conceived as an introduction to his vast and somewhat unruly body of work—his mind at play. It is designed as a continuous illustrated narrative, with a series of interspersed visual essays with an integrity of their own. The early essays in this volume trace the colonial circumstances that propelled Prakash to pursue

A birthday "working drawing" created collectively by the staff of the Chandigarh Capital Project for Pierre Jeanneret. Unlike Le Corbusier, who came across as haughty and aloof, Jeanneret was well-loved by much of the Indian staff whom he supervised.
Photo credit: Fonds Pierre Jeanneret, Canadian Centre for Architecture, Montréal; Gift of Jacqueline Jeanneret

architecture as a vocation, first in New Delhi and then in London, repressing his personal desire to become an artist. The life and professional relations of the officers of Chandigarh Capital Project team, which young Prakash joined in 1952, as the "junior-most of the junior architects", are described in the third essay, re-tracing the path of Prakash's absorption of the Chandigarh modernist idiom. His learning of and subsequent transformation of the Le Corbusier Modulor is described as a pivotal moment in his "education" as an architect. This is followed by a discussion of some of Prakash's key early modernist works in Chandigarh, in particular, Tagore Theatre, his "signature" building. The middle essay, titled 'Designing the Agricultural Revolution', identifies Prakash's work in Ludhiana as the architect of the three universities that were built to usher in the "Green Revolution" of the 1960s. This was arguably his most productive period, when he not only built extensively, but he also started to paint, sculpt, and do photography. This essay also describes how Ludhiana set him on the path of his search for an Indian self-sustaining urban planning model. The following essay on Chandigarh College of Architecture describes Prakash trying to build a culture of academic research in the 1970s in the context of the decaying Nehruvian nation-state and Indira Gandhi's infamous "license Raj." It documents the early successes and later frustrations of his life as an academic, and the alternative "hobbies" of theatre, art, and intellectual gathering he pursued to keep his spirit going. It ends with a discussion of Prakash's arguments against the turn to postmodernism in Indian architecture of the early 1980s. The last two essays of the book document Prakash's work as a private practitioner and painter, most of which was produced after his retirement from government service in 1982. This is the most interpretive section of the book, where I have attempted to parse the various threads that constituted the weave of Prakash's aesthetic universe from his love of the Modulor to his emotional investment in the animal, to the exploration of the erotic in form.

The book concludes with a polemic on the life and legacy of Prakash's oeuvre, considered both in the context of its times and today. There, I have also engaged with the concept of entangled histories, and subjectivity as a diffractive agential process as embodied in his life-work, and as representative of the processes that produced, and may yet produce, something like a "global modernism." If there is a "thesis" to this book, the reader can find it there. This thesis is also quietly alluded to throughout the text.

Today, in the age of globalization and its discontents, the legacy of the mid-century, postcolonial modernist world is both at risk and subject to nostalgia. Many structures from the 1950s, 1960s, and even the 1970s—and not just

Prakash's—have already been destroyed and replaced with the latest icons of globalization. The problem is not only the age and potential outdatedness of the structures, but also a sense of hostility cultivated by strong, nationalist political forces against the Nehruvian age and its values. This is the case not just in Chandigarh, but throughout India where the rush to join the new global economic order is the new religion of the times. Prakash's modernist age seems to have passed. At least two of Prakash's iconic structures in Chandigarh—KC Theatre and Tagore Theatre—have been destroyed, and many others are at risk.

At the same time, one can argue that Prakash's life and work were well ahead of the times, embodying ideas that are coming to fruition only today, with our contemporary commitments to concepts like ecological design, food security, and sustainable architecture and urbanism. Even modern Indian art, and mid-century modernist furniture and architecture of the kind that Prakash and his ilk practised are back in vogue, eagerly sought after in galleries and art auctions. The value of the mid-century moment is only just beginning to be known, and so much of the work and ethos of that time remains unknown.

It is my hope that this book will provoke other scholars and enthusiasts to engage with Aditya Prakash's oeuvre via their own interests and points of contention. In general, I have tried to keep my text as un-interpretive as possible, focusing more on documentation and suggestion, and less on close readings and nuance. *Even so, I am writing about my father, and so any claim to dispassionate commentary would be remarkably disingenuous. I am sure that my biases, Oedipal and others, must inevitably creep in, for which I beg the reader's indulgence in advance. Periodically, I have in italics inserted my direct voice as a son, whenever I have felt that a personal memory might illustratively complement the main narrative. These are clearly marked and called out.*

NOTES

1 "Punjab Agricultural University Some Thoughts: Some Memories," In *Advance: The Punjab Magazine* 37, 2 (1988): 12-15

2 For a more through discussion of the making of Chandigarh in terms of the exigencies of postcolonial India see Prakash, V. (2002). *Chandigarh's Le Corbusier: The Struggle for Modernity in Postcolonial India* (Studies in modernity and national identity). Seattle: University of Washington Press.

3 Aldous Huxley was one of Prakash's favourite authors, and while several of his books were in Prakash's library, *The Doors of Perception* was not one of them. Although Prakash was always very interested in expanding his perceptual universe, particularly via painting, there is no evidence that he was ever interested in, or used, psychedelics of any sort.

FROM MUZAFFARNAGAR TO LONDON

A young Aditya Prakash in one of his tailored English suits, APF

Aditya Prakash was born in Muzaffarnagar, a small town in colonial north India. It was 1924, and the British empire was at high noon, but so was the Indian Independence movement, spearheaded by the likes of Mahatma Gandhi, Jawaharlal Nehru, Subhash Chandra Bose, M. A. Jinnah and Sardar Patel. The Indian nationalists were focused on a concept of Independent India based on self-reliance and rapid progress, with the aspiration of not only catching up with the West, but surpassing it. Two competing visions of this future India filtered through the Indian imagination—Nehru's cosmopolitanism and liberalism, influenced by a school-learned vision of future socialism, and Mahatma Gandhi's self-styled individualism, carefully inculcated via a practice-based adaptation of utopian writings of John Ruskin, Leo Tolstoy, and Henry David Thoreau. The tension between these two visions dominated Aditya Prakash's life and work, most of which was done for the newly-independent Indian nation-state.

Prakash's father, Ram Chander Das, was one of the few educated Indian clerks of the time, but he eschewed the opportunity of a lucrative career in the British imperial administration to work for *swadesh*, or "self-rule."[1] Das was for a long time the sole bread winner of the extended family, and so his choice was actively contested by many relatives. For the most, "sacrificing for the nation" won the day. Eventually, Das secured an opportunity with the Birla family, one of the rare industrial houses of British India that was run by a Hindu, rather than by a small minority community such as the Parsis. Das had embraced the Arya Samaj movement, a 19th century colonial ideology-influenced reform effort that sought to cleanse Hinduism of what it considered to be superstition and ritual and return the religion to its imagined roots in the 1st millennial BCE world of the Aryas. An earnest believer in the principles of the Arya Samaj, Das performed *yagna* (fire sacrifice) every morning and evening, insisted on the *janaeu* (sacred thread) ceremony for all his coming-of-age sons and grandsons, and educated all the girls in the household. For the last two decades of his life, he laboured daily to translate into English sections of the *Vedas*, the 3000-year-old Arya texts that were canonized by the Arya Samaj in the 19th century as the fountainhead of Indic thought.

R. C. Das was a teacher. He retired as Headmaster of New Delhi's Birla High School, one of the "progressive" non-missionary schools of India, meaning that its curriculum imitated the English missionary schools, substituting Shakespeare and canonical English texts with Hindi equivalents. The core philosophy of such schools was to embrace the advances offered by the colonial model of education, but to try and find local replacements, to think of Indian ways of imparting the same pedagogical lesson.

Mahatma Gandhi,
acrylic on canvas,
17 x 21 inches, 2000s,
APF (17_5_18)

In some respects, this would remain Prakash's abiding project as well—to find a truly "Indian" modernism.

Prakash studied at the Birla School as well, as did all his siblings and cousins. They lived in the area called Subzi Mandi, located in the early 1940s at the edge of Delhi, right next to the Birla Cotton Spinning and Weaving Mills. Years later as Prakash would pore over a new map of this area he would be surprised to see that both the High School and the Mills were erased and replaced by housing as the cotton industry fell on hard times in the 1970s.[2] But at that time, just before Independence, they were big.

Because his father was the headmaster, Prakash did not have to pay any fees to go to the Birla School. There is an unpublished essay titled "Reminiscences of Education in Pre-Independence India" in the AP Archives that describes life in "a school"[3]—*takhti*s (writing boards) pasted with *multani-mitti* (a specific kind of dried clay), much sought-after "G" nib penholders dipped in ink, slates cleaned by fingers wetted by saliva, and learning by rote done to the accompaniment song. It also describes strict teachers with the inevitable cane in their hands terrifying the classroom, with students routinely being kicked and made to stand on the benches as punishment.

Although never explicitly religious, Prakash's work can be seen as a repetition of the Arya Samaj's ethic, an attempt to rethink Chandigarh and modernist aesthetics through an Indic lens. In becoming an academic and founding a new college of architecture in Chandigarh, Prakash exhibited an Oedipal desire to emulate and outdo his father's work. The same logic can be seen at work in his desire to reinvent Le Corbusier's Chandigarh in the form of a linear self-sustaining city. At the core of India's postcolonial dilemma, like that of every new generation, was the challenge of how to define itself against, while taking on the very forms, of the authority figures of its recent past.

Prakash's mother, Kala Wati, died young, when he was only eight years old. She had gone for a visit to her mother's, her *maikai*, or so Prakash was told, when she suddenly succumbed to an unknown ailment. Sudden deaths were common in colonial India; usually from childbirth, or contagious diseases such as smallpox, measles, and tuberculosis. Polio was widespread. Urban India was affected most significantly by tuberculosis, exacerbated by the coal-run cotton ginning mills that were deadly not only for those who worked in them but also for those who lived around them. Two of Prakash's brothers who worked in these mills died in their twenties from TB, as most likely did his mother.

Following his mother's death, his grandmother, Lado Rani, seems to have assumed a critical role in Prakash's life. This is how he recalled her:

Mahatma Gandhi,
charcoal on paper,
13.25 x 17 inches, 2000s,
APF {16_(46)}

> After the death of my mother, Dadi [grandma] was the sheet anchor for running the household. She did it with great aplomb. She carried all the responsibilities on her shoulders as a matter of fact. Whenever, wherever there was need of an extra feminine hand it was Dadi who was immediately called. She always responded and took on the job in hand. She could cook for the entire household in one sitting. Indeed[,] she appeared to enjoy feeding one and all.[4]

By contrast, Prakash recalled his grandfather, Munshi Ram, who was a *zamindar* (landowner) in their ancestral village, as a man of pomp and circumstance, and aloofness:

> Whereas Dadi was at all places our grandfather—Babaji—always stayed in the village—our village Kharar. That is where he breathed his last... His cremation after his passing away was not an ordinary affair. Tailors were requisitioned to set up a proper vehicle for his journey to the heaven. This was made in the form of a chariot with colourful cloth. He was carried with a band playing...in front. Of course the cremation was the usual affair, but his passing away was registered as something that any old man would wish for, that is to say, a well established progeny in good circumstances with children and grand children, and great grand children.[5]

Not unexpectedly, his mother's and two brothers' early deaths from industrial pollution left a fundamental void in Prakash's psyche, a hole that he arguably spent the rest of his life trying to fill by the actions of his own life. He described the Birla Cotton Spinning and Weaving Mills as the "boon and the bane of our life" because the mills, while they took the lives of many in the family, were also the source of his father's employment and income, enabling opportunity for the family.[6] The utopian, self-sustaining urban planning principles that he came to champion so passionately can be seen as compensations for the loss of his siblings and mother, and an attempt to reconcile the contradiction of the Birla Mills by making an urbanism that was both productive and humane. The latter was of course the classic problem that was tackled by modernism in the late 19th century in the context of industrializing Europe.

After his mother's death, Prakash was raised by his aunts and grandmothers in an extended joint family. This too was to leave a lasting impression on him as he felt both mercifully tended to, but also spurned and discriminated against—once describing himself as "defenceless"[7]—with no recourse to object or complain. It inculcated in him a reserved personality that in outward appearance learned to privilege the necessary and the authoritarian over the self-expressive and assertive. In response, painting and the joy of

Bent iron sculpture of a bull, part of the zodiac designed by Prakash in the 2000s, APF

creativity, both solitary inward-looking activities, became his lifelong refuges.

The lives of the women of the household introduced Prakash to the virtues of handicraft, and their productive and social value in the community. He would later describe this with nostalgia:

> Our grandmother (Dadi) used to say: *Saton kate kukde, ghar ubba-ubba, saton kate teekde, ghar dubba-dubba* (if one spins seven spindles of cotton then the house prospers, but if one eats seven *chapatis* only then the house goes down). The spindles of cotton (*chinchli*) were then made into a sort of bundle on an "*atarun*" and when enough spun thread had been put together it was given to a weaver for weaving into the prescribed cloth. I have often seen these weavers at work. They would stretch the thread given to them between two sticks which were set apart according to the length of cloth to be woven. On this they would sprinkle water by blowing it from their mouth and then smoothen the thread by running a big brush along its length. That would form the "*taana*" the stretched yarn ready for the loom. Then there would be the thread put in shuttles for the "*baana*" that is for weaving. The loom would be operated by a pair of levers by the two feet so that in one go the shuttle would be thrown from one side to the other, and then in the next go the threads would have changed positions and the shuttle would go in the other direction. When one operates a handloom there is a rhythmic sound. The *charkha* also produces a rhythmic sound. At any rate spinning was then a leisure time activity. It was a social occasion like what later became in the manner of knitting sweaters with the ladies. Now even that has given way to the ready-mades. Why am I saying this? It is because I wish to distinguish between handwork and factory work.[8]

Untitled, acrylic on canvas, 1990s, APF (17_6_23)

In search of opportunity, Prakash's extended family had to repeatedly move from their ancestral home in Kharar in the state of Uttar Pradesh, to Shamli, to Muzaffarnagar and then to Panipat. Panipat seems to have been a happy time of his childhood that Prakash remembered nostalgically as full of kite flying and idolizing his older brothers.[9] But then the school his father was teaching in closed, and so the family moved one final time in the early 1940s to Lutyens' New Delhi when it was still an empty landscape. Although driven by economic hardship, the repeated dislocations inculcated in Prakash an appreciation of the resilience of the familial order, and the key role of self-sufficiency as the family ethic, ensuring that they were not completely subject to external forces. Later, he would repeatedly cite in his papers the role played by a "productive" household, in which all the members of the family—from the kids to the elderly—were expected to contribute in some way to ensure their daily needs were met.

Animals were always around in the childhood house, loved and respected not as pets but as critical members of an extended concept of the productive family. On festival days, specific religious ceremonies were devoted to the household animals. As a young adult, Prakash's assigned chore was to milk the cow twice a day, early in the morning and again in the evening, a task he resented at the time as an unfair expectation of him compared to his cousins. But he later recalled with fondness the critical role it played in the family's well-being, and the intimacy it engendered in him for the cow. The cow always recognized him when he came home in the evening, and had been waiting for him, Prakash felt, transferring onto the domestic animal the child's desire to feel wanted. This transference became a vital part of Prakash's psychological universe, with animals, like so many other aspects of his childhood, occupying a prominent place in his urban planning proposals and paintings.

Architecture was not Prakash's chosen profession. Looking for a career in art, Prakash showed up at the Delhi Polytechnic in 1945, amateur paintings and drawings in hand. The school was run by British administrators at the time, and the admissions faculty suggested that he try architecture. Prakash had never heard of architecture, nor had any one in his family. He had hoped for something more "respectable" like engineering, as had his family, but admission to that required influential connections, which the family had so demonstrably not cultivated. And so, he went to architecture school.

The Delhi Polytechnic (which later became the School of Planning and Architecture, New Delhi) was essentially a vocational training institution, intended to produce graduates who would apply for jobs in the various Public Works Departments (PWDs) that were responsible for building the vast infrastructure of the colonial economy of India.[10] Architecture in colonial India was taught as a sub-discipline within engineering with education focused on producing standardized designs that could be rapidly deployed wherever needed. The priority of the colonial PWDs was to design durable structures, cheaply built and as comfortable as possible, which they did with fabled efficiency and success. While their tendency to rely on the tried and tested opened them up to the charge of monotony, the PWD's architecture can retrospectively also be argued as being a kind of a proto-modernism that was extremely climatically responsive.[11]

Across the road, at the College of Art, one of colonial India's most privileged schools,[12] there were signs of an ongoing battle for influence between the powerful schools of engineering, with architecture as a sub-discipline, and the small host of schools of art that were staffed by arts and crafts enthusiasts. Supported from London by Henry Cole and his Department of Science and Art, these art schools were created as "reform" institutions after the rebellion of 1857, intended to represent the Empire as more sympathetic to the indigenous cultures of the sub-continent.[13] While architecture and engineering were considered to be vocational disciplines responsible for constructing the infrastructures of the Empire, art education, like the teaching of English literature, was charged with the cultivation of taste, a supposedly key marker of civility and modernization, necessary for legitimizing the colonial project as a "civilizing mission."[14] But some of the art schools also taught architecture as a sub-discipline of art, and the arts and crafts enthusiasts who staffed these new schools castigated the PWD engineering schools for running roughshod over Indian crafts. The mission of their own arts and crafts-motivated architecture schools was to cultivate the traditional craftsmen of India and harness their crafts to develop an Indian style of architecture that came to be known as the Indo-Saracenic.[15]

In other words, in the Delhi Polytechnic in the mid-1940s, there was competition between a kind of a colonial modernist approach focused on form and function, and an early postmodernist perspective focused on appearance and cultural identity—architecture as a sub-discipline of engineering and rationalization versus architecture as a sub-discipline of art and cultural identitarianism. Prakash's unwavering commitment to the modernist, rational architectural aesthetic throughout his life, especially in the face of trenchant postmodern critiques of the 1980s that insisted that the architecture of India must cultivate an Indian historicist aesthetic, can be seen as an outcome not just of his association with Le Corbusier and the modernists, but also his early proto-modernist training at the Delhi Polytechnic. One can compare the career of Aditya Prakash to that of his peer Balkrishna V. Doshi, the renowned Indian modernist, who studied architecture at the Sir JJ School of Art in Mumbai.[16] While both were closely associated with and deeply influenced by Le Corbusier, Prakash's architecture remained rigorously devoted to a modernist formal aesthetic, while Doshi, in the wake of the critiques of postmodernism, happily and very successfully embraced the investigation of Indic historicist sources and mythological narrative in his search for architectural form starting in the early 1980s.[17]

Throughout his time at the Delhi Polytechnic, Prakash frequented the art school, starting a collateral relationship with art education that was to continue through his career. The College of Art mostly taught naturalistic painting, with a focus on still life, although some modernist abstraction was also present. As Prakash later recalled, all the examples were of European artists, though some of the new Indian artists, like Raja Ravi Verma, who painted naturalistically were also celebrated. Prakash specifically recalled that he liked the work of the Bengal school artist Jamini Roy—but he was denigrated by the faculty, because he built on Indian folk themes. Part of the Eurocentrism of the colonial ideologues was that while they championed Indian crafts, the arts and crafts enthusiasts saw no merit in Indian art, which they considered to be degenerate because of its lack of naturalism.[18] Naturalistic painting never came to interest Prakash. Later in life, as he developed into a full-fledged painter, Jamini Roy would remain an important reference point for Prakash.

***RMS Franconia* (1922–1956), Cunard Line, at West Circular Quay in Sydney**, photographer unknown

Creative Commons https://www.flickr.com/photos/anmm_thecommons/8266248782/

The Franconia

At the stroke of the (in)famous midnight hour on 14–15 August 1947, while the world slept, the British left India peaceably. But in their wake, they left a bloodbath of communal violence amid the Partition of British India into the independent nations of India and Pakistan. Although he did not know it at the time, Partition would ultimately be the genesis of Chandigarh, the locus of Prakash's aesthetic and professional *Weltanschauung*. As India burned in 1947, Prakash realized that all his British professors at the Delhi Polytechnic were also leaving, which left him feeling bereft.

His choices were either to stay at the Delhi Polytechnic and see what happened, or apply for admission to one of the other Indian schools of architecture. The departing English faculty offered a third possibility by inviting him to join them in London, but that was the most prohibitively expensive option. Prakash took his fate into his own hands, and forced his father to "beg"[19] the Birlas for a loan to go to London. After much cajoling, the Birlas gave him a loan of Rs 2,000. Half of it went into the steamer passage. With the other half, Prakash bought two suits, a handful of supplies, some instruments, and saved the rest for expenses.

In 1947, Rs 2,000 was a mini-fortune, particularly for a family that essentially lived from hand to mouth. That loan, and the thought of turning his back on a precarious, newly-independent India, was to remain a heavy load on Prakash through his five-year tenure in the UK. Then there were the expectations of the extended family that the special privilege that Prakash was about to enjoy was going to have to be repaid in kind. It is symptomatic of the contradictions of the colonial condition that a scion of a struggling but successful and strongly nationalistic middle-class Indian family nevertheless thought it worthwhile to take on significant financial liability and risk for the chance of a "proper" British education. All prospects of advancement in colonial India were closely guarded by title and education. A title being unavailable, the best available education was—and in many ways still is—burnished as the only path to success in life.

On 8 August 1947, just days before India's independence, as the RMS *Franconia* steamed away from Bombay port, Prakash felt his spirits lift. The *Franconia* was long and sleek—601 feet long with a beam width of only 73 feet, a classic interwar cruise ship built for the Cunard Line in 1922, similar in design to the *Queen Elizabeth* of 1939. The Cunard Line was known for the speed with which it accomplished the Atlantic crossing and all its ships had that windswept modernist look with a piercing bow, narrow profile, and low-slung superstructures. One of the prides of the Cunard Line, the *Franconia* was requisitioned as a troop ship in World War II and had served as the headquarters for Winston Churchill during the Malta conference. It had been damaged in the war and so in its post-war career was used by Cunard in the Asian sector rather than the Atlantic.

Prakash recorded every day aboard the *Franconia* in his journal. He found himself cavorting with British and Indian young men and women on the ship—all of whom were headed for an adventure into the heart of the Empire. Prakash was particularly keen to note that class divisions between the English and Indian passengers suddenly seemed to disappear, and that the women (even Indian women) were more flirtatious and that some unfortunate souls suffered from seasickness almost instantly, while others, like him, were completely unaffected.[20] The crowning moment of the journey was the passage through the Suez Canal, with Asia on one side and "Europe" (actually British-controlled Egypt) on the other, "one side set with beautiful gardens, the other desert."[21] Seeing the fabled pyramids and the sphinx was a special treat. In Prakash's journals, as in his later imagination, the *Franconia* retained a special hold as something like a ship of dreams.[22]

London

Post-war London was a trying place even for the natives, and more so for fresh-off-the-boat, cash-poor Indians. Rationing was *de jour*, energy was scarce, heating had to be paid for with pennies inserted in meters, and steady employment was a luxury enjoyed by few. To cover his fees, room and board, Prakash had to find a job. His erstwhile professors from the Delhi Polytechnic had secured him admission, but could not offer him employment. Fortunately, other opportunities were at hand as London bustled with reconstruction projects, and Prakash found work with the office of Peter Moiret and Leslie Wood. It was a small office, consisting of seven people in all (including the principals).[23] Work was satisfactory. Moiret and Wood made

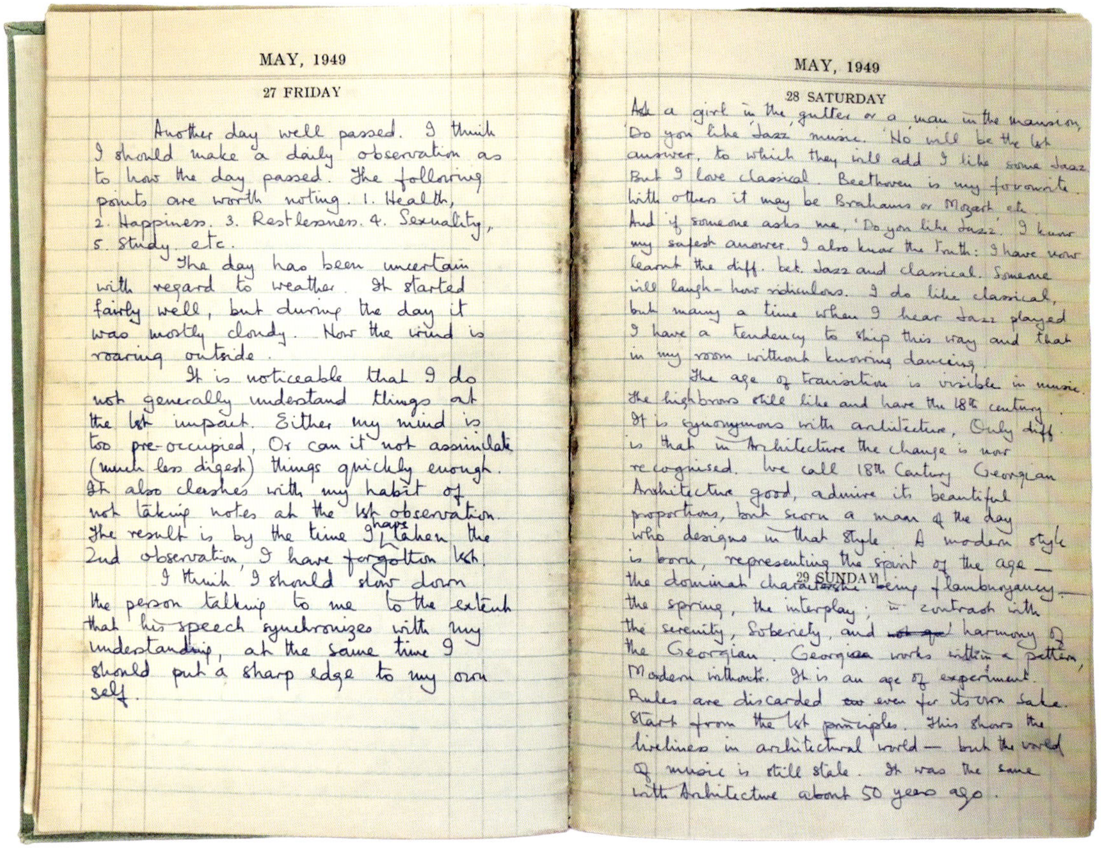

MAY, 1949

27 FRIDAY

Another day well passed. I think I should make a daily observation as to how the day passed. The following points are worth noting. 1. Health, 2. Happiness. 3. Restlessness. 4. Sexuality, 5. Study. etc.

The day has been uncertain with regard to weather. It started fairly well, but during the day it was mostly cloudy. Now the wind is roaring outside.

It is noticeable that I do not generally understand things at the 1st impact. Either my mind is too pre-occupied, Or can it not assimilate (much less digest) things quickly enough. It also clashes with my habit of not taking notes at the 1st observation. The result is by the time I've taken the 2nd observation, I have forgotten 1st.

I think I should slow down the person talking to me to the extent that his speech synchronizes with my understanding, at the same time I should put a sharp edge to my own self.

MAY, 1949

28 SATURDAY

Ask a girl in the gutter or a man in the mansion 'Do you like Jazz music.' 'No' will be the 1st answer, to which they will add I like some Jazz But I love classical. Beethoven is my favourite. With others it may be Brahams or Mozart etc. And if someone asks me, 'Do you like Jazz.' I know my safest answer. I also know the Truth: I have now learnt the diff. bet. Jazz and classical. Someone will laugh - how ridiculous. I do like classical, but many a time when I hear Jazz played I have a tendency to skip this way and that in my room without knowing dancing.

The age of transition is visible in music. The highbrows still like and have the 18th century. It is synonymous with architecture, Only diff. is that in Architecture the change is now recognised. We call 18th Century Georgian Architecture good, admire its beautiful proportions, but scorn a man of the day who designs in that style. A modern style is born, representing the spirit of the age — the dominant character being flamboyancy — the spring, the interplay, in contrast with the serenity, soberety, and harmony of the Georgian. Georgian works within a pattern, Modern without. It is an age of experiment. Rules are discarded too even for its own sake. Start from the 1st principles. This shows the liveliness in architectural world — but the world of music is still stale. It was the same with Architecture about 50 years ago.

29 SUNDAY

A page from one of Prakash's handwritten journals that he maintained continuously from 1946 to 1954, APF

a successful practice out of designing public projects, in particular schools and housing, at very reasonable rates. They were gracious and open with Prakash, and he found something of a family in the office environment.[24]

Finances were always very scarce, and Prakash constantly found himself making difficult choices. Typing was expensive, so he hand-wrote his final papers for the ARIBA exams, which was against the explicit instructions. In his journal he secretly feared that his entire education could be for naught if his exams were rejected on this technicality. But they were not. This sense of the necessity of having to negotiate between the desired and the real would feel like a persistent dichotomy in his life, even after he came to be aligned with the some of the most famous modernists of the time.

There was also the general problem of being expected to behave like an Englishman. Prakash obsessed in his journals over this question. While language and dress soon ceased to be an issue (he bought more suits, and learned the local cockney), the political/racist challenge of having to defend India's freedom was more complicated. What was he doing in London seeking an education, if it wasn't for the superiority of English culture and civilization? And if so, why did India really want freedom? Prakash was determined not to hang out only with fellow Indians, but the persistent threshold of civilizational judgement structured his relationships with even the most liberal English people.

Even so, Prakash later noted that although everything was scarce, spirits were high at that time in London. Moiret and Wood's office was located in Bridge House above the Blackfriars Underground Station. From his desk Prakash could see the Hungerford Rail Bridge with the "soupy" water of "Father Thames" flowing beneath. During lunch recess, Prakash loved to walk along the

Prakash at his ARIBA graduation formal banquet in London, 1952, APF

Watercolour of Thames River with St. Paul, London, one of two drawings submitted by Prakash for an exhibition at the Architectural Association, 5 x 8 inches, c. 1950, APF

A greeting card designed by Prakash, of the view from his window, 1949, APF

river, past the Shot Tower and the Lions Brewery, watching the barges being pulled along the river by horses on the banks (the barges had to lower their funnels when they went under the bridges).[25] These horse-drawn barges he loved in particular. A greeting card that he made in 1949 recorded the view from his room where he lived as a paying guest. What appears like a bleak urban landscape, with industrial chimneys as background, is rendered by Prakash in pen and India ink with undeniable, if optimistic, romanticism.

Central to the gaiety of London was the state-sponsored free access to the institutions of high art and culture. This greatly impressed him and went a long way in terms of inculcating affection for England and feeling like a British citizen.[26] Most evenings and weekends, Prakash found himself pulled into the world of post-war London museums, theatres, symphonies and operas, most of which he often attended alone. Royal Albert Hall was one of his favourite venues. He was enthralled by the comic operas of Gilbert and Sullivan, particularly *The Mikado* as performed by the D'Oyly Carte Opera Company, as also by Offenbach's bizarre *Tales of Hoffman*, which he saw repeatedly. He took classes and read books to cultivate and get a feel for English culture, taste, and language.[27]

Prakash's entries in his journals suggest that the workday was mostly to be endured until it was over, and the evening's charms and classes became available.[28] Prakash had joined the evening course at the Regent Street Polytechnic (located on Little Titchfield Street), so that he could work during the day. The classes at this Polytechnic were vocation oriented, like the ones at the Delhi Polytechnic, designed to enable its students to pass professional exams. All the excitement around modernism seemed to be at the AA (Architectural Association) at Bedford Square, which Prakash regularly visited mostly to attend lectures such as Hugh Casson's at the centenary celebrations in 1947. Le Corbusier, whose first Unité d'Habitation was being built at the time, was the rage among the student community, while the faculty seemed divided about him.[29]

Much of Prakash's education came from studying the *A&B News and Architects' Journal* which was available to students at a concessional rate. Each edition published detail sheets that Prakash carefully cut out and filed for future use. Theatre design became a preoccupation for Prakash, triggered by the big design event of the time, the 1951 Festival of Britain held at South Bank. Intended as a sign of a resurgent Great Britain, modern architecture was showcased in the festival's Dome of Discovery, the Skylon and most importantly in the Royal Festival Hall designed by the Scottish architect Sir Robert H. Matthew (with Peter Moro and Sir Leslie Martin). Prakash was

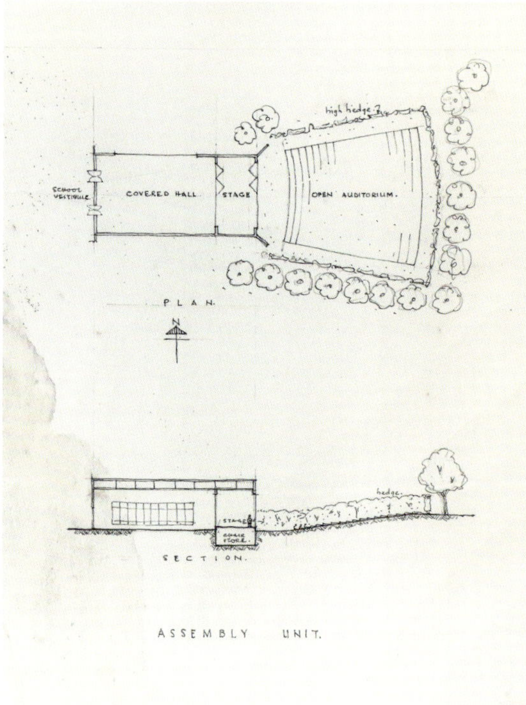

Assembly Hall design submitted by Prakash as part of his final thesis paper for his ARIBA exams, 1951, APF

A colour-coded cross-section of the Tagore Theatre, APF

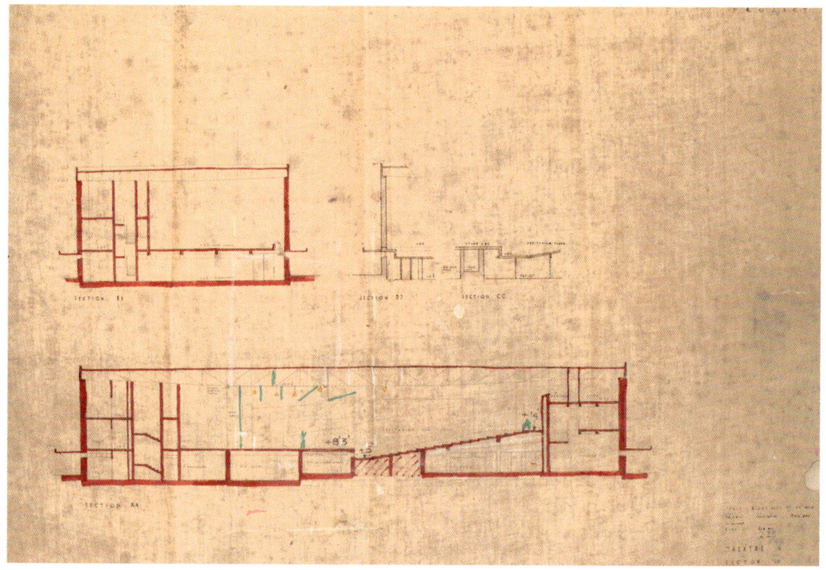

fascinated by the Dome with its extraordinary engineering, but it was the Festival Hall that most interested him. There was spirited debate on the Festival Hall's acoustics at the AA at the time. While they were engineered to perfection to ensure that there was no reverberation, many claimed that the Festival Hall felt dead precisely because of that. This made a significant impression on Prakash; he was fascinated by the technical achievement of the Festival Hall, but admitted that he preferred the acoustics of the old Royal Albert Hall. He also noted there was a debate on the design of the roof of the Festival Hall, that was curved to "reflect" the acoustic character of the main one, but not an actual part of the hall. This was a distinction that clearly stayed with him, and would come to haunt him later in his career as he tried repeatedly to design—and repeatedly failed to execute—theatres whose external form was dictated by their internal acoustic requirements.[30]

Return to India

In July 1951, Prakash submitted his final paper for the ARIBA exams, a handwritten 60-page document on "Primary Schools for North India."[31] Although Prakash noted that he did not think that a school should be designed as "a machine for teaching in", he argued that climatic considerations should be paramount in designing for India. He proposed that the design be very simple and low cost, designed for traditional modes of teaching,

Photograph of sculpture in the Glasgow School of Art found in the Prakash archives, APF

with students sitting on the floor cross-legged, but with better ventilation and solar exposure. His classrooms were designed as simple rooms with pitched roofs and high ceiling, not unlike colonial rest-houses. He put all his effort into the design of the assembly hall, organized around a simple rectangular stage that opened on two sides, accessible to a covered hall on one side, and an open auditorium (surrounded by a high hedge) on the other.[32] In conception, and also in form, the design of this assembly hall is remarkably similar to Le Corbusier's *La boite à miracle*, or The Miracle Box, a little-known, never-built project of the 1950s. It can also be seen as the generative design DNA of Prakash's signature building to come—the 1961 Tagore Theatre in Chandigarh.[33]

In October 1951, almost immediately after passing his ARIBA exams, Prakash took a job in Glasgow and left London looking for a new start. His journals note that work at Moiret and Wood had become extremely tedious, and that some of his personal relationships had become too convoluted. He applied to a number of firms in London, and also to London Transport and the London County Council ("places [he] thought he would go to only as a last resort").[34] But none of these panned out. As soon as he could, Prakash resigned, set off for a month-long holiday to France and Italy, and then returned to Glasgow to join the firm of Launcelot Hugh Ross. Ross was an associate of Thomas Tait (the lead designer of the Glasgow Empire Exhibition of 1938), who worked

Vintage heavy vinyl LP disks of the kind Prakash brought back with him to India from London, Photograph by author

mostly on schools. A domineering personality, whose promising career had suddenly been curtailed by the War, Ross was struggling to re-establish himself. He immediately rubbed Prakash the wrong way and they clashed. Fortunately, Prakash discovered the Glasgow School of Art just a block away from where he was living on Hill Road, and enrolled in evening classes in "Clay Modelling" and "Art for Life". He enjoyed the clay modelling and noted that his teachers thought that he could make a great sculptor.[35] These classes and the friends he made there became the centre of Prakash's life. The Glasgow School of Art "saved his life," as he would often recount.

Prakash's big break came in the summer of 1952, when he learnt that Le Corbusier was designing Chandigarh, the famous postcolonial capital city commissioned specifically by Jawaharlal Nehru, the first Prime Minister of India, as a symbol of the aspirations of the independent nation. Nehru specifically sought to make a "modern" city, and put his reputation behind it. The making of Chandigarh thus was a prestigious project and attracted the attention of architects and planners worldwide. Initially, Nehru had commissioned Albert Mayer, an American planner who was already in India working on a model village project at the behest of Mahatma Gandhi, to design the new city. An exponent of the garden city planning principles, Mayer was a close associate of Lewis Mumford, the trenchant historian and critic of American urbanism. At Mumford's suggestion, Mayer had brought a young Polish émigré architect, Matthew Nowicki, to design the large public buildings, but unfortunately Nowicki died in an air crash over Egypt in September 1950. Hired simply to replace Nowicki and execute the Mayer master-plan, Le Corbusier had managed to take over the entire project, re-design the master plan, and establish a brand new design and planning team headed by his cousin Pierre Jeanneret and the British modernist architectural couple, Maxwell Fry and Jane Drew.

Fry and Drew had just returned from West Africa, where they had developed the principles of what they would eventually come to term

"Tropical Modernism."[36] They knew Le Corbusier well from the CIAM meetings, and admired him, though Fry was also wary of Le Corbusier's overbearing and dominating character. Even so the making of Chandigarh was a historic project, much heralded (and also sharply contested) in the architectural media, and they agreed to pack up their lucrative practice in England and move to India for a contracted period of three years.

The main reason that Fry and Drew were required to move to India to work on Chandigarh by the Indian government—a requirement that Le Corbusier had managed to sidestep by recommending Pierre Jeanneret in his stead—was the expectation that they were to "train" local Indian architects and planners so that they could eventually take over. A team of seven Indian architects and planners had already been assembled, along with a host of draftsmen and administrative staff. On an impulse, Prakash wrote to Maxwell Fry asking if he could join the team. After seeking approval from India, Fry, during one of his visits back from Chandigarh, interviewed Prakash on 27 May 1952 in London and soon after, offered him the job with the handsome take-home pay of Rupees 700 per month (along with passage to India). On Monday 29 September 1952, Prakash set sail in another steamer for India, leaving behind friends, friendships, and a formative period of his life.

Later, Prakash would look back on his tenure in the UK with mixed feelings. While he had earned the prestige of being an "ARIBA," he felt that the education had been too conservative and had to be completely unlearned once he started working on Chandigarh. While he became very close to some of his friends and girlfriends, in general, he felt discriminated against and taken advantage of.[37] And while he came to greatly love the cultural life of London and the entire caboodle of symphony, opera, theatre, and vaudeville would remain a lifelong passion for him, he was quick to give up English manners and customs and happily resettle into the daily informality of Indian life.

Before leaving, Prakash expended all his remaining funds on a state-of-the-art Gerrard multi-disk changer, along with a collection of Decca LPs of his favourite symphonies, operas, and plays. This journey back on the steamer was much shorter than the passage there, and there is no mention in his journals of the name of the boat or its passengers, or what Prakash did to while his time away when he was on board.

NOTES

1 As described by Prakash in Aditya Prakash "A slice of my life" email to his children dated June 16, 2000. *APFA_D86.*

2 Aditya Prakash "A slice of my life" email to his children dated May 20, 2000, *APFA_D86*. I have abridged all references to the holdings in Archives of the Aditya Prakash Foundation as "APFA_##", where ## refers to the folder number where the document can be found.

3 "Reminiscences of Education in Pre-Independence India" *APFA_D3a*.

4 Aditya Prakash "A slice of my life" email to his children dated June 02, 2000, *APFA_D86*.

5 Aditya Prakash "A slice of my life" email to his children dated June 02, 2000 *APFA_D86*.

6 "Bane and Boon of our life" is part of the subject line of one of his memoir emails, Aditya Prakash "A slice of my life" email to his children dated May 19, 2000, *APFA_D86*.

7 Aditya Prakash "A slice of my life" email to his children dated July 1, 2000, *APFA_D86*.

8 Aditya Prakash "A slice of my life" email to his children dated June 16, 2000. But it seems that handcraft was only considered appropriate for women, and not for men. For men to spin would be considered reducing themselves to the status of a lower-caste person, a *julaha*. This is why Mahatma Gandhi spinning cotton himself was both an affront to the colonial mills and also to the caste- and gender-normed Hindu society. See Aditya Prakash "A slice of my life" email to his children dated June 24, 2000, *APFA_D86*.

9 Prakash wrote a detailed description of his house in Panipat in his emailed memoirs to his children:

Prakash was very good at it. The kites had to have a perfect balance if they were to fly straight and obey the commands of the flier. Otherwise they would go haywire. Kite watching and kite flying were our childish passions which were resented by all the elders. One of the stories often told about the evils of kite flying was that one boy while flying kite got so absorbed in the act that he kept on moving backwards and fell off the roof into a large frying pan (*kadhia*) in which *kachoiries* were being made. I think the story was made up to frighten us.

Aditya Prakash "A slice of my life" email to his children dated June 11, 2000, *APFA_D86*.

10 The architecture cohort seems to have been very small. Aditya Prakash's journals only mention a handful of students: B.P. Mathur, Farooqi and a Ms. Dutta. *Eagle Table Diary No. 2 1947*, *APFA_Journals*, entry dated January 11, 1947. W. W. Wood of W. W. Wood and Sons and Partners, reputedly the personal architect to the British Viceroy, ran the Delhi Polytechnic at that time. They also did most of the projects for the Birlas. Aditya Prakash "A slice of my life" email to his children dated May 27, 2000, *APFA_D86*.

11 As Peter Scriver has persuasively argued. See Scriver, P. (1994). *Rationalization, standardization, and control in design: A cognitive historical study of architectural design and planning in the Public Works Department of British India, 1855-1901*. Delft: Publikatieburo Bouwkunde, Technische Universiteit Delft. See also Peter Scriver's essay in Scriver, Peter, & Prakash, Vikramaditya. (2007). *Colonial modernities: Building, dwelling and architecture in British India and Ceylon* (Architext series). London; New York: Routledge.

12 This is the College of Art that is now located on Tilak Marg in New Delhi.

13 For a critical history see Dutta, A. (2007). *The bureaucracy of beauty: Design in the age of its global reproducibility*. New York: Routledge.

14 See for instance Watt, C., & Mann, Michael. (2011). *Civilizing missions in colonial and postcolonial South Asia: From improvement to development* (Anthem South Asian Studies). London; New York: Anthem Press.

15 See the work of Thomas Metcalf in this regard, particularly Metcalf, T. (2002). *An imperial vision: Indian architecture and Britain's raj*. New Delhi; New York: Oxford University Press.

16 B.V. Doshi recently won the 2018 Pritzker Prize for architecture.

17 See for instance my conversation with Balkrishna Doshi recorded for *ArchitectureTalk*. www.architecturetalk.org, conversation recorded on December 4, 2017, released on January 31, 2018. For a broader discussion of the contexts of Indian modernism and postmodernisum, see Scriver, P., & Srivastava, Amit. (2015). *India: Modern architectures in history (Modern architectures in history)*. London, UK: Reaktion Books.

18 See Mitter, Partha (1992). *Much maligned monsters: A history of European reactions to Indian art*. Chicago: University of Chicago Press.

19 "Beg" is the term Prakash used to describe it as. See, Aditya Prakash "A slice of my life" email to his children dated July 5, 2000, *APFA_D86*.

20 Prakash's journal contains a long list of friends and their addresses in London, all collected onboard the Franconia. *Eagle Table Diary No. 2 1947, APFA_Journals*. Some are underlined; a "very rich Sikh gentleman going to the U. K. with his family on a pleasure trip" and a Sarala Bakaya, introduced to Prakash as a "poetess" and an expert in Russia. Sarala Bakaya, a nurse by training, and Prakash seemed to have remained friends for a while in London, but then drifted apart. She later married one Robin Kumar Basu in 1953, according to an online memoir by her brother, Ravi M. Bakaya. *The Life and Times of Kamla Bakaya*, https://archive.org/stream/TheLifeAndTimesOfKamlaBakaya1900-1973/kamlabakaya_djvu.txt, accessed Tuesday, January 16, 2018.

21 *Eagle Table Diary No. 2 1947*, APFA AP Journals, journal entry dated Thursday July 17, 1947.

22 Aditya Prakash never really took to air travel, particularly after the introduction of the jet-engine, that required flying at a high altitude.

23 Prakash's journals record the member of the practice as Peter Moiret, Leslie Wood, Rita (Moiret), Caroline, Cathy and Nicholas (no last name recorded for the last three). *The University Desk Diary 1948 APFA_AP Journals*, entry dated February 28, 1948.

24 Prakash seems to have enjoyed a somewhat close personal relationship with Peter Moiret and in particular with his wife Rita (Henrietta?) Moiret, who was also a part of the practice, and whom Prakash described in his journals in glowing terms. See *The University Desk Diary 1948 APFA_AP Journals*, entry dated March 03, 1948.

25 All these descriptions are from the unpublished article titled "Royal Festival Hall" *APFA D3b*.

26 Prakash in fact still held a British passport at this time, which he surrendered only after he returned to India in 1952.

27 Catalogues of several art exhibits still survive in the Archives of the Aditya Prakash Foundation.

28 Prakash was constantly worried that he would lose his job, and that he was too slow at his work—"In India I was supposed to be having a good speed of work—was among the fast workers. Here I feel I am slow amongst the slowest." *The University Desk Diary 1948 APFA_AP Journals*, entry dated March 16, 1948.

29 As noted in "Royal Festival Hall" *APFA D3b*

30 "Royal Festival Hall" *APFA D3b*.

31 "Primary Schools for North India" original manuscript, *APFA D165*.

32 "Primary Schools for North India" original manuscript, *APFA D165*, p.47.

33 For a discussion of the Miracle Box see Massilia 2012. Annuaire d'études corbuséennes *La boite à miracles - Le Corbusier et le théâtre* Fondation Le Corbusier, Paris; Éditions Imbernon, Marseille, 2012.

34 *Diary 1951 APFA AP Journals* entry dated August 16, 1951.

35 *Diary 1951 APFA AP Journals* see journal entries for October and November 1951 for AP's observations on entry into Glasgow.

36 A topic which they started and taught for years at the Architectural Association in London during the 1960s, and which they published as Fry, M., & Drew, Jane. (1964). *Tropical architecture in the dry and humid zones*. New York: Reinhold Pub. See also: Jackson, I., Holland, Jessica, (2016). *The architecture of Edwin Maxwell Fry and Jane Drew: Twentieth century architecture, pioneer modernism and the tropics* (Ashgate studies in architecture series). London; New York: Routledge, Taylor & Francis Group.

37 In 1971 Prakash went to Edinburgh for a conference, and on his way back stopped over in London for a couple of days to meet old friends. He later noted in a journal how superficial and perfunctory those meetings were, and how glad he was that they were over. See "Musings on a Flight to London," *APFA D88*.

Prime Minister Jawaharlal Nehru during one of his many state visits to the Chandigarh Capital Project site, meeting the architects (left to right): Jeet Malhotra, Aditya Prakash, A.R. Prabhawalkar
Photo credit: Fonds Pierre Jeanneret, Canadian Centre for Architecture, Montréal; Gift of Jacqueline Jeanneret

THE CHANDIGARH CAPITAL PROJECT TEAM

Prakash (far left) and the Capital Project team
Photo credit: Fonds Pierre Jeanneret, Canadian Centre for Architecture, Montréal; Gift of Jacqueline Jeanneret

Isolated from normal life and building a utopian new city in the countryside, the culture of the Capital Project team was a heady mix—very intimate and personalized, but also a minefield of intrigue and competitiveness. Lifelong friendships developed among many of the young Indian architects, planners, and administrators who made Chandigarh. The team comprised a very small community, and all the families relied on each other for friendship and support in the absence of the usual Indian extended family and social networks. Most of the Indian architects were young when they joined the Capital Project, and as they got married, one by one, everybody attended these big events. And then, as the families grew, there were frequent gatherings, festivals were observed and celebrated together, and the children often became best friends if only due to a lack of choice.[1]

In May 1953, six months after joining the Capital Project team, Aditya Prakash married Savitri Gupta in a ceremony that took place in the Karol Bagh neighbourhood of New Delhi. Savitri Gupta was a university educated, English-speaking woman nine years younger than him. The prospect of moving to the middle of nowhere, married to a man in a profession she had barely heard of, frightened her. Savitri's mother assured her that family would be on hand to help, and that an officer of the Government of India, working on a Nehruvian

Prakash and Savitri's wedding in New Delhi, attended by Maxwell Fry and Jane Drew, May 1952, APF

Savitri with one of her daughters in front of their first home in Sector 22, APF

project, was an exceptional match. And so, she took the Kalka Mail train to Chandigarh, and arrived at midnight on a platform that showed no signs of urban civilisation for miles around.

The first thing the Chandigarh architects had to do was to build houses for themselves. The Capital Project was born in open agricultural fields, and while there were several thriving villages at the site, the new city was planned and laid out in accordance with a modernist reading of the site which was usually, though not always, at odds with the existing inhabitants and their patterns of living. While the plan, famously, took Le Corbusier just a weekend to outline, the city itself took a long time to take hold; construction was slow, inhabitants slow in coming. For years, even the drainage system stayed incomplete and so the roads turned into canals during the rains. Sand was everywhere, settling on the sun-breakers and blowing into the houses and offices with the wind.[2]

Jeanneret had designed and built the very first building at the site, the project's office itself, which the team occupied on 15 December 1951. The row of houses for the staff were built on the V4 street in front of the main markets of Sectors 22 and 16. These took time and were built on demand. When Prakash took charge of his position on 31 October 1952, there was no house for him. Fortunately, Bhanu P. Mathur, one of his old classmates from the Delhi Polytechnic, was working in the office and offered to host him for the three months it took to build Prakash's house. Finally, in December 1952 Prakash was able to move into House No. 12, located right on the V4 directly opposite the main market in Sector 22.

Socially speaking, a clear distance was kept between the foreign architects and Indians. Jeanneret spoke broken English and was a confirmed bachelor, which made the women wary of him. Fry and Drew were very social, but they left after two years. Prakash's journals note that there were frequent "official" parties, usually hosted by Jeanneret, particularly in the winter months when Le Corbusier was there. Solan No. 1 was the whisky of choice. There was no heating of course, so wood bonfires were lit, and occasionally local folk performances like *swangs* were held.[3] A *swang* or *saang* is a folk song-and-dance routine, native to the state of Rajasthan, far from Chandigarh. But many of the migrant labourers working on the Chandigarh Project were from Rajasthan (like the famous veiled woman featured in Le Corbusier's oeuvre), and it seems that they also provided some of the entertainment.

The Chandigarh site
Photo credit: Fonds Pierre Jeanneret, Canadian Centre for Architecture, Montréal; Gift of Jacqueline Jeanneret

Scan image with the **BooksPlus** app

The Chandigarh Capital Project team; and **the official IDs issued to Prakash** (facing page), APF

Name ADITYA PRAKASH
Designation SENIOR ARCHITECT
Department SENIOR ARCHITECT
Registrar PAU
Punjab
1. Name ADITYA PRAKASH
2. Father's Name Ram Chandra Das.
3. Designation Architect
4. Full Address Capital Project Department of Architecture Chandigarh.
6J/15 E Sector 7.
7 Age 36 years
8. Height 5ft 10 ins.
9. Visible Distinguishing Marks
Birth mark on left
Signature of the holder
Dated 22. 4 1956
Govt. Punjab.

Pierre Jeanneret with Jawaharlal Nehru
Photo credit: Fonds Pierre Jeanneret, Canadian Centre for Architecture, Montréal; Gift of Jacqueline Jeanneret

Pierre Jeanneret with Jawaharlal Nehru and Jeet Malhotra
Photo credit: Fonds Pierre Jeanneret, Canadian Centre for Architecture, Montréal; Gift of Jacqueline Jeanneret

Le Corbusier and Nehru at the High Court

The social pecking order was determined strictly by the rank of the officers; even the wives and families adhered to the expected norms of deferring to seniority. While the "seniors" were expected to go out of their way to try and make their "juniors" as comfortable as possible, there was a certain comfort in the clarity of social order.[4] Everyone knew "their place," so uncomfortable social entanglements were few and far in between. There were occasional scandals—a shotgun wedding or two, and an affair documented famously in the novel, *Storm in Chandigarh* by Nayantara Sehgal, Jawaharlal Nehru's niece—and the scars from these events could induce pain long after.[5] The tensions in the team came from the hierarchy and differences in opinion among the senior architects. Right from the beginning, the European leaders of the Capital Project team did not gel. Jeanneret and Fry in particular continually clashed on design principles. Fry felt that he had the experience of working in tropical climates, while Jeanneret asserted that he had the backing and authority of Le Corbusier, which officially made him "head" of the entire team. This tangle was resolved by having Fry and Drew return to London in 1955, one year before their contract was up, leaving Jeanneret in charge.

The anointed spearhead of the entire team, with the august backing of Jawaharlal Nehru, Le Corbusier in Chandigarh was a strange mix of the bullishly arrogant and the defensive. Having secured his biggest project ever, he designed the Capitol with great fervour. But he also felt denied, curtailed at every turn. Dealing with the engineers was particularly frustrating for Le Corbusier, and he continually threatened to rain down Nehru's authority on them, and very often did. The residual colonial culture also stoked tensions between the architectural team and the engineers in charge of the actual construction. The engineers were used to wielding authority from colonial times and assumed that everybody at the site would answer to them. That a 'prima donna' architect, even with Nehru's backing, could overrule their decisions was unpalatable. Fortunately, P. L. Varma, the chief engineer who had been instrumental in selecting Le Corbusier for the job, developed a close friendship with the architect. Supported by Jeanneret's conciliatory demeanour, Varma ensured that the architects, engineers, and administrators worked reasonably well together.[6]

Letter from Prakash to Le Corbusier, dated 21 July, 1959, APF

Jawaharlal Nehru speaking in front of Secretariat, APF

Le Corbusier felt oddly estranged from his own architectural team as well. In one instance he accused Jeanneret of having "betrayed" him, even though the latter was clearly the main reason that the former's buildings were executed on site with such attention and care. The main point of contention seems to have been housing. Le Corbusier had hoped to build at least some of his "Unités" mass-housing schemes in Chandigarh, but that was never on the agenda, and neither Jeanneret nor any of the other team members seem to have supported that idea. Ultimately, Le Corbusier did not design a single housing unit in Chandigarh; all the signature "Chandigarh-style" government housing was designed by Jeanneret, Fry, and Drew.[7]

In the midst of these scuffles and simmering tensions, the junior Indian architects and town planners on the team found themselves jostling to develop their own skills and modes of expression. The competition for access to the "masters" and for promotion in rank coloured all interactions. It was essential to show that one had developed the expertise to design and manage projects by oneself. Already, there was competition among the senior European designers to see who could design the better house, with the same budget, and the Indian architects often joined the fray and even took sides. Certain Indian architects came to be identified with particular "masters," and this caused tensions with understated charges of favouritism.[8]

In his early days at the office, Prakash felt intimidated by the jargon thrown around—words like "Modulor," "Brise-Soleil," "Grid Climatique," "Monsieur," and "the Vs" were used as self-evident concepts of the holy gospel.[9] Being the youngest and least experienced on the team, the "junior-most of the Junior Architects " (as the rest of the staff ragged him), Prakash initially felt wary of the culture of one-upmanship. Perhaps, having earned his credentials in the UK, he had expected to be treated with more respect. It took some time before he could overcome his natural shyness and reserve and resolve to compete.

For Prakash, the competition amongst the ranks of the Capital Project team translated into an active search to try and understand the modernist concepts being floated in Chandigarh via what he called "first principles." What he meant by "first principles" was that rather than just mastering the vocabulary established by the "masters," Prakash decided to study the underlying questions of climate, materials, and urban organization that were deployed to develop Chandigarh. To understand these, and not just the forms of buildings, was for him the core contention of the modernist design ethic.

This was, as it quickly became clear, a Herculean ambition. The ARIBA training in London had barely schooled him in the idioms

238

Retour Septembre

P1-18

IMMEDIATE:

BY AIR MAIL

D.O. No:330-Arch-59/3920

Office of the Senior Architect,
Capital Project, Chandigarh.

Dated the 21st July, 1959.

Reçu le 27 Juillet 1959

Répondu le

Subject: Audio Visual Training Institute.

My dear Mons. Le Corbusier

A recent meeting was called by the Chief Engineer to which the Directorof Industries, and Principal of the School of Art were invited to discuss the possibilities of realising the above scheme. I am enclosing a plan showing their proposal of omitting the auditorium in the first instance and extending the garden further. The plan also shows the proposed distribution of spaces as desired by them.

Could you kindly send your approval or comments to this scheme as soon as possible? The minutes of the above meeting will be sent to you shortly.

Yours sincerely,

A Prakash

(Aditya Prakash 21/7/59.

Mons. Le Corbusier,

35, Rue - de - Sevres,
Paris-6.

E
LC

D.A/a.a.

The Chandigarh site
Photo credit: Fonds Pierre Jeanneret, Canadian Centre for Architecture, Montréal; Gift of Jacqueline Jeanneret

and ideologies of modernism. On the other hand, Le Corbusier at this point in his career was a learned reader of form, order and history—the lightning rod of the modernist movement for a reason. In the early days, the task of "translating" Le Corbusian modernism for the Indian team had been left to Jeanneret, Fry, and Drew. Their contracts explicitly stated that the senior architects had to "train" their junior Indian charges, and get them ready to take over the project themselves. In the old colonial culture, the expectation would have been just that—to "train" the juniors to exactly reproduce what their seniors had done. But since the advertised culture of modernism, with its foundational investment in first principles and causality-driven design, was different, the task of "training" the Indian team was approached as a kind of mentorship. Le Corbusier was impatient and in a hurry to get his projects built. He brooked little discussion and left the task of "training" to Drew, Fry, and Jeanneret, all of whom were patient and indulgent schoolmasters, but were understandably more focused on executing the project as cheaply and efficiently as possible than on "training" their Indian charges.

To try and learn things from first principles, thus, Prakash had to swim against the current, and strike out on his own. At the outset, Prakash was put to work under Jane Drew when she was designing a dispensary in Sector 22 and the main general hospital for the city in Sector 16. The social culture of the Capital Project team was decidedly male in character. Jane Drew and U. E. Chowdhury were the only women on the team, and after Drew left, Eulie Chowdhury held fort singlehandedly her entire career. Chowdhury had a distinguished career, eventually retiring as Chief Architect of Punjab. She maintained an iron facade and reportedly did not brook any behaviour by her peers or juniors that discriminated against her based on her gender.[10] Socially, she behaved like "one of the boys," drinking and smoking like the best of them.[11]

There is little in Prakash's journals of his professional relationship with Drew or her mentorship, although later, in 1989, after Drew had returned to Chandigarh one last time, Prakash followed up with a letter to her noting:

> One phrase of yours I always remember: It is "NEVER SAY DIE." May GOD bless you for the inspiration you provided when you were with us. I remember with gratefulness and nostalgia the time we spent with you, Max

> Fry, Pierre Jeanneret and Le Corbusier when the whole team was with us. You helped us to discover ourselves.[12]

And then, on learning of Drew's death in 1996, Prakash described her with some admiration and noted her connection with the "Modern Architects Club:"

> Jane was a "modernist" to the core. She would say, "Is it modern, or not quite?" and would be on the lookout for a wholly modern solution. When we started an architects club, she desired that it be called "Modern Architects Club." It was. She had great sympathy for the indigenous building practices. Corbusier introduced "brut" concrete, Jeanneret brick and stone facing, Max a mixture of both, but Jane had plastered surfaces as was the local tradition. She created homely atmosphere by locating low-cost housing around a central common space where children can still be seen playing in safety... She had great sympathy the building labour of which there was quite a large number carrying baskets on their heads. Looking at the female labourers in their flowing colourful dresses doing the hard work, she would say "Queens are building Chandigarh."[13]

Aditya Prakash's first major effort at establishing an independent identify took the form of the making of a "Modern Architects Club." He did this in 1954, barely a year-and-a-half into his term with the Capital Project team. In a note written "On behalf of the Modern Architects Club" he noted the core motivation:

> We Indian Architects who have been associated with the foreign geniuses found ourselves pulsating with life, for such opportunity is very rare in the lives of most Architects. We saw the eyes of the world focused on us. We have been absorbing the ideas given to us by our visiting Architects, but not only that, we have always had our own contribution, not a small one, to make the most of the buildings built or being built in Chandigarh. Thus, we are proud to say that we proved ourselves worthy of standing up to the world's most renowned Architects. It is amply verified by what the visiting Architects have said time and again.[14]

One imagines that the being able to "stand up" to the "world's most renowned Architects" while the "eyes of the world" were focused on them would have been a significant source of anxiety for the young Indian architects. It certainly seemed to have been for Prakash. He responded by setting high and lofty goals for the Club—nothing less than "discovering" the fundamentals of architecture:

> [T]wo things are foremost in our minds: First, the co-ordination of the professions of Architecture and Engineering. This is not to

suggest that there is any discord. It is only that since Architecture is a new profession in India, it has to find its right place in the midst of other people who deal with the buildings. The Second... is to "Discover" the function of man in the house. This sounds so simple, yet when you come to solve it, it is the most difficult problem of Architecture. We have been moved to do this on account of the varied criticism and appreciation we got of the houses we built in Chandigarh. The research is to find out the fundamentals of house design, a research which has always been going on, and will always be going on.[15]

Little is known about the Modern Architects Club, particularly in terms of any research it may have conducted.[16] Its only concrete outcome was the idea of making a school of architecture in Chandigarh. Surprisingly, the Chandigarh brief included an art school, but not one for architecture. Based on the colonial model, architecture was considered a sub-set of art or closely allied to art as a discipline. Prakash made the case for a separate school of architecture, which Jeanneret supported, even though the famously anti-academic Le Corbusier was more reluctant. Eventually, after the college was built and ready, and A. R. Prabhawalkar, his favourite Indian associate, was established as its principal, Le Corbusier did come to deliver a few lectures to the students at the Chandigarh College of Architecture (CCA).[17]

By the summer of 1954, the differences among the senior team were such that Drew and Fry left to return to London, one year before their contract was up. After Drew's departure, Prakash turned to Jeanneret for mentorship and over the years the two developed a close bond. For his role as a mentor, and for his long years of patient hard work in Chandigarh, Prakash later described Jeanneret as a "saint." Prakash in fact credited Chandigarh's—and Le Corbusier's—success, that could easily have been a "failure," to Pierre:

Let it be stated, while I deliberate on Jeanneret
That the success of Chandigarh,
And of Corbusier in Chandigarh
Is due very very largely
To the saintly nature
Of Pierre Jeanneret.
He absorbs many shocks
Of opposing opinions—confrontation
with rare equanimity.
It could be that Corbusier
Would have quit the scene in a huff
Because of his fiery temper
In the face of opposition
To his futuristic projections,
And added "Chandigarh" to his list of failures.
It could be that the infant team
Of architects and planners
Would have wilted and dissipated

The newly created Sukhna Lake, APF

In the face of administrative problems.
Only the serene personality of Pierre Jeanneret
Could sail smoothly
Over rough and calm seas
And carry the ship to its desired destination,
And itself perish in the effort.[18]

Jeanneret's "saintly" character, as Prakash describes it here, manifested in Chandigarh by the work he did in smoothing over the "rough and calm seas" generated by Le Corbusier's "fiery temper" even though it meant that he himself had to "perish in the effort." This portrait of self-sacrificing resilience in the interest of the larger good may have been as much a characterization of how Prakash felt about his own role in life, as the critical life lesson he learnt from Jeanneret. By the time he came to Chandigarh, Jeanneret of course had had a long and complex relationship with Le Corbusier, having started out as partners and then falling out during World War II.[19] One of the main reasons that Jeanneret likely took the Chandigarh job was that it offered the perfect arrangement where he could both continue to work with and represent Le Corbusier, and at the same time keep some distance between them and maintain his own independence. In fact, Prakash later recalled that when Le Corbusier was around Jeanneret seemed to be half the man he was otherwise. He would cower and was seen taking frequent toilet breaks.[20] All this in spite of the fact that Jeanneret repeatedly played the role of the mediator between Le Corbusier and the Indians and painstakingly figured out the working drawings and the techniques that would allow the "master's" designs to be executed in the challenging circumstances of an impoverished India building with 19th -century colonial construction methods.

Having lived most of his life in Le Corbusier's shadow, one imagines that Jeanneret must have felt a certain sympathy for the underling Indian staff. Jeanneret in fact became a good mentor to many of the Indian architects on the Capital Project team. This was likely one of the main reasons that he stayed on until 1965, running the Architect's office like an atelier, or even something like an "ashram."

Jagat Theatre and District Courts, Chandigarh
Photo credits: *Architectural Design*, October 1965, p. 513, and APF respectively

Interrogating the "Modern Style"

Prakash's independent work done as part of the Capital Project team sought to interrogate that very pragmatic architectural idiom that came to be called the Chandigarh style. The idiom of this so-called "Chandigarh style" consisted of exposed load-bearing brick walls, concrete lintels and floor slabs, and the occasional rubble masonry wall that characterized all residential structures. Institutional and public buildings were built in concrete, their dimensions based on standard grids and floor heights. Solar shading, natural ventilation, and the honest expression of materials and forms were de rigueur.

Chandigarh was made by very simple means, technologically speaking. This is how Prakash remembered it:

> What was the technology when the building of Chandigarh was undertaken? It was "brickwork," and carpentry, and that is about all. The craftsmen were the Mason and the Carpenter. Between them they did all the work. Besides brickwork, a mason also did concrete work, plastering, flooring, drain laying, etc. A Carpenter did shuttering, making doors, windows, and other filaments in which not only wood but metal was also used. The tools were only hand tools e.g. trowel, brick hammer, plumb line, hand saw, planer, screw driver, chisels and adze. Human labour or the donkeys was the basic power.[21]

For Prakash, there was virtue in the simplicity of means and methods employed in Chandigarh. This did not always sit well with the "modern-city" expectations of the Chandigarh project. Early on in his tenure in Chandigarh—possibly as a part of the "research" of the Modern Architects Club— Prakash proposed experimenting building with a mud-brick wall. Jeanneret had set the example by using large river rock, available plentifully in the intermittent rivers around Chandigarh, to construct beautiful rubble masonry walls. These became extremely popular in Chandigarh. Prakash felt that the long history of mud-construction in India could, in a similar experimental vein, also be harnessed to build cheaply. But the first test wall that was built in the yard of the Capital Project Office collapsed, and the experiment was immediately shut down. As Prakash recounted later, the main reason why mud was not experimented with was not its lack of structural strength, but because it tied Chandigarh to the "past" and its villages, which did not fit the expected image of a "modern" city.

Even so Prakash's early work in Chandigarh belonged clearly to the "Chandigarh style", but always with a twist, and usually connected to the expression of programme and structure. For Prakash, function and structure generated form. From this, he tried to make a poetics of form by pushing the idea as far as it would go, but only as far as could always be rigorously defended in the court of purpose and programme. In this sense,

Sector 17, Chandigarh, frame design by Le Corbusier, APF

Prakash tried to actualize the "form-follows-function" modernist orthodoxy in his work. At the same time, however, one can detect a distinct painterly sensibility to his work, not in terms of the search of emotionally expressive gestures (as in Le Corbusier's grand Capitol buildings, for instance), but in the sense of a deep investment in the staging of the formal composition of the building. Prakash's buildings were always composed from a small set of elements—they were minimalist in this sense—but were richly composed as if they were lines in a painting.

One of the first projects assigned to Prakash was the District Courts building in Sector 17, the commercial heart of the city. The 17 feet 3 inches wide concrete frame grid, devised by Le Corbusier as the architecture's domino-frame, was implemented with military rigour in Sector 17. Prakash's design tried to break with these specifications, and explored the possibility of expressing the grid in double- and triple-heights. As a consequence, his design generated a sense of volume and openness missing from the rest of the sector. In the District Courts' design, we also find his early interest in the bounding frame in the form of blank end walls.

A strong frame, in the form of parallel, thick, load-bearing exposed brick walls, also defines Prakash's designs for Neelam and Jagat theatres, the first two of the three cinema halls he designed in Sector 17 in the mid-1950s. Before he left, Maxwell Fry had built the very first of Chandigarh's cinema halls, Kiran Theatre in Sector 22. Fry's Kiran is a strongly gestural work, with simplified art-deco motifs arrayed to generate the front facade as a public spectacle. In contrast, Prakash's Neelam and Jagat have massive side-walls—utilitarian constructs with little impact on the facade other than as a bounding frame. An old sectional drawing shows that the front facades of Neelam and Jagat were intended to be a continuation of the acoustic curve of

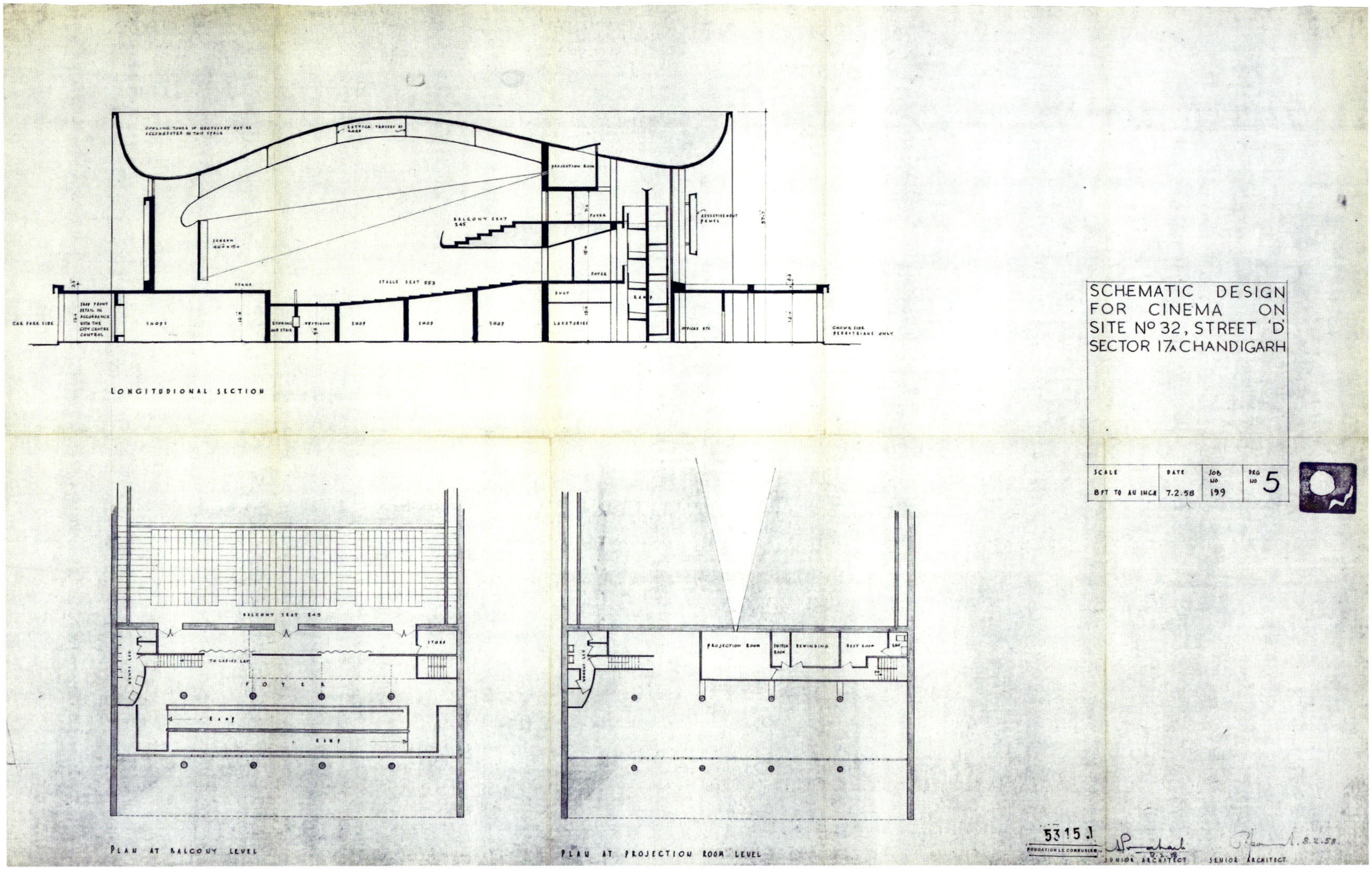

Schematic section of Neelam theatre by Prakash, APF

their internal ceilings. Although on the outside the upward-turning concrete volume bears a distinctive gestural similarity to the portal of Le Corbusier's Assembly building, in fact it is a direct extension of the interior space, and not an external stand-alone element as in Le Corbusier's Assembly.

Born of his theatre experiences in London and the controversies of London's Royal Festival Hall, the acoustic curve as a figural form became a lifelong obsession for Prakash. The fact that a free-flowing architectural form could be so viscerally generated by the logics of sound and its propagation attracted his painterly interests. One can think of the acoustic curves in the intended sections of Neelam and Jagat as figures of desire, straining against the confines of the frame, while continuing to be contained within. Curves straining against the frame was to become a recurrent theme in his paintings and drawings as well.

Painting with Arcs,
acrylic on canvas,
23 x 44 inches, 1998,
APF (17_4_38)

These acoustically informed formal tendencies were finally liberated in Prakash's design of KC Theatre from the early 1970s, which has no frame at all. In KC Theatre, the acoustic curve of the roof continues to become the overall form of the structure, determining the elevation, section and trapezoidal outline of the plan. According to Prakash, KC Theatre was intended as an object in space, while Neelam and Jagat were conceived in the context of a row of buildings.[22] This may well be how Prakash remembered it, but it cannot be denied that the continuous curve of KC Theatre projects a sense of freedom that is not available to the profiles of Neelam and Jagat.[23]

KC Theatre's continuous curve—distinctly visible from Madhya Marg, the main circulatory spine of Chandigarh—quickly established itself as an iconic structure of Chandigarh. Its singular form was completely unlike anything else in the city. Later, when KC Theatre was demolished to make way for a mall in 2005, the city's residents

Sector 17 petrol pump with KC theatre in the background
Photo courtesy Arjan Singh, Chandigarh

KC theatre aerial view

KC theatre with signboard
Photo courtesy Arjan Singh, Chandigarh

Petrol pump in Sector 17, Chandigarh, with dramatic curving inverted beam roof, 1957
Photo courtesy Arjan Singh, Chandigarh

protested and the chief architect's office hastily mandated that the new structure maintain the original outline and form. When asked to support this preservation order, however, Prakash demurred. While the form was important, the fact that the internal function of the structure was completely altered no longer justified the external form for Prakash, however poetic or iconic it may have been.[24]

The joy of the continuous curve also translated into the beautiful sweeping upward curve of Prakash's standard design for the petrol pumps of Chandigarh, one of which was built right next to KC Theatre. (There is a great old photograph that shows the two of them together!) This time, the logic was not acoustic but structural. The long span required to cover the pumps without support called for an inverted beam structure, with the steel acting as a tie member, functioning like an inverted bow truss. In their final form, the petrol stations were like birds with their wings outstretched right at the moment of flight.

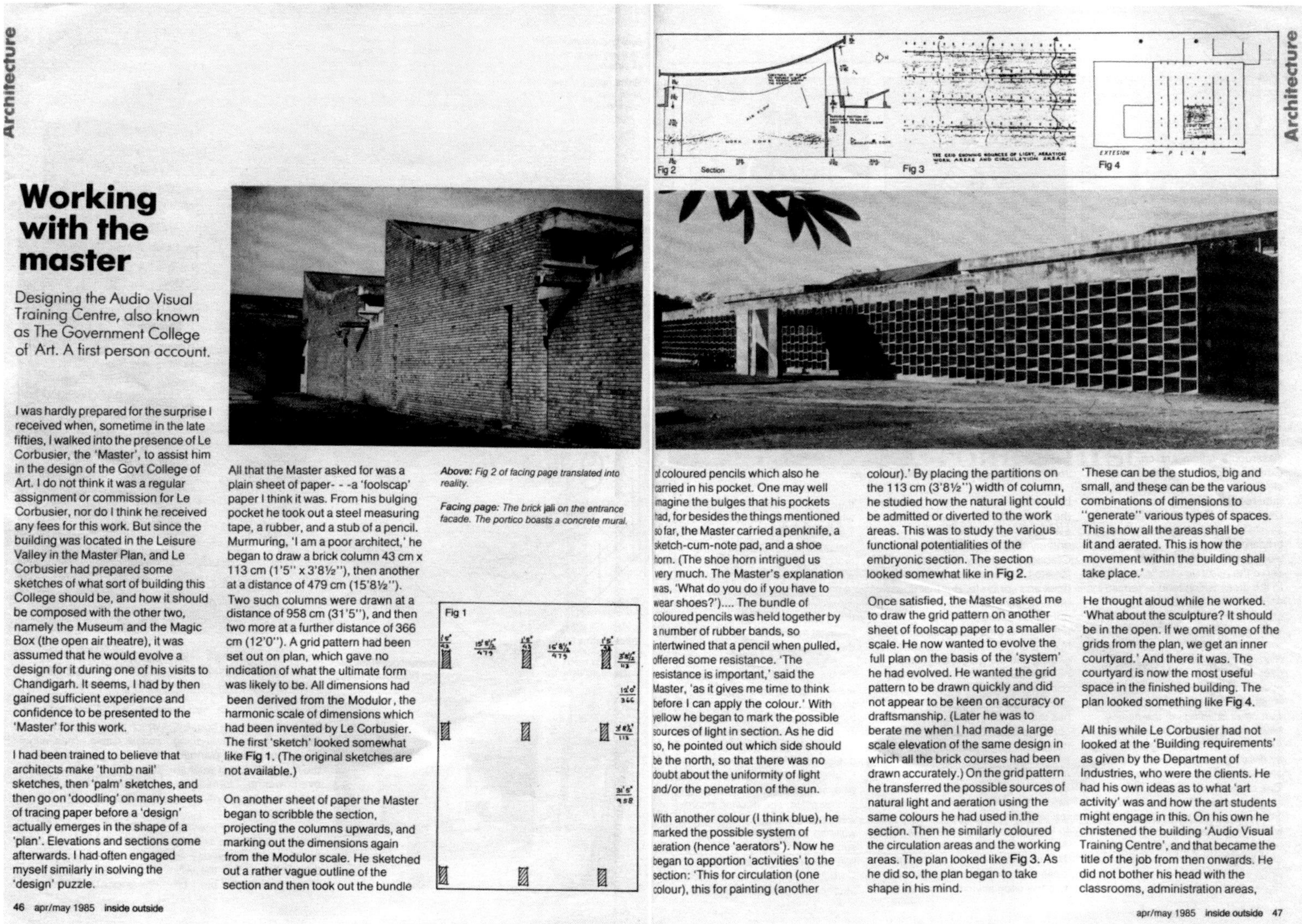

Architecture

Working with the master

Designing the Audio Visual Training Centre, also known as The Government College of Art. A first person account.

I was hardly prepared for the surprise I received when, sometime in the late fifties, I walked into the presence of Le Corbusier, the 'Master', to assist him in the design of the Govt College of Art. I do not think it was a regular assignment or commission for Le Corbusier, nor do I think he received any fees for this work. But since the building was located in the Leisure Valley in the Master Plan, and Le Corbusier had prepared some sketches of what sort of building this College should be, and how it should be composed with the other two, namely the Museum and the Magic Box (the open air theatre), it was assumed that he would evolve a design for it during one of his visits to Chandigarh. It seems, I had by then gained sufficient experience and confidence to be presented to the 'Master' for this work.

I had been trained to believe that architects make 'thumb nail' sketches, then 'palm' sketches, and then go on 'doodling' on many sheets of tracing paper before a 'design' actually emerges in the shape of a 'plan'. Elevations and sections come afterwards. I had often engaged myself similarly in solving the 'design' puzzle.

All that the Master asked for was a plain sheet of paper- - -a 'foolscap' paper I think it was. From his bulging pocket he took out a steel measuring tape, a rubber, and a stub of a pencil. Murmuring, 'I am a poor architect,' he began to draw a brick column 43 cm x 113 cm (1'5" x 3'8½"), then another at a distance of 479 cm (15'8½"). Two such columns were drawn at a distance of 958 cm (31'5"), and then two more at a further distance of 366 cm (12'0"). A grid pattern had been set out on plan, which gave no indication of what the ultimate form was likely to be. All dimensions had been derived from the Modulor, the harmonic scale of dimensions which had been invented by Le Corbusier. The first 'sketch' looked somewhat like **Fig 1**. (The original sketches are not available.)

On another sheet of paper the Master began to scribble the section, projecting the columns upwards, and marking out the dimensions again from the Modulor scale. He sketched out a rather vague outline of the section and then took out the bundle

Above: Fig 2 of facing page translated into reality.

Facing page: The brick jali on the entrance facade. The portico boasts a concrete mural.

Fig 1

of coloured pencils which also he carried in his pocket. One may well imagine the bulges that his pockets had, for besides the things mentioned so far, the Master carried a penknife, a sketch-cum-note pad, and a shoe horn. (The shoe horn intrigued us very much. The Master's explanation was, 'What do you do if you have to wear shoes?').... The bundle of coloured pencils was held together by a number of rubber bands, so intertwined that a pencil when pulled, offered some resistance. 'The resistance is important,' said the Master, 'as it gives me time to think before I can apply the colour.' With yellow he began to mark the possible sources of light in section. As he did so, he pointed out which side should be the north, so that there was no doubt about the uniformity of light and/or the penetration of the sun.

With another colour (I think blue), he marked the possible system of aeration (hence 'aerators'). Now he began to apportion 'activities' to the section: 'This for circulation (one colour), this for painting (another colour).' By placing the partitions on the 113 cm (3'8½") width of column, he studied how the natural light could be admitted or diverted to the work areas. This was to study the various functional potentialities of the embryonic section. The section looked somewhat like in **Fig 2**.

Once satisfied, the Master asked me to draw the grid pattern on another sheet of foolscap paper to a smaller scale. He now wanted to evolve the full plan on the basis of the 'system' he had evolved. He wanted the grid pattern to be drawn quickly and did not appear to be keen on accuracy or draftsmanship. (Later he was to berate me when I had made a large scale elevation of the same design in which all the brick courses had been drawn accurately.) On the grid pattern he transferred the possible sources of natural light and aeration using the same colours he had used in the section. Then he similarly coloured the circulation areas and the working areas. The plan looked like **Fig 3**. As he did so, the plan began to take shape in his mind.

'These can be the studios, big and small, and these can be the various combinations of dimensions to "generate" various types of spaces. This is how all the areas shall be lit and aerated. This is how the movement within the building shall take place.'

He thought aloud while he worked. 'What about the sculpture? It should be in the open. If we omit some of the grids from the plan, we get an inner courtyard.' And there it was. The courtyard is now the most useful space in the finished building. The plan looked something like **Fig 4**.

All this while Le Corbusier had not looked at the 'Building requirements' as given by the Department of Industries, who were the clients. He had his own ideas as to what 'art activity' was and how the art students might engage in this. On his own he christened the building 'Audio Visual Training Centre', and that became the title of the job from then onwards. He did not bother his head with the classrooms, administration areas,

Fig 2 Section

Fig 3

Fig 4

46 apr/may 1985 inside outside

apr/may 1985 inside outside 47

"Working with the Master", written by Prakash in *Inside Outside*, April/May 1985

Learning from the "Master"

In 1958, six years after he had started working with the Capital Project team, Aditya Prakash finally graduated to work directly with Le Corbusier, who by then was finalizing his design for the Government Museum complex in Sector 10. The Museum Complex—with its ancillary, the Museum of Knowledge, in the Capitol Complex—was the last set of buildings that Le Corbusier was to design for Chandigarh. This was a landmark opportunity for Prakash. Le Corbusier was a celebrity, even for the Chandigarh staff. In 1949, when he was still a student at the London Polytechnic, Le Corbusier's name was mentioned in the halls in hushed tones and with awe, and so he decided to go down to Paris to see his office and visit his buildings. Later, in an essay titled "Reminiscences of Le Corbusier" (1987), Prakash wrote that that even though he visited his office at Rue de Sevres,

> I did not meet him them. I was too afraid and self-conscious to try it. His office people said, "he is too busy, and does not like to meet anyone like that." That was enough to keep me off the master. But I did find out what work of L.C. I could see in Paris...and ...whatever I looked at was more with trying to understand the MAN behind the building rather than trying to find fault.[25]

In other words, while working with Le Corbusier, Prakash, like the rest of the Capital Project team, was self-conscious of working with what we would today call a "starchitect," something like a

Le Corbusier's Portrait by Prakash, pencil on paper, 8.75 x 13.75 inches, 1997, APF [2_(11)]

Le Corbusier's Portrait by Prakash, ink on paper, 11 x 17 inches, 1997, APF [3(13)]

Scan image with the **BooksPlus** app

"once-in-a-lifetime" opportunity, and a frightening one at that. "That was some experience," Prakash later noted, "a feeling which still brings sweetness to my being."[26]

Prakash made detailed mental notes of Le Corbusier's working process, which he later published under the title "Working with the Master."[27] Le Corbusier was starting work on the School of Art in Sector 10 at the time. Prakash noted how Le Corbusier came to his desk ready to design, without any concept sketch, thumbnail or programme. He started with dimensions taken straight from the Modulor, which he instructed Prakash to draw. These gradually metamorphosed into a plan grid and section. Converting the grid into a functioning plan via partitions was Prakash's task.

From this experience evolved Prakash's credo that designs emerge not through a magical process of the magnification of a "thumbnail" sketch, but by clear systemic thinking. Building designs had to have an underlying order or system. And, although he never explicitly stated it, it seems clear that Prakash was very impressed by the Modulor as manifested by Le Corbusier's ability to generate exact dimensions from inside his head with a sense of certainty.[28] From here onwards Prakash used the Modulor to dimension not only all of his buildings but also a lot of his paintings.

Unlike his intimate relationship with Jeanneret, Prakash worked closely with Le Corbusier only this one time, and that too through the very strict filter of a professional assistant and apprentice. Le Corbusier was always aloof, probably by plan, and did not brook much discussion, far less any questioning, even at an ordinary inter-personal level.[29] Even so, Prakash was to later repeatedly characterize Le Corbusier as a "master" or "guru:"

> What I want to say is that a guru, in my concept, does not teach, but only inspires you to learn. You may or may not be in the presence of a guru, but if you place him in your heart then you receive inspiration to learn, to discover your own potential to acquire skill and to create through your own genius. Corbusier did not teach me. For a long time, I had no direct contact with him. Yet his presence in Chandigarh and his work in Chandigarh and by direct contact with his disciple Pierre Jeanneret I was able to discover my own potential of design and creativity, of comprehension and analysis.[30]

The unabashed reference to Le Corbusier as a "master," even very late in his life, can give

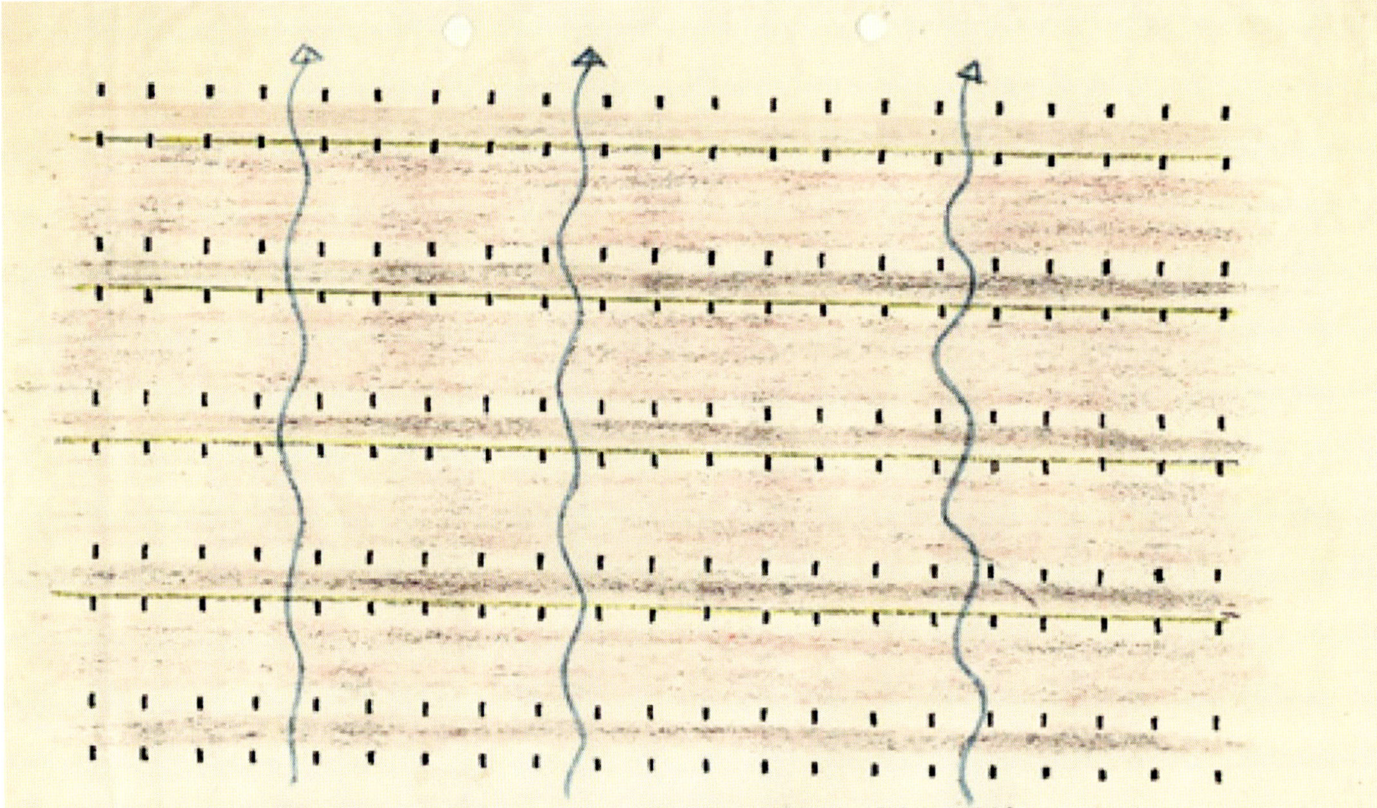

FIG. 3 THE GRID SHOWING SOURCES OF LIGHT, AERATION WORK AREAS. AND CIRCULATION AREAS.

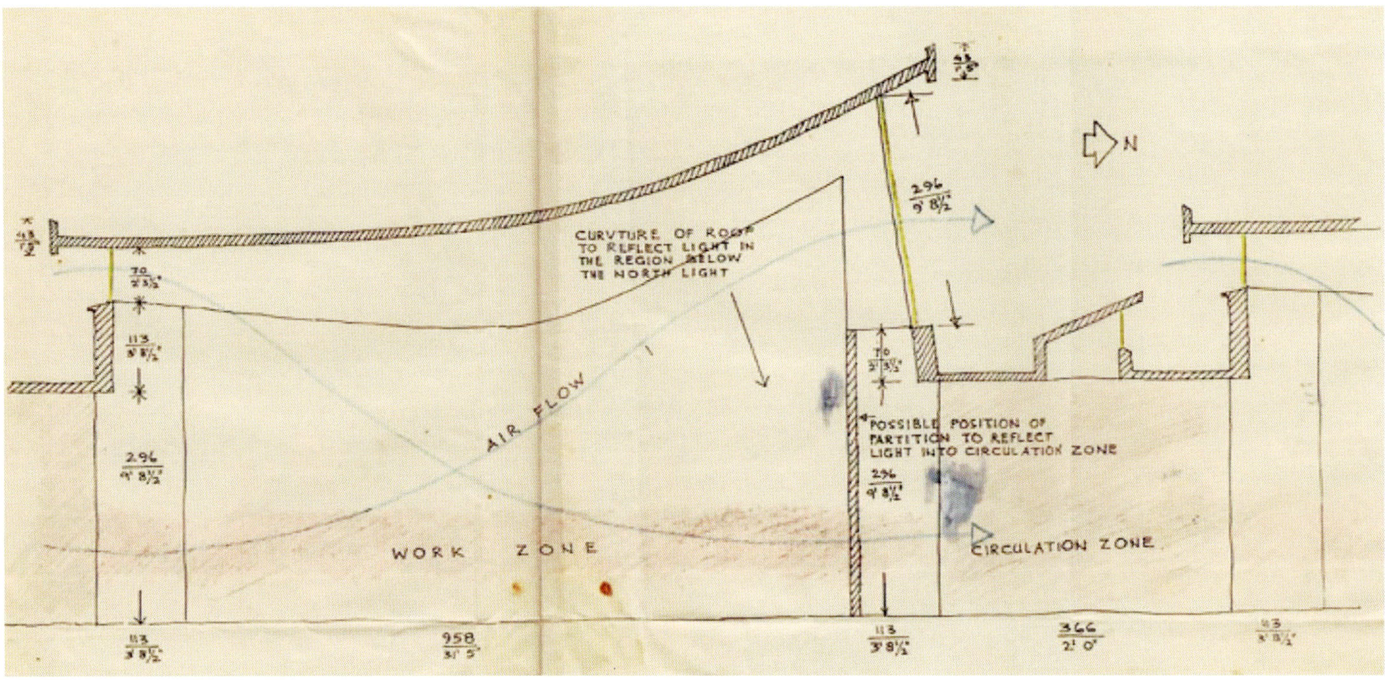

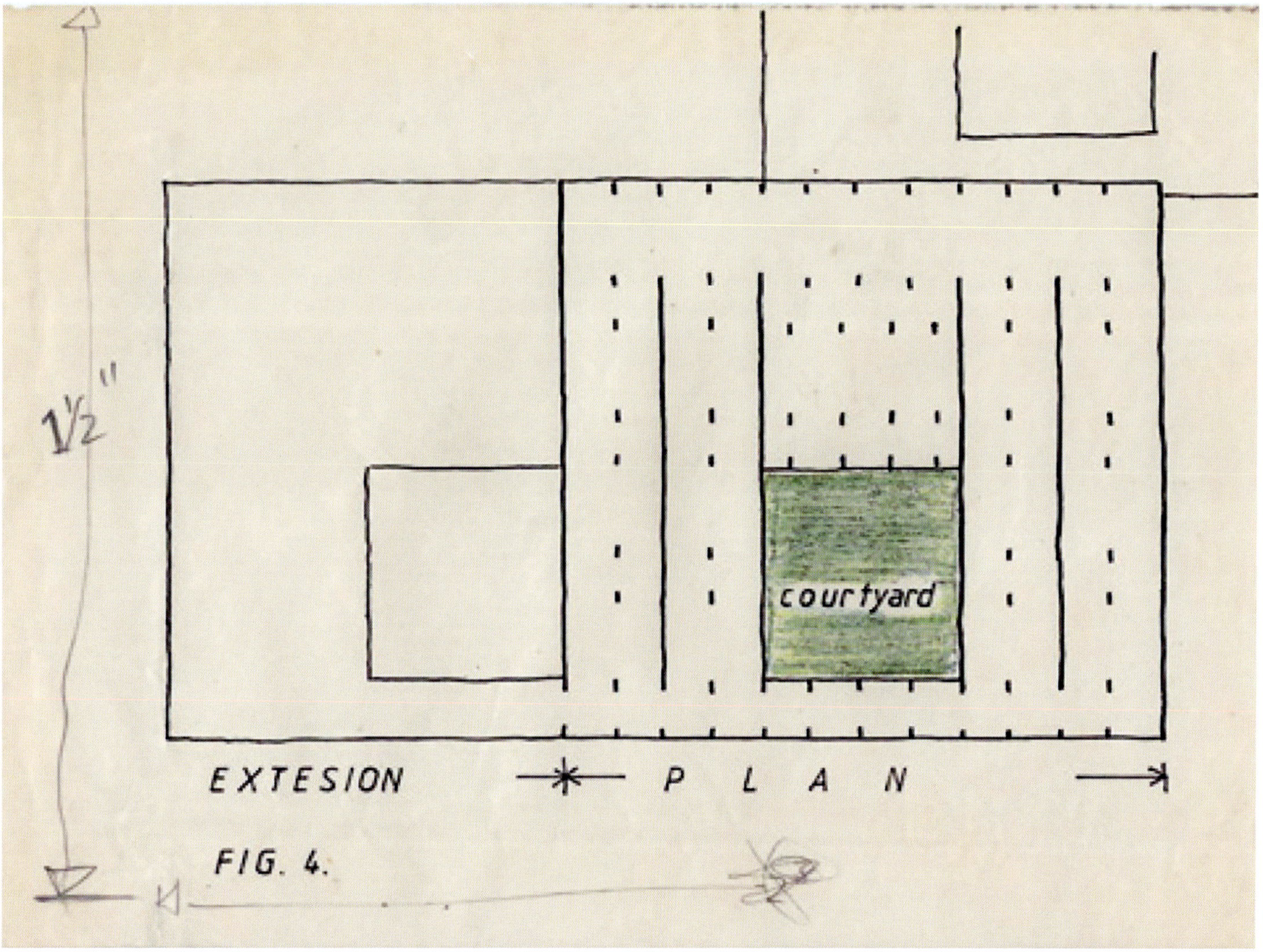

Sketches by Prakash, dated 1984, retrospectively recalling the design process of the School of Art while working with Le Corbusier, APF

one reason to pause, and wonder about the postcolonial persistence of the institution of "guruvada"—the unquestioned deference to the teacher—engrained in Indian culture.[31] One can think of the descriptions of schools that Prakash went to as a child as a reference—where the teacher and the headmaster exert absolute authority.

At the same time, if one wanted, the very same text can be read as a critique of the authoritarian institutions of education. Not only is there a simmering sentiment of resentment—a "guru...does not teach"—there is also a sense that the teacher should be able to "earn" his authority such that you "place him in your heart." After Prakash himself became an academic, he took pains to be accessible and available to all the students. He worked hard to earn his authority as a teacher, as testified repeatedly by many of his students, though not always successfully.[32]

In spite of all his later critiques of modernism, Prakash continued to respect Le Corbusier (as he did Jeanneret), as a guru until the end of his life. The respect Prakash maintained for his gurus also took the form of critique. He would often say, "I have learnt everything I have from Le Corbusier, even if it is in going against him." In the same paper where Prakash characterized Le Corbusier as a "guru" he also described his reaction to a visit to the Capitol Complex, where he criticized the attempts by the Chandigarh administration to faithfully execute all that remained to be built without any reflection or amendments. The Capitol should be modified and not just executed as per the last set of drawings, Prakash maintained.[33]

Prakash explaining the model of the Secretariat to a visiting dignitary (probably Giani Zail Singh)

Frame Control and the Indian Modulor

The investment in "system" as the generator of form resulted in Prakash's most visible contribution to the architectural image of Chandigarh—the idea of urban "frame control." As the city's first privately-owned shops and houses began to be constructed in the early 1950s, their architectural language derived from a persistent Indo-colonial imagination, replete with pedimented porticoes, articulated column capitals, and the occasional *jharokha* balcony. Prakash instead proposed, and Jeanneret and Le Corbusier agreed, that all smaller privately-owned plots, particularly in commercial zones, should be sold with the stipulation that they had to follow a modernist aesthetic of uniform heights, clearly defined frames and an apprehensible structural aesthetic vocabulary. This was called "frame-control."[34]

In the December 1961 issue of the Indian art and culture journal *Marg* devoted entirely to Chandigarh,[35] Prakash argued for the necessity of frame control in terms of the "urban-picture," with visual arguments that would seem familiar to later more postmodern urban designers such

Modulor 19, acrylic on canvas, 15 x 40 inches, APF

Scan image with the **BooksPlus** app

Shops designed by Prakash using the frame control, APF

as Kevin Lynch. In many ways, the frame-control system was exactly that—a systematic control of the frame. The external frame was specified, the dividing frame of the facade was specified, and even the shapes and sizes of windows were controlled. A Prakash drawing that articulated the first set of frame-control rules shows the 18 standard windows (and 11 "additional" ones) that were allowed; a perspective view showed the variations within the frame that were possible.[36]

Frame control was a controversial idea, even in its time. Many argued that the private sector should be allowed to develop the city in their own image. Nonetheless the idea stuck, and throughout the 1960s and 1970s most privately developed houses acquired the sparse look of the "Chandigarh style." Indeed, many of the new developments that took place in the areas around Chandigarh, well beyond any frame-control rules of the city, also began to aspirationally resemble buildings in the city. Today, the idea of frame control, both within the city and without, is rapidly on the decline as new "global" references take over the aesthetic imagination of its citizenry.

Modulor Painting,
acrylic on canvas,
8.5 x 47.5 inches,
APF (17_4_27)

All the dimensions of the frame control Prakash of course took from the Modulor. In Chandigarh, a design practice of the 1950s and '60s was to use a complete set of Modulor dimensions to articulate the individual openings in a window wall. Le Corbusier had used this strategy in many of his buildings, including in the Lake Club and the Secretariat in Chandigarh. Many of the Indian architects tried their hand at the same window strategy, although Prakash, for reasons unknown, never did.

Prakash's full-fledged infatuation with the Modulor took flight in the process of designing one of his last buildings as a part of the Capital Project team, the Chandigarh College of Architecture (CCA) in 1961. Having worked on the School of Art with Le Corbusier, and having proposed the program for architecture, Prakash was the natural choice to design CCA. Here, Prakash made an unusual proposal. Instead of designing from "first principles," he proposed that the design DNA—the grid and the north-light section—of Le Corbusier's School of Art be cloned for the College of Architecture. Le Corbusier himself often cloned his own designs, as in the case of the various museums he made during his career. Since these were projects with closely connected programmes, Prakash argued that the School of Art could be cloned as the College of Architecture.

It seems this was done with Le Corbusier's assent; and it certainly had Jeanneret's approval.[37] However, the cloning hit a snag—the assigned budget for the College of Architecture was smaller than that of the School of Art. Rather than truncate the building and make it smaller, as was suggested, Prakash decided to literally shrink the building (since the majority of the cost of the building, then as now, was materials). The precedent for this once again had been set by

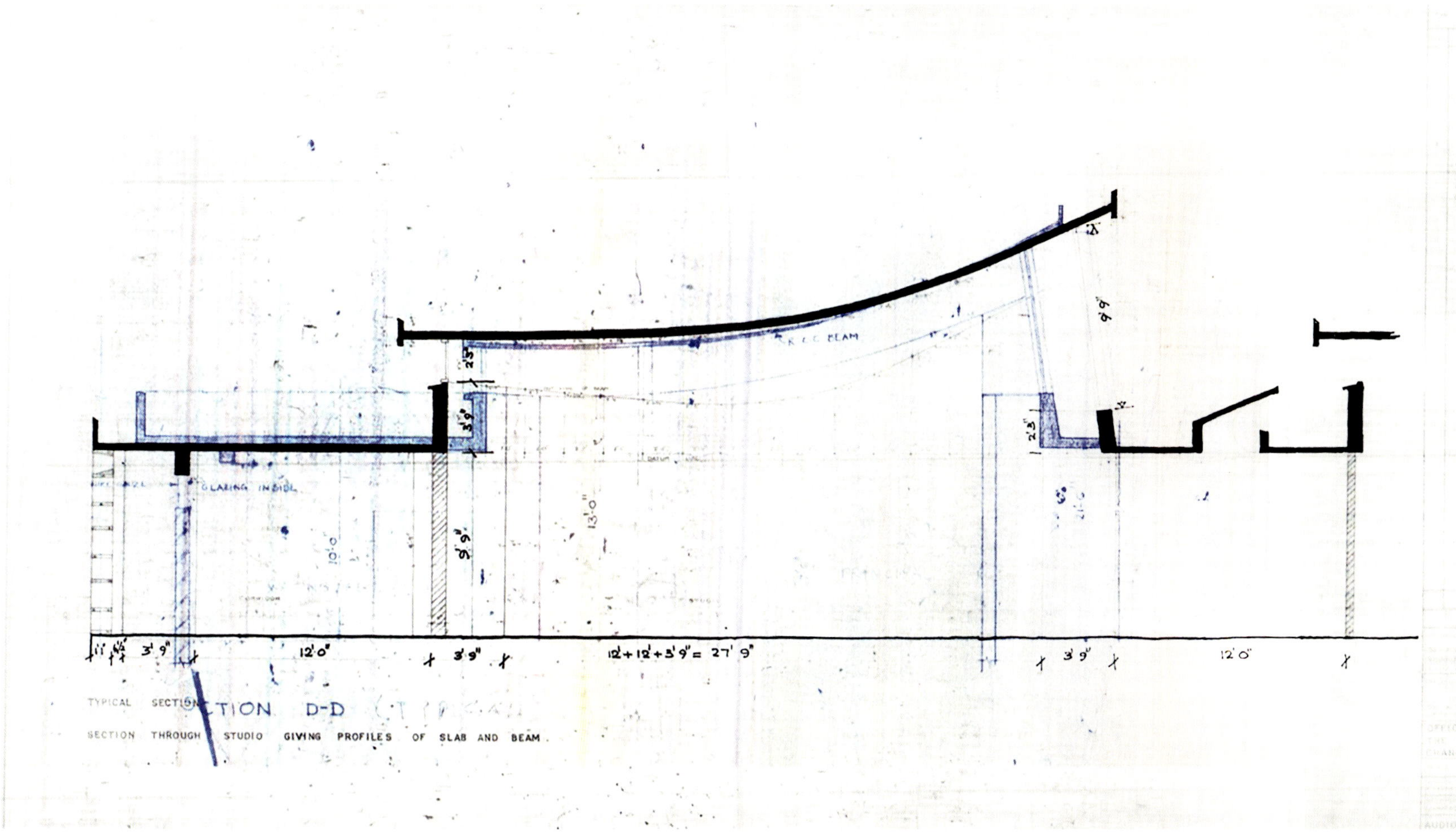

Section of the Chandigarh College of Art and Architecture overlaid for comparison. Overlay drawing by James Donaldson, Chandigarh Urban Lab, University of Washington
Photo courtesy James Donaldson

Le Corbusier. The Governor's Palace as initially proposed proved to be much larger than its budget would allow. Le Corbusier simply shrunk it using the instrument of the Modulor, without altering the design.

This shrinking-to-fit exercise introduced Prakash to the intricacies of the Modulor. Using the Modulor to scale the building down would not result in every dimension being reduced proportionately, but the Modulor scale would enable each dimension to be "stepped-down" so that they all retained a harmonic relationship. Prakash used this opportunity to study the Modulor from Le Corbusier's recent publication on the idea.

Eventually, Prakash developed his own adapted "Indian" Modulor. Le Corbusier's Modulor had a flaw; its dimensions were extremely idiosyncratic. Since it was rigorously derived from a series of geometric expressions, Le Corbusier's Modulor specified very precise dimensions that were supposed to be mathematically harmonic, but were unconnected to the world of construction. In India, all construction was ultimately based on whole number multiples of the standard brick size, which of course rarely, if ever, added up to the exact Modulor numbers. And so, Prakash generated a modified version of the Modulor that consisted of whole-number multiples of Indian brick dimensions. This Indian Modulor could not of course be defended on the grounds of mathematical precision, confirming the divinity of exact numbers. Rather, as a practical working system, Prakash's Indian Modulor—with its 6 feet 9 inches tall doors, 2 feet 3 inches sill levels and 3 feet door widths—can be seen as a manifestation of the ideal of pragmatic regionalism in modernism, an idea that started to come to the fore with Team X from the 1960s onwards.[38] We shall return to this discussion in the final essay of this book.

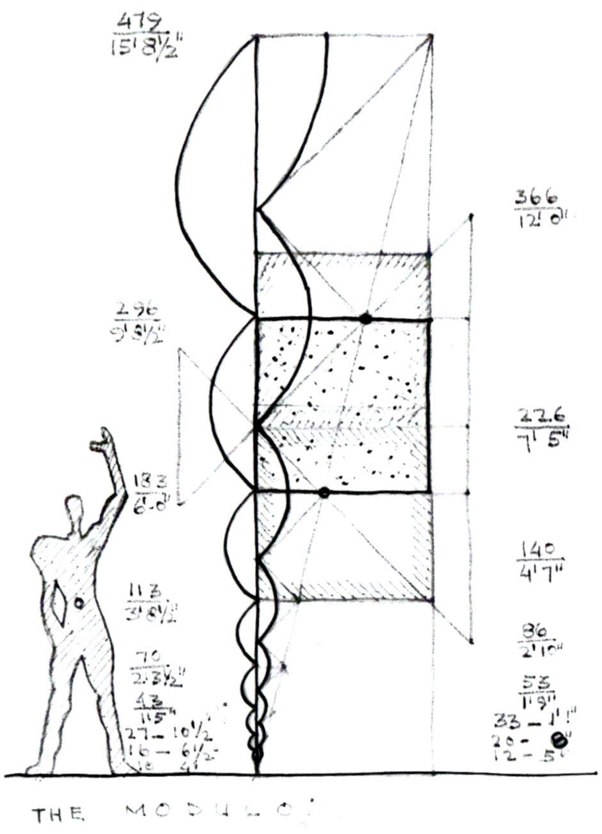
THE MODULOR

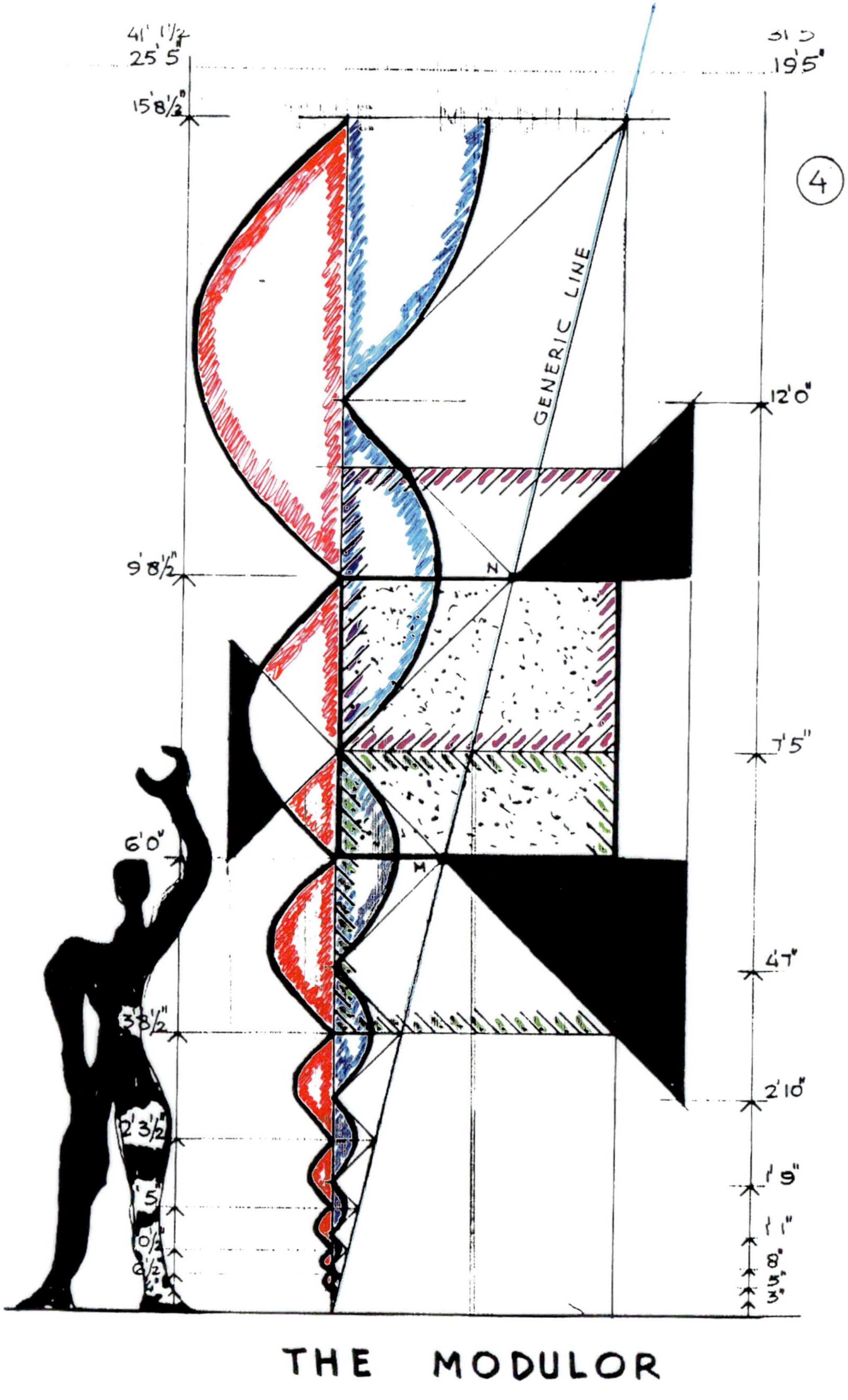
25'5"
19'5"
15'8½"
4
GENERIC LINE
12'0"
9'8½"
N
7'5"
6'0"
M
4'7"
3'8½"
2'10"
2'3½"
1'9"
1'1"
8"
5"
3"
THE MODULOR

Modulor studies (left and below) **with the important "variations"** (following pages) **adopted by Prakash**; these drawings were made by Prakash for an illustrative lecture on the Modulor using overhead projections, APF

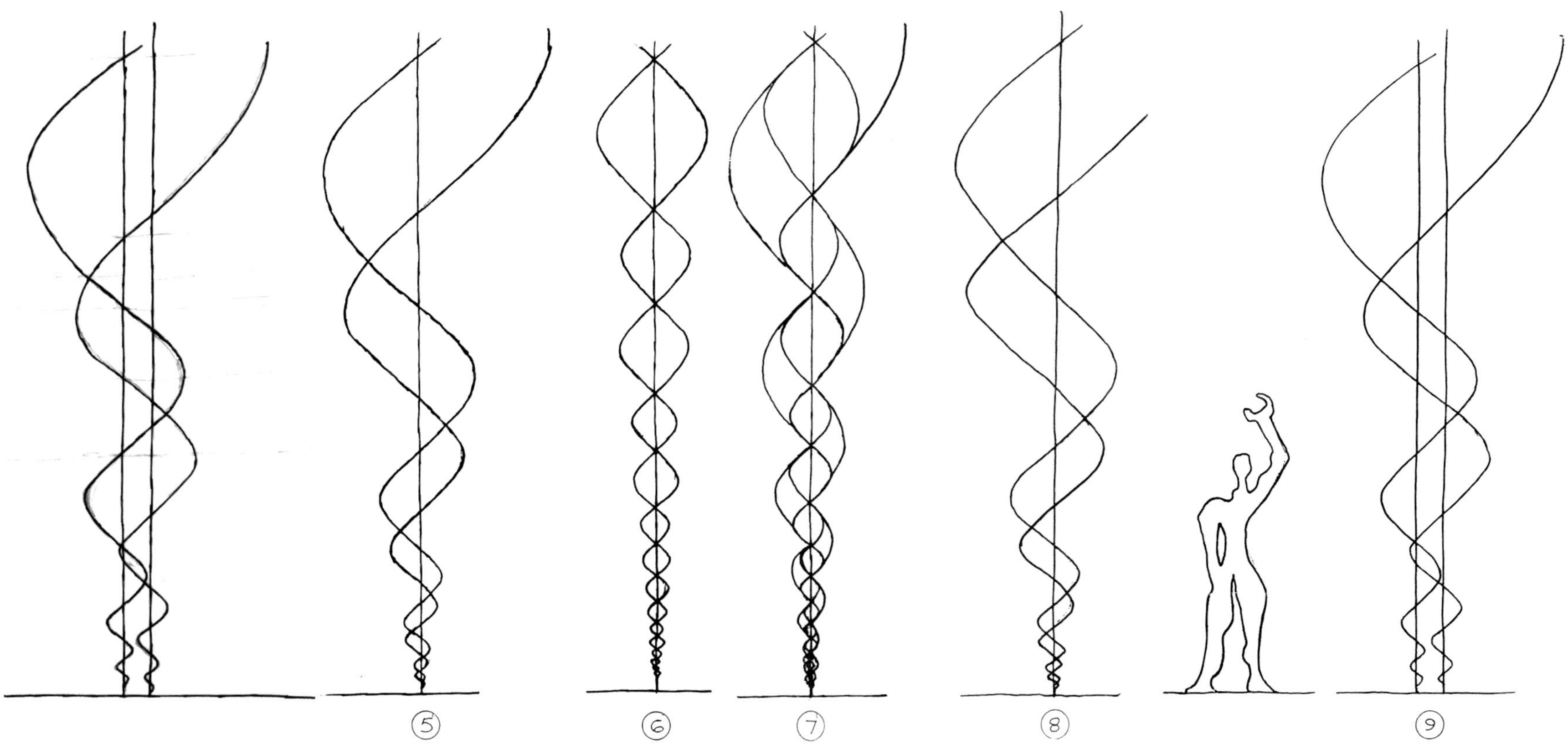

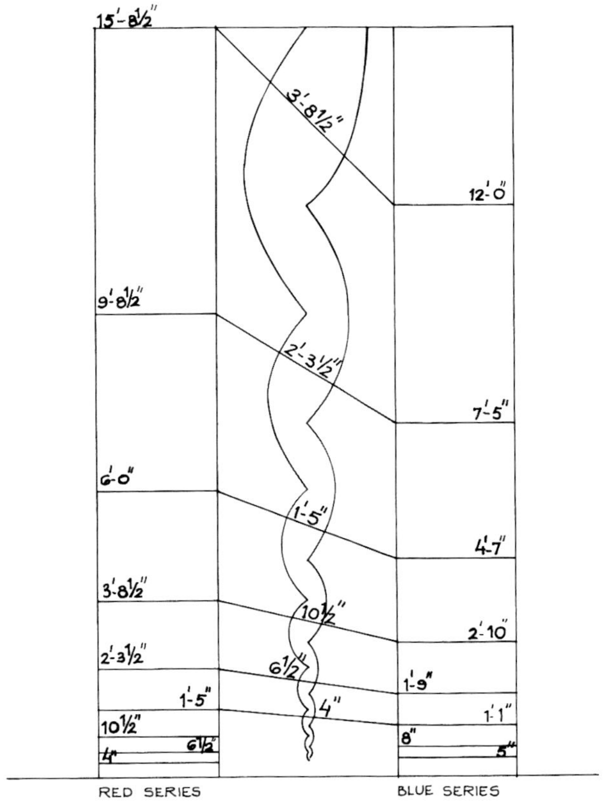

SUBTRACTION OF DIMENSIONS IN TWO SERIES STILL RESULTS IN MODULOR DIMENSIONS

SOME DIMENSIONS WHICH DO NOT FIND PLACE IN EITHER SERIES MAY USEFULLY BE INCLUDED AS VARIATIONS

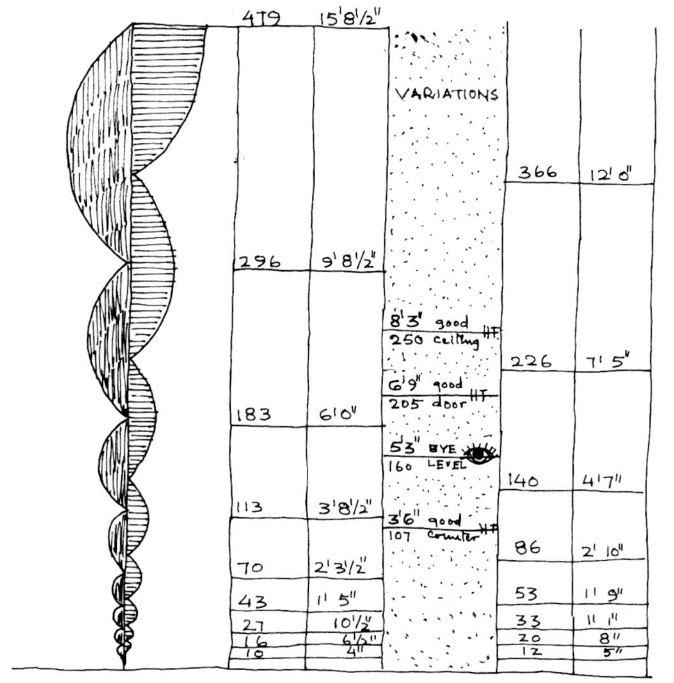

VARIATION TO MODULOR DIMENSIONS.

18.4.68

SUM OF ANY TWO SUCCESSIVE DIMENSIONS IN ANY SERIES IS EQUAL TO THE NEXT HIGHER DIMENSION IN THAT SERIES

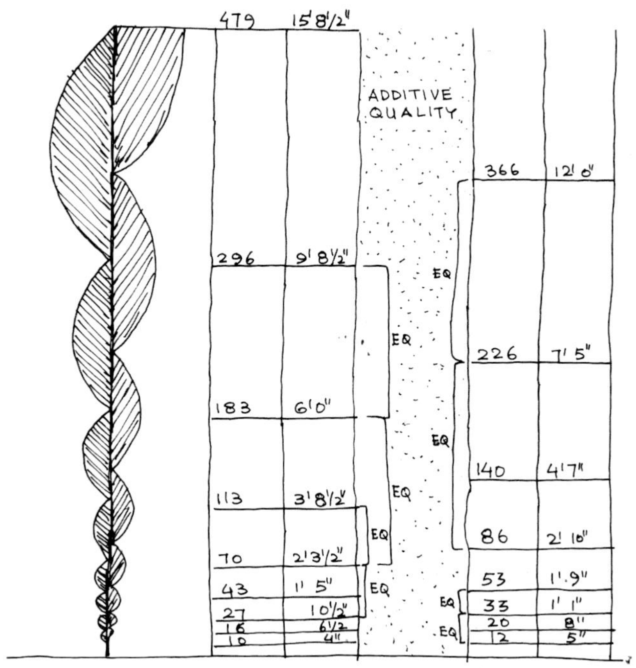

SOME CHARACTERSTICS OF MODULOR DIMENSIONS

18.4.68

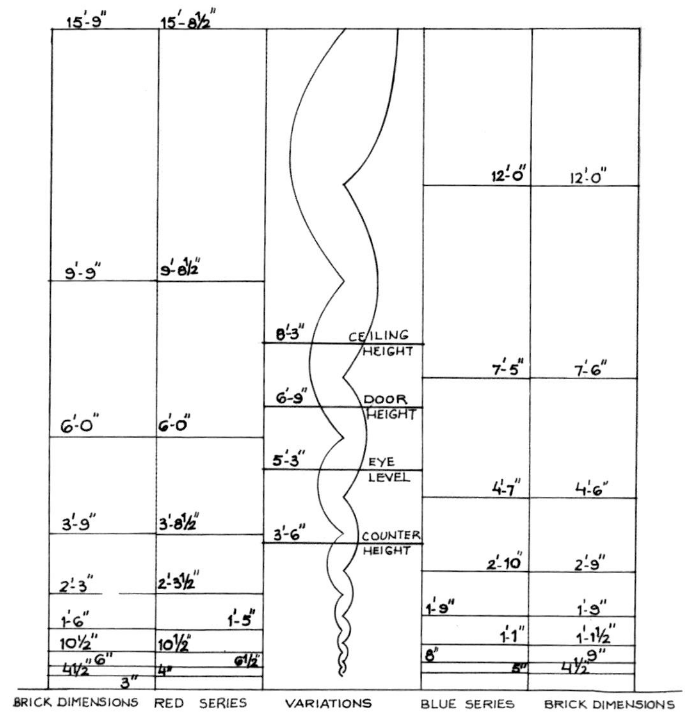

DIMENSIONS ADOPTED IN CHANDIGARH TO SUIT THE BRICK DIMENSIONS AND SOME VARIATIONS

Scan image with the **BooksPlus** app

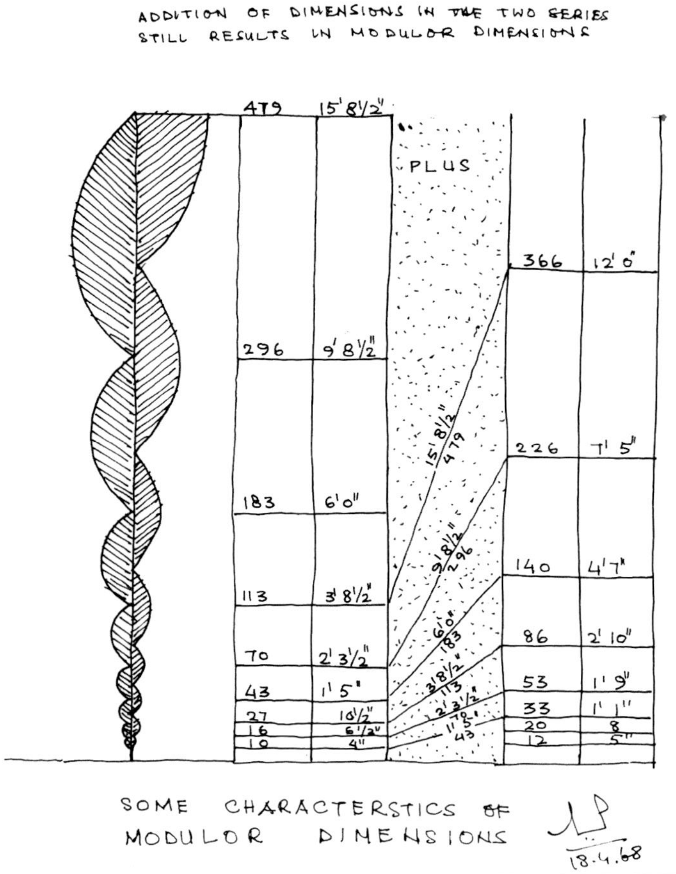
ADDITION OF DIMENSIONS IN THE TWO SERIES
STILL RESULTS IN MODULOR DIMENSIONS
PLUS
SOME CHARACTERSTICS OF
MODULOR DIMENSIONS
18.4.68

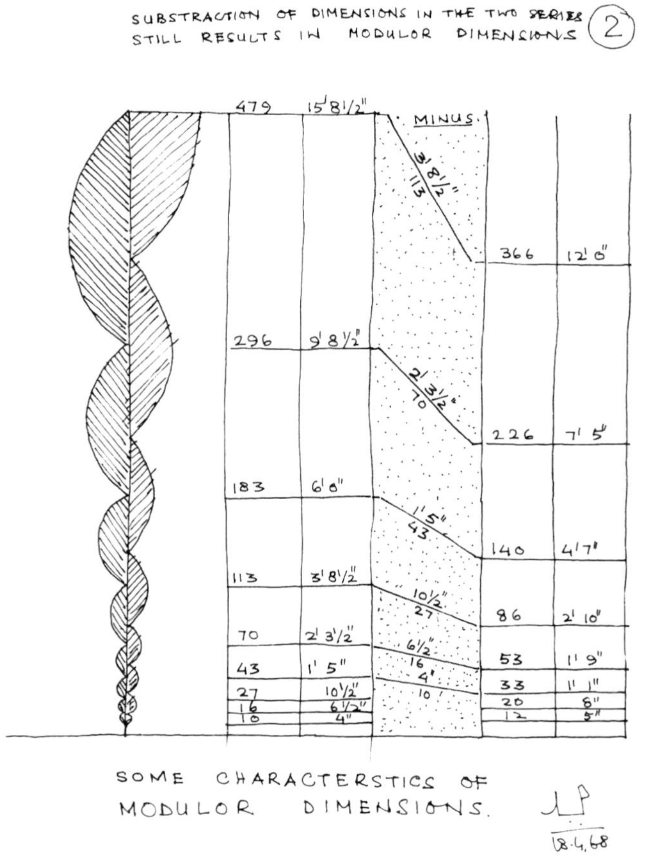
SUBSTRACTION OF DIMENSIONS IN THE TWO SERIES
STILL RESULTS IN MODULOR DIMENSIONS
2
MINUS
SOME CHARACTERSTICS OF
MODULOR DIMENSIONS.
18.4.68

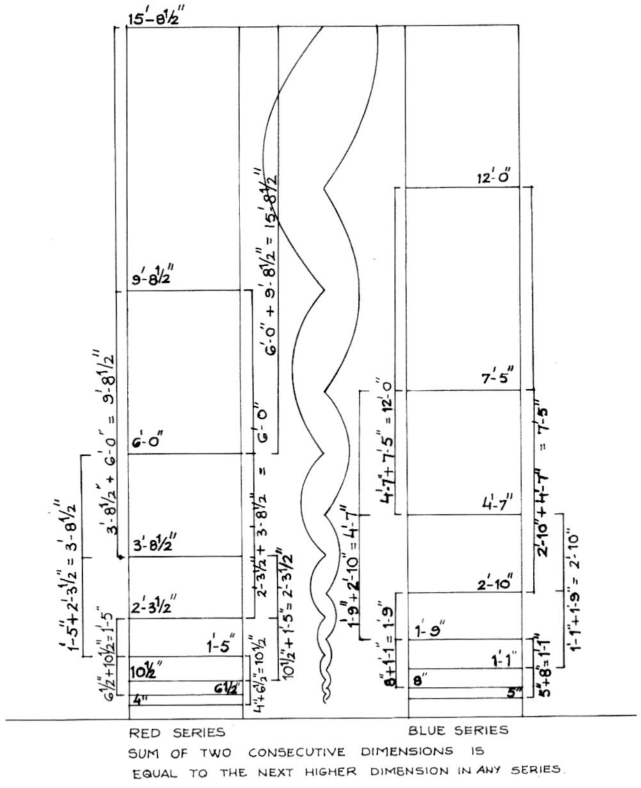
RED SERIES
BLUE SERIES
SUM OF TWO CONSECUTIVE DIMENSIONS IS
EQUAL TO THE NEXT HIGHER DIMENSION IN ANY SERIES.

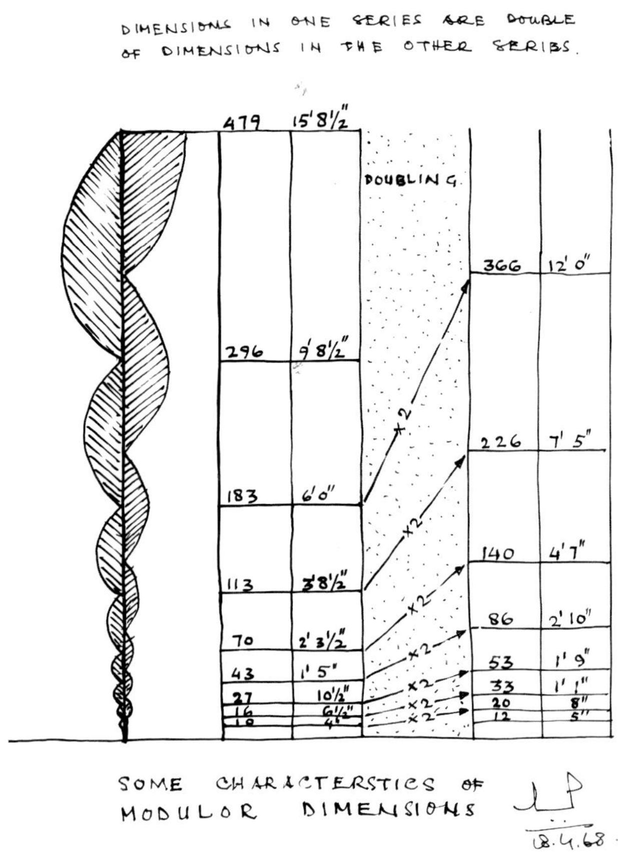
DIMENSIONS IN ONE SERIES ARE DOUBLE
OF DIMENSIONS IN THE OTHER SERIES.
DOUBLING
SOME CHARACTERSTICS OF
MODULOR DIMENSIONS
18.4.68

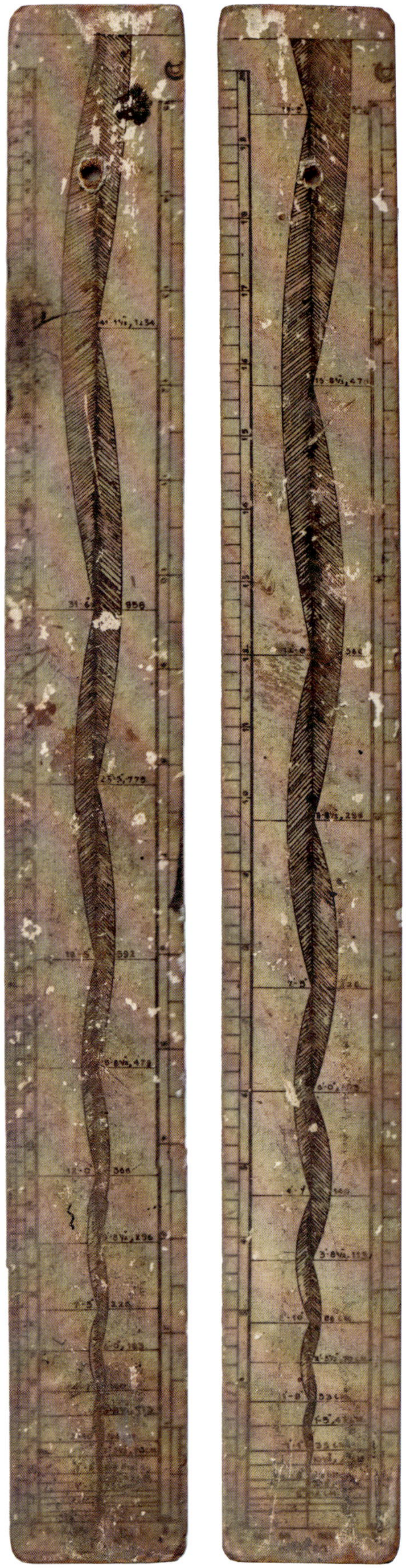

Scale based on Modulor, handmade by Prakash, APF

Cover design by Prakash, APF

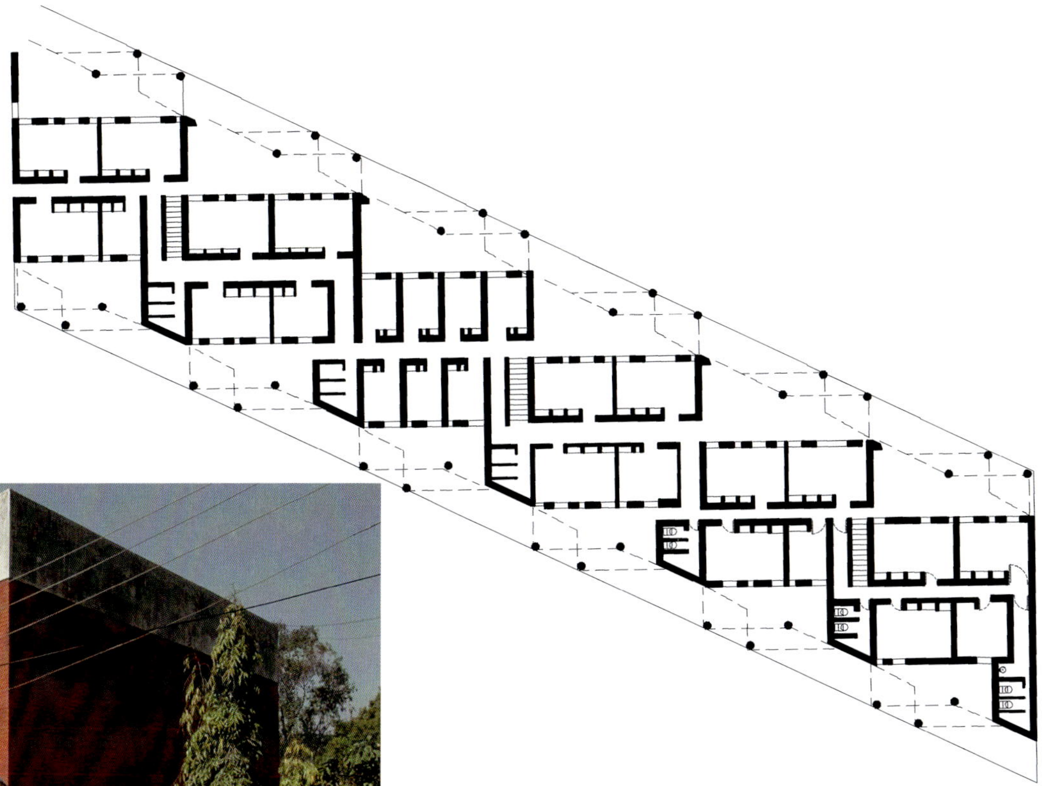

Corbu House, boys' hostel, Chandigarh College of Architecture, APF and Photo courtesy Ariadna Garreta

For the Chandigarh College of Architecture, Prakash also designed a boys' hostel, named Corbu House. This was accompanied by a dining hall that, using the British military nomenclature as is still the norm in India, was known, without irony, as the "Corbu Mess". Corbu House was Prakash's attempt at reinterpreting the Jeanneret-Mathur Chandigarh hostel grammar. But rather than a straight line, Prakash made the central, doubly loaded corridor zig-zag down the building. This enabled him to develop unusually large, solar-protected, outdoor sleeping balconies with rooms that still have access to direct daylighting. Against the norms of efficiency, Prakash supported each set of balconies with its own free-standing column. This set up an alternating double- and triple-height free-standing columns which made for an actively playful facade, unusual in Chandigarh's austere urban landscape. A thick parapet band at the roofline tied the whole structure together.

Distant view of Tagore Theatre exterior (below), **juxtaposed with Le Corbusier's Miracle Box sketch** (right), APF

Tagore Theatre

The crowning moment of Prakash's tenure at the Capital Project Office arrived when he was assigned to design Tagore Theatre for the centenary celebrations of the nationalist literary laureate, Rabindranath Tagore. The structure had to be readied within a year. A site had been quickly created at the centre of Sector 18, carved out of an institutional plot. Jeanneret had outlined a design, but when he saw a sketch proposal from Prakash, the former immediately liked it and put aside his own design without even sharing it.[39] Prakash immersed himself in the theatre's design with abandon. Besides being the largest commission he had yet received, it brought a set of diverse interests together for him—his love for the theatre, his fascination with acoustics, his history with the Royal Festival Hall and his interest in Rabindranath Tagore and the Santiniketan school of painters, in particular Jamini Roy. Until the end of his life, Prakash thought of Tagore Theatre as his signature work of architecture.

Tagore Theatre's form was generated from the plan—two 80-feet squares interlocked at the corner, with the stage straddling the intersection. One square was for the audience and the other for the actors and their props. The plan was extruded to make the elevation, its defining visual element, a massive window-less unadorned exterior load-bearing brick wall. Le Corbusier's unbuilt design for the *Boîte à Miracle* (the Miracle Box) may have been a reference, for its window-less big box design bears remarkable similarity to that of the completed Tagore Theatre. But then Tagore Theatre also repeats Prakash's design of the auditorium in his 1951 ARIBA thesis.

By Prakash's own telling, his design derived entirely from the precise analysis of acoustics, sightlines and the ergonomics of the human body. All the materials of the theatre, every detail of the structure, all the infrastructure, the red and yellow curtains, the broad swoop of the thrust stage—everything, in Prakash's retelling, was designed to conform to the modernist orthodoxy that form must follow function.

Tagore Theatre exterior with continuation lines drawn by Prakash in photo album, APF

Famous photograph of model of Tagore Theatre site with roof held up by Giani Rattan Singh, the modeller of the Capital Project, APF

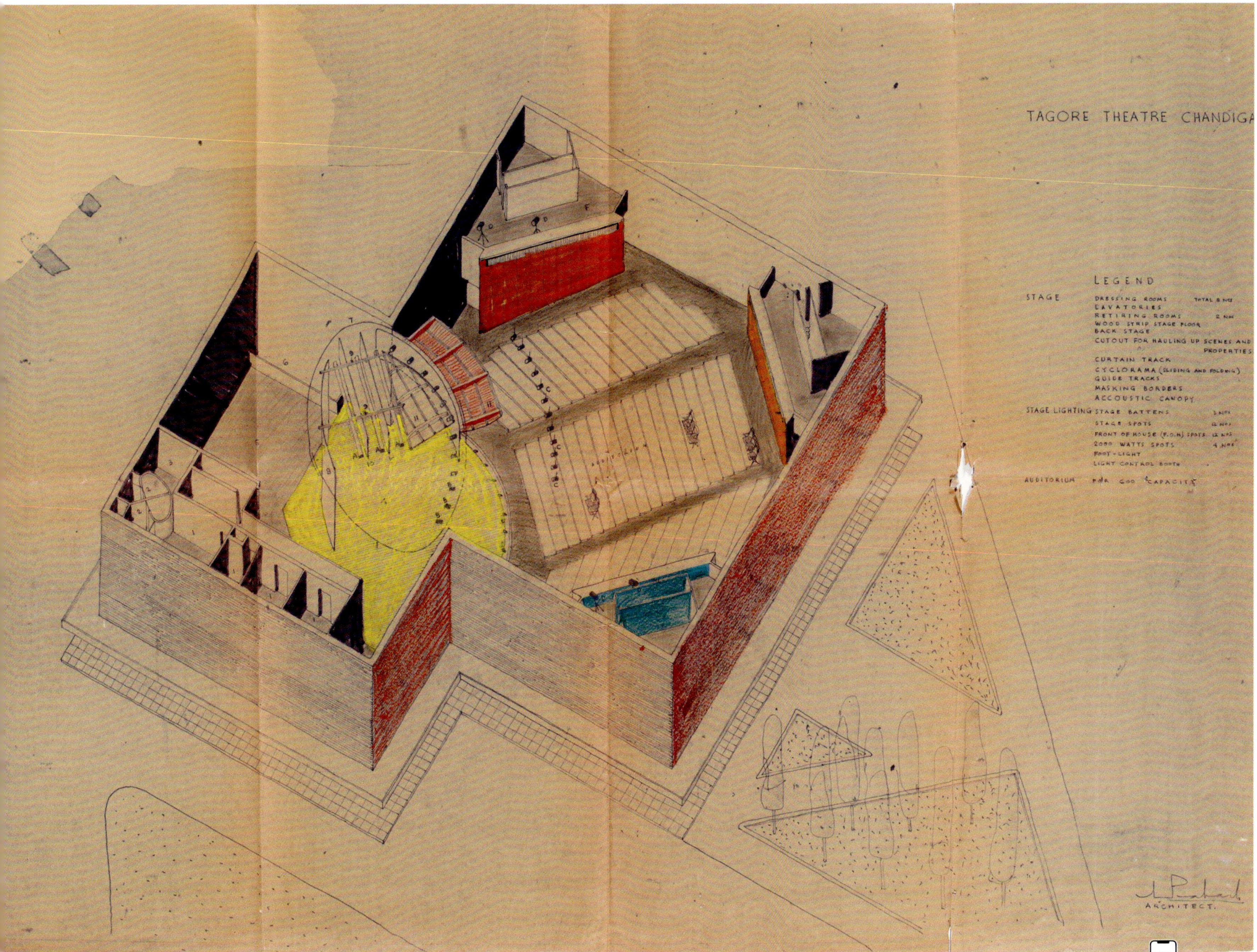

Scan image with the **BooksPlus** app

Tagore Theatre axonometric view, blueprint hand-coloured by Prakash to study interior, APF

View of auditorium from the stage; the original "space-frame" roof is partially visible, APF

Stairs to the auditorium at the Tagore Theatre, APF

View of the corridor, APF

Perforated acoustic panelled wall, APF

In the Tagore Theatre, the entire experience was in the interior space.[40] The exterior wall, like shrink wrapping, was there just because an enclosure was required.[41] Prakash was careful to avoid the experience of the Royal Festival Hall, whose acoustics were considered to be too perfect with insufficient reverberation. He designed the end walls, the reflective canopy and the overall dimensions to ensure that a single actor standing anywhere on the stage could be heard clearly at the furthest seat without amplification, while music and complex sounds maintained richness of tone. Prakash's anxiety to get this right knew no bounds. He consulted a variety of acoustic engineers, and after the Theatre was built he invited an independent acoustic engineer to objectively measure all the qualities of sound. The resultant paper, published in the *Indian Concrete Journal* in 1965, gave the Theatre high marks, and the lead author of the paper, Dr. M. Pancholy became a lifelong friend of Prakash's.[42]

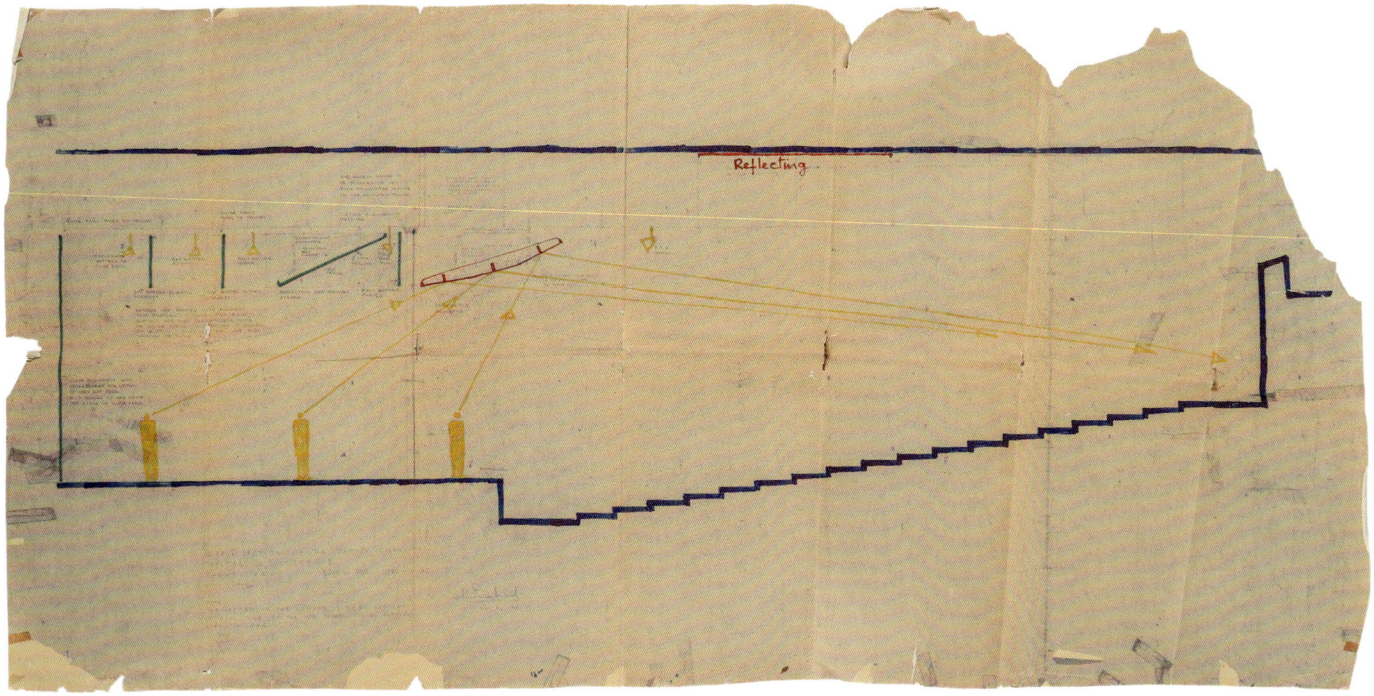

A colour-coded section illustrating how the acoustic canopy functioned, APF

Auditorium interior, Tagore Theatre, APF

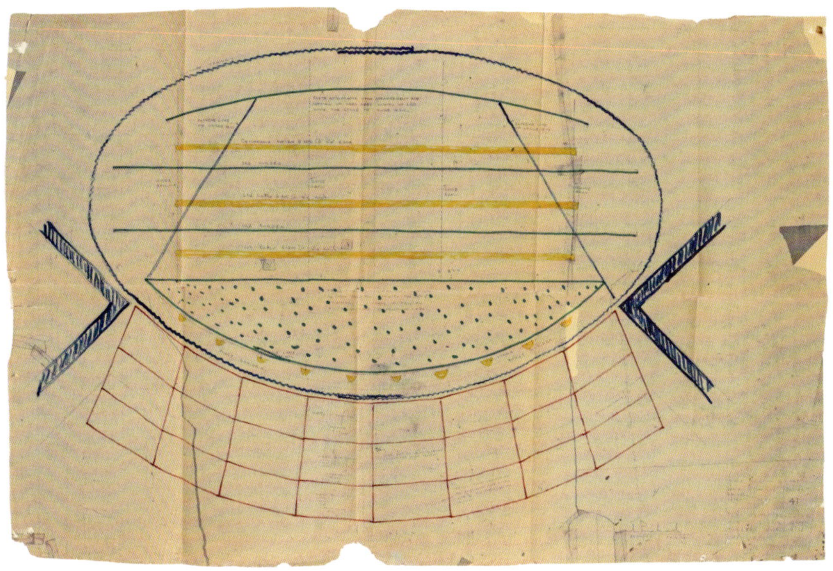

Stage plan in colour

Top view of the model revealing arrangement of two dissimilar squares overlapping at the stage, Tagore Theatre, APF

One of Prakash's great joys about being able to author Tagore Theatre was that it enabled him to engage with the world of theatrical personalities. Prakash had consulted with Prithviraj Kapoor, the patron of Bombay's Prithvi Theatre and arguably the most famous Indian film star of his time, on the design of the Theatre and he became a lifelong friend, showing up frequently in the architect's house unannounced. Similarly, the Bombay theatre actor Zul Vellani, whose troupe put up Tagore's play *Dak Ghar* (The Post Office) as the inaugural performance at Tagore Theatre, regularly started showing up in Chandigarh and Prakash's house, to talk theatre and life.[43] Vellani's wife Nimmo was from Nilokheri, a small town not far from Chandigarh, where the two of them were establishing a rural theatre workshop. This brought them frequently to Punjab, and to Chandigarh. Other film and theatre personalities that Tagore Theatre brought into Prakash's life included Chetan Anand, Priya Rajvansh and Balwant Gargi.

In the end, Tagore Theatre, though connected to many of "Chandigarh style's" concepts and convictions, did not look like any other structure in the city. It was a distinctive work, by a man seeking to establish himself as an independent thinker, which was a daily struggle, surrounded as he was by a plethora of strong-willed individuals organized by a strictly hierarchical pecking order.

Scan image with the **BooksPlus** app

Propped open roof of the theatre resembling a grand piano during a presentation, APF

Colour plan with seating

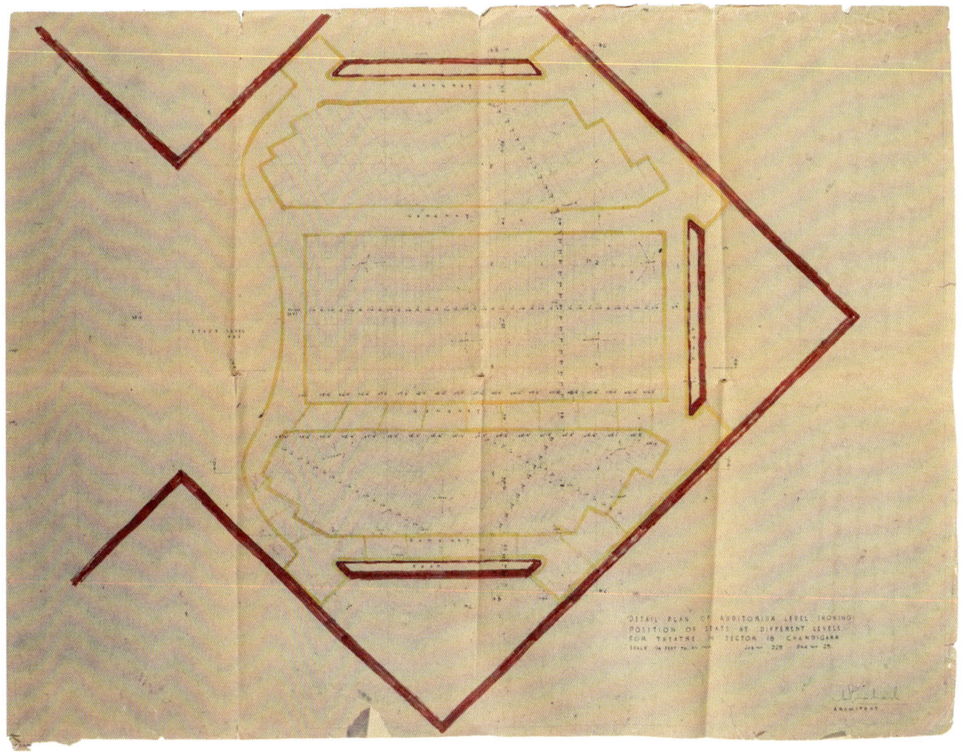

Plan view: Tagore Theatre model, APF

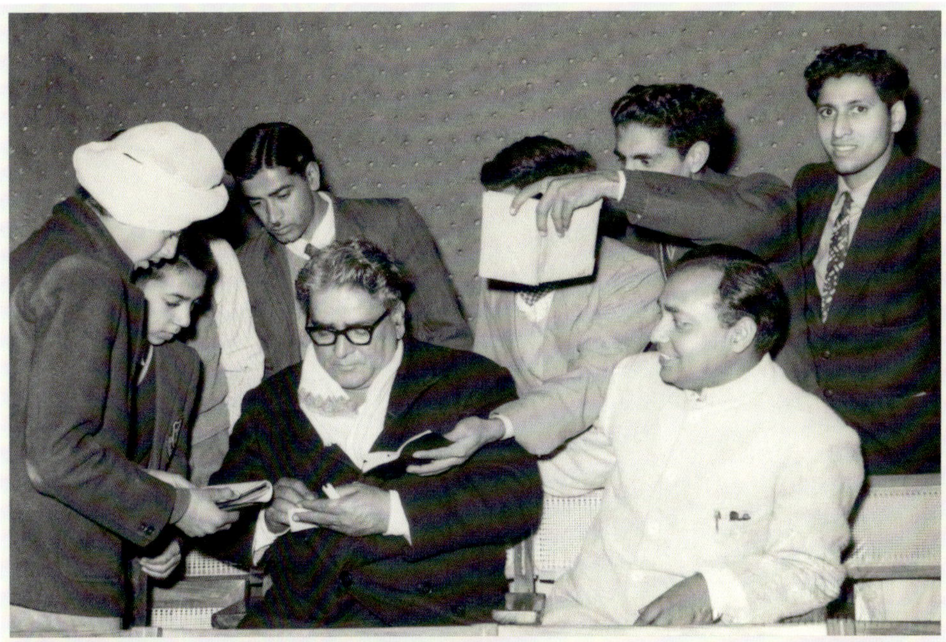

Prakash and renowned actor Prithviraj Kapoor at Tagore Theatre, APF

Prakash presenting the model of the Indo-Swiss Training Centre to Chief Minister Partap Singh Kairon, along with Swiss experts, APF

Structure and its Expression

In general, Chandigarh's modernist vocabulary presumed "honesty" in the expression of structure and materials, i.e. they were to be left exposed as is and not covered over or clad.[44] Fry and Drew certainly felt that the Chandigarh buildings should be plastered and painted white; from their experience, this added to the thermal performance of the structure and contributed to the modernist "look" of the building. Pierre Jeanneret left the exteriors of his buildings exposed, but completely plastered the interiors, and carefully developed techniques to conceal all the plumbing so that it would not interfere with the clean look of the building. Le Corbusier left his concrete as naked as possible using the shuttering pattern as its organic ornament.

Exploring new structural possibilities was a passion with Prakash.[45] In 1959, before he was assigned Tagore Theatre, Prakash had designed the Indo-Swiss Training Centre, a technical institute for which the expertise was supplied by the Swiss government. Leading the Swiss team was a Mr. Lenzlinger, an engineer from Zurich.

Model of the Indo-Swiss Training Centre, APF

Entrance cantilever, Indo-Swiss Training Centre, 1958, APF

For this building Prakash wanted a folded-plate structure for the roof, to bring north light into the workshops. Lenzlinger immediately supported the idea, and the Indian engineer on the job, J. S. Gill, took on the challenge to figure out how to pour the slab at 45° and still have a clean finish with minimal 'slumping', so that it could be left exposed. The process developed in the Indo-Swiss Training Centre was then repeated in several other buildings of Chandigarh such as the Textbook Press in the Industrial Area and the Industrial Training Institute in Sector 28. Later, Prakash would use the engineering innovations developed with the Swiss for his buildings in Ludhiana as well.[46]

When it came time for the structural design of Tagore Theatre, Prakash specified a bi-directional space frame for the roof structure, given that the plan was a square. Space frames were new and had never been attempted in Chandigarh before then. But when the structural drawings came in, he realized that the engineers had simply designed a steel truss in one direction, and then added in equivalent-looking struts in the other direction to make it look like a space frame! This battle Prakash lost to the engineers.

The same sleight-of-hand was deployed in the construction of Prakash's designs for his cinema halls, the Neelam and KC theatres. Both were conceived as cylindrical shells, with Prakash trying to marry his acoustic and structural interests. In both cases, which were privately executed, the engineers, and presumably the owners, refused to take on the risk and the learning curve that thin-shell construction involved. They spanned them with tried and tested trusses instead, and only made the exteriors look like shells.[47]

***Janj Ghar* (marriage hall)**, Chandigarh, 1962, APF

Indo-Swiss Training Centre, 1958, APF

Exterior of the Indo-Swiss Training Centre, 1958, APF

Such negotiations between making things "look" modern and having them "be" modern were not limited to Prakash's works. They defined the relationship between the engineers and the architects, and were negotiated daily. Despite Nehru's explicit decision to hire outside expertise to build Chandigarh, the Capital Project Office only brought in architectural and town planning experts, leaving all the engineering in local hands. The Indian engineers and the Indian Administrative Services officers in charge of the project were both trained in colonial institutions and considered themselves up to the task. The Roorkee College of Engineering, where most of them trained, was a fine institution, but their pragmatic ethos sought the most expedient structural ways to build things to both "look" and "perform", with no necessary causality between the two.[48]

Later in life, Prakash would often recall a significant moment of tension connected to structure and its expression: whether or not the steel truss of the Tagore Theatre roof should be covered over with an artificial ceiling. It was not required for acoustic purposes, so Prakash was opposed to it. "We cover our bones with skin," P. L. Varma, the chief engineer reportedly insisted, arguing his point to Jeanneret. Although Jeanneret was usually supportive of Prakash's designs, he deferred to the senior Varma and asked Prakash to reconsider. But Prakash persuaded Le Corbusier to visit the theatre under construction to settle the matter, and he summarily ruled in Prakash's favour, without any explanation.[49] "Do you want a signed certificate from me?" Le Corbusier offered. "No thank you, Monsieur," replied Prakash, "Your word is my certificate," and thus it was decided. In the mid-1980s, three decades after it was built, a local bureaucrat decided to install a false ceiling beneath Tagore Theatre's truss anyway.

Prakash attending a play at Tagore Theatre, c. 1982, APF

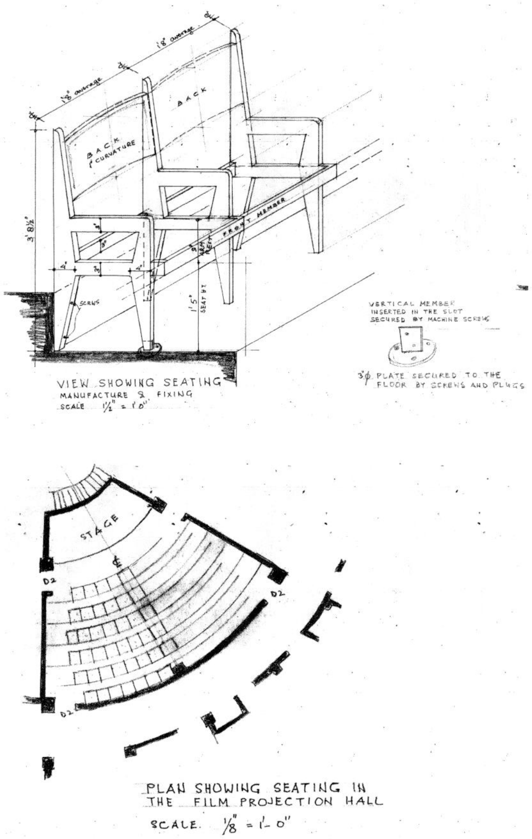

Furniture design drawings by Prakash, APF

Furniture

Prakash also designed the furniture for Tagore Theatre. A routine expectation of the Capital Project in the 1950s was that architects would have to also design all the required furnishings for their buildings. This was the cheapest way to furnish buildings, for ready-mades were very expensive when compared to on-site work employing local carpenters. In this sense, furniture design was simply a part of the process of detailing the building.

Under Jeanneret's leadership, the architects borrowed from his and Charlotte Perriand's collaborations in wood furniture design—that occurred mostly late in the 1930s well after Perriand had left Le Corbusier's atelier—and reinvented them to suit the local conditions of production and use in Chandigarh. This meant first of all designing for local construction techniques and materials. The local furniture shops were skilled, but relied on a handful of joinery details that could be executed by hand. Cost was the paramount consideration, and materials constituted the lion's share of the overall cost.[50] Hard woods were prohibitively expensive, and teaks were reserved only for the most important pieces. The "luxury" factor of the designs lay in an interpretation of ergonomics and the preservation of a modernist "look." Like the trusses used to hold up "shells," Jeanneret's furniture was made to look modern, but was crafted simply and reliably.[51]

Prakash studied the section of the chair for Tagore Theatre by drawing it at full size on one of his office walls that he had painted with blackboard paint (presumably imitating a similarly painted wall in Le Corbusier's atelier in Paris). Micro changes required complete re-drawing. The goal: to enable spectators to pay attention to the performance and be "comfortable", but not so comfortable that they would fall asleep—a kind of somatic ergonomics![52]

Eventually, Prakash designed several chairs and tables, most of which drew from Chandigarh's modernist vocabulary. Chairs for the living and dining rooms, side and centre tables and even a dressing vanity went through their full-size vetting process on the blackboard. One of his best designs, however, came out of his own idiosyncratic interests in the form generative possibilities of the continuous line. Looking for a cheap way to make an outdoor lawn chair

Tagore Theatre chair drawn full size on wall painted with blackboard paint in Prakash's office at the Capital Planning Office, Chandigarh, 1963, APF

Continuous line bent steel chair designed by Prakash, photograph by the author

Dining chair designed by Prakash, photograph by the author

Lounge chair by Prakash, photograph by the author

for personal use, Prakash designed a chair that was made by repeatedly bending and welding a single 5mm steel rod. Deftly, the rectangle of the back of the chair slid down to make the legs which returned upward to form the seat before swivelling down again to form the intermediate reinforcing members. A few small pieces had to be added at the end to close the loop at a couple of places and to ensure long-term structural strength; but the 'miracle' of watching how one continuous rod of steel could be made to turn and spin to generate a complete chair never ceased to bring joy to Prakash.

Side tables with paintings by Prakash, photograph by the author

NOTES

1 For another account of the early days of the Chandigarh Capital Project see Sharma, M. N. (2016) *Making of Chandigarh: Le Corbusier and After Chandigarh*, India; Chandigarh Administration.

2 "Chandigarh - In Retrospect", *APFA D17, p.16*.

3 See Prakash's journal entries from late 1952, particularly of December 11, 1952. *Collins Royal One Day Diary 1952 APFA AP Journals*.

4 Oral conversation with my mother, Savitri Prakash, July 2017.

5 Sahgal, N. (1969). *Storm in Chandigarh*. New Delhi, India; New York: W. W. Norton.

6 Varma's retirement in 1956 was an event much feared by the architects. His replacement could completely upset the balance. By some reckoning, their fears were not unfounded.

7 The housing is beautifully documented in Joshi, K. (1999). *Documenting Chandigarh: The Indian architecture of Pierre Jeanneret, Edwin Maxwell Fry, Jane Beverly Drew*. Ahmedabad, India: Mapin Publishing; Chandigarh College of Architecture.

8 A. R. Prabhawalkar was often considered to be the 'favourite' of Le Corbusier, and this caused a lot of friction. See my discussion with Maristella Casciato in "The Life and Work of Pierre Jeanneret with Maristella Casciato" *ArchitectureTalk* Podcast, architecturetalk.org, published January 3, 2018. See also: "Chandigarh—In Retrospect", c. 1975, *APFA D17*.

9 Aditya Prakash notes this in his journal entry of November 1, 1952.

10 Based on my conversation with P. L. Luthra, June 2017.

11 For more discussion on women architects of India see Woods, M. N. (2016), *Women architects in India: Histories of practice in Mumbai and Delhi*. Taylor and Francis, and Desai, M. (2016), *Women architects and modernism in India: Narratives and contemporary practices (Visual & media histories)*. Milton Park, Abingdon, Oxon: Routledge, Taylor & Francis Group, and

12 There is a great photograph of her with Aditya Prakash and P. L. Varma, standing beneath the Open Hand Monument, which was published in the local newspaper.

13 Typewritten noted by Aditya Prakash dated 6th November 1996, *APFA Img_7232*.

14 I imagine that an allusion to the MARS group that hosted the CIAM Summer Schools is inevitable here. The International CIAM Summer School was held in London in 1949, when Aditya Prakash was living there, and Maxwell Fry attended, though there is no record of it in the APF Archives.

15 "On behalf of the Modern Architects Club" *APFA D14*.

16 The APF Archives do contain one line drawing, published under the name of the "Modern Architects Club" for a Typical Primary School. It identifies A. Prakash and R. Bose as the architects. It has an inverted swastika-shaped plan, centred on an open-to-sky courtyard. I have not been able to conclusively identify who were the official members of this Club, though I assume that the entire architectural team was.

17 Prakash wrote about Le Corbusier's disinterest in the "academic spirit" but support of CCA, and the mission of CCA in "Le Corbusier and Later Development in Chandigarh" (1988) *APFA D16*.

18 "Chandigarh—In Retrospect", *APFA D17, p.21*. Until 1960, Pierre Jeanneret, like Le Corbusier, worked on yearly contracts. In 1960, the chief architect and chief town planner's offices were established as permanent post in the Government of Punjab, with Jeanneret as head of both.

19 For this discussion see Weber, N. (2008). *Le Corbusier: A life*. New York: Alfred A. Knopf.

20 As described by Prakash in "Chandigarh—In Retrospect", *APFA D17, p.20*. Amongst others, Shivdatt Sharma also specifically identified Jeanneret as his mentor. See Prakash, V., & Sharma, Shivdatt. (2012). *The Architecture of Shivdatt Sharma* (Modernism in India series). Ahmedabad: Mapin Publishing. Jeanneret had his bones and ashes after cremation immersed in Sukhna Lake, not only so that he could permanently be enjoined to Chandigarh, but also as an embrace of the Hindu tradition by which the ashes after cremation are to be immersed in water, preferably that of the river Ganges. In this sense, Jeanneret adopted Sukhna Lake as his modern Ganges.

21 By "Chandigarh style" I am referring to the architectural vocabulary established by Jeanneret, Fry and Drew, in the early 1950s as used for all the government housing and official buildings. Later, this vocabulary was of course also used widely in the private housing in Chandigarh as well, which can be considered to be an extended manifestation of the "Chandigarh style".

22 "K.C. Theatre" APFA D109.

23 It is interesting to speculate if the curve of KC Theatre was inspired by the controversy around the external curve of the Royal Festival Hall in London that appeared to be informed by acoustic consideration but was actually not. Although not actually built as it was supposed to have been, the upper "roof" part of the curve of KC Theatre was intended to be the actual acoustic curve of the roof, which was then continued down to the ground.

24 "K.C. Theatre" *APFA D109*.

25 "Reminiscences of Le Corbusier" 1 Oct. 1987, APFA D16.

26 "Lessons from Chandigarh" c. 1985, *APFA D16*.

27 *A+D* Magazine, April-May 1985, New Delhi, p.46-7.

28 The Modulor was Le Corbusier's system of proportions based on the right-angle, golden proportion and the Fibonacci series. Le Corbusier had published his first book on the Modulor (1948) just before the Chandigarh project started, and the second, which contained a section on the Capitol Complex, came out in 1955. Le Corbusier used the Modulor dimensions everywhere in his own projects and strongly suggested that it be used the default system of dimensioning in all designs executed by the Capital Project Office. Le Corbusier published *Le Modulor* in 1948, followed by *Modulor 2* in 1955, both in French. They were first published in English as *The Modulor* in 1954 and *Modulor 2 (Let the User Speak Next)* in 1958.

29 Aditya Prakash often narrated an alleged incident when Le Corbusier was looking for his measuring tape and could not find it and so Prakash lent him his own. When Prakash went to ask for it back the next day, Le Corbusier denied any knowledge of it and retorted—"Are you accusing me of being a thief?"—as he dismissed Prakash.

30 "Art in Architecture" 13 January 1986, *APFA D6b*

31 The noted postcolonial critic Gayatri C. Spivak directly criticized this persistence of "guruvada" in the Chandigarh culture when she came for the *Theatres of Decolonization* conference in 1995. See Gayatri Chakravorty Spivak "City, Country, Agency" in Prakash, V. (1997). *Theatres of decolonization: (architecture), agency, (urbanism): Proceedings: The second "Other Connections" Conference: Chandigarh, India, January 6—10, 1995*. Seattle, Wash.: Office of the Dean, College of Architecture and Urban Planning, University of Washington.

32 Late in Prakash's tenure at Chandigarh College of Architecture there were a series of strikes by the students in the late 1970s which, in spite of the general context of political unrest in the country at that time, have to be interpreted as a rejection of his administration.

33 "Art in Architecture" 13 January 1986, *APFA D6b*

34 For a detailed documentation of Chandigarh's entire system of construction and frame control see Bakshi, I.J.S. (2002) *Chandigarh: Aesthetic Legislation: Documentation of Urban Controls in Chandigarh (1951-2001)* Chandigarh: Chandigarh College of Architecture.

35 Prakash, Aditya "Architectural Control—Shops, Flats, etc." *Marg: A Magazine of the Arts*, Mumbai, Vol XV No 1, December 1961, pp. 39-41. This was a landmark issue of *Marg*, as it was the first full-length publication on Chandigarh, and contained writings by almost all the primary architects and planners who worked on the city.

36 Of course, the idea of urban street facade control was not original as such. Even Haussman's new streets of Paris in the mid-19th century were effectively frame controlled. Urban preservation movements in Europe in the mid-century also championed a kind of frame control.

37 Prakash specifically notes that it had Le Corbusier's permission in the address he prepared for the 25th anniversary celebrations of CCA in 1986. See: "Random Thoughts on Architectural Education," *APFA D6b*.

38 I am thinking here of the argument outlined by Tzonis and Lefaivre in the 1960s, though they did not publish on it until much later. See Lefaivre, L., & Tzonis, Alexander. (2003). *Critical regionalism: Architecture and identity in a globalized world* (Architecture in focus). Munich; New York: Prestel.

Another way to interpret Prakash's Indian-Modulor can be found in the core differences between Western and Indian classical music. While Western music works with a strictly defined scale, and a broadly recognized pattern that inevitably circles back to its origin, Indian classical music derives from an infinite series of shifts from a nominal standard, depending on the instrument, the type of music, and even the musicians and their various schools of music. Variation or regionalization, in other words, is the only standard in Indian classical music, an idea that has yet to find its full appreciation. Credit to Eashan Chaufla for this observation.

39 See Prakash's description of this event in "Mere Jeevan Ka Chamatkaar," *APFA D3b*.

40 See "Tagore Theatre" *APFA D18*. Other than the broad sweep of the thrust stage, surprisingly there were no curves in Tagore Theatre. Unlike KC and Neelam theatres,

Tagore Theatre was not derived from a section. The self-imposed expectations of the structure's design perhaps did not permit Prakash to explore the more sensuous aspects of his design thinking.

41 Prakash discusses the idea that the Tagore Theatre was "austere" on the exterior in part also not to compete with the "gaiety" on the interior. See "Form and Architecture," *APFA D1812*.

42 M. Pancholy, A. F. Chhapgar and Davinder Singh "Acoustics of the Tagore Theatre, Chandigarh" *The Indian Concrete Journal*, December 1965.

43 Aditya Prakash wanted to have Zul Vellani appointed as the director of Tagore Theatre. He made the case for him in a paper simply titled "Tagore Theatre" in which he noted, "I can only say that from amongst the performance done in the theatre recently, Shri Zul Vellani, who has established a theatre Centre at Nilokheri, sacrificing an attractive income from Cinema industry in Bombay, is the only man who showed [the] grit" for the job. *APFA D18*.

44 The expression of structure is an abiding discussion in twentieth-century modern architecture. In some cases, such episodes produce fascinating structures, as in Mies van de Rohe's German Pavilion in Barcelona, where, as Robin Evans discusses, the tension between the suggestion of structure in the cruciform steel columns, and its dissimulation—covered in reflective chrome—generates a fascinating sense of weightlessness and ethereality. But in other cases, it is dissimulation. See Evans, Robin "Mies van de Rohe's Paradoxical Symmetries" *AA Files* 19, London, 1990.

45 This may have its roots in the friendship he developed with Mr. (First Name Unknown) Iyer, the engineer who built the hyperbolic paraboloid of the Assembly building. While he was in Chandigarh building the Assembly paraboloid, he lived next door to Prakash, and became a good friend. Prakash always referred to his times with Mr. Iyer fondly.

46 The Indo-Swiss Training Centre has been significantly altered and the original structure is barely recognizable. But the ITI building by Prakash in Sector 28 in Chandigarh is well maintained and shows the how the rivers of light bathe the massive workshop space in light. "Technology and Chandigarh," *APFA D17*.

47 "In that," Aditya Prakash noted describing KC Theatre, "lies the cause of cracks appearing in its roof. A shell is always in compression and therefore does not crack" and thus does not leak. See complete discussion of structure and design in Chandigarh in Prakash's fascinating paper "Technology and Chandigarh," *APFA D17*.

48 Gargiani and Rossellini have also reported how once the Indian engineer offered to "improve" Le Corbusier's structural design, he chafed at their suggestion. Gargiani, R., Le Corbusier, Rossellini, Anna. (2011). *Le Corbusier: Béton brut and ineffable space, 1940—1965: Surface materials and psychophysiology of vision* (1st ed., Essays in architecture). Lausanne, Switzerland: Abingdon, Oxford; New York, NY: EFPL Press; Distributed by Routledge. In general, Le Corbusier carefully ensured that his buildings only used very basic structural techniques which could be faithfully expressed. He made the 'big' structural move to build the main hall of the Assembly as a hyperbolic-paraboloid only after he had seen one being built in Ahmedabad and was assured that the same contracting company would come and build the one for his Assembly. But there is the curious case of the 'arches' of the High Court. Whereas from the elevation they appear structural, designed to hold up the second roof of the building, they are in fact hung with steel rods from the upper roof. Perhaps Le Corbusier had envisaged some kind of a hyperbolic parabolic shell (perhaps based on the kinds of shells that Xenakis designed for the Brussels Pavilion, and of the kind he was developing for the roof of the Museum of Knowledge in the 1960s). The drawings in Chandigarh are vague about the intended structure; they certainly do not show the arches hung with steel rods; they seem to imply a shell. How the decision came to be made to hang them, remains to be researched.

49 "Reminiscences of Le Corbusier" 1 Oct. 1987, *APFA D16*.

50 This was true of all the building construction as well. Labour was a very small percentage of the overall cost, and land acquired via eminent domain was almost "free".

51 Which raises a question regarding the re-sale in auction of the same furniture in the recent past. The crudely made so-called "Jeanneret furniture" is completely re-constructed with new joinery and finishes in Swiss and French workshops before being sold as "originals." See the film titled "Provenance" by Amie Siegel. http://amiesiegel.net/project/provenance, accessed Tuesday, 6 February 2018.

52 As described by Aditya Prakash in "Form and Design: Analysis of the Process of Solving Problems of Architecture" *APFA D8_12*.

DESIGNING THE AGRICULTURAL REVOLUTION

The agricultural college, Ludhiana, aerial view, photograph by Prakash, APF

Prime Minister Jawaharlal Nehru visits Punjab Agricultural University, Chandigarh, c. 1964, APF

In 1961, India faced a severe food shortage, and closely avoided a famine by importing grains, largely from the United States. In response, Nehru's government refocused its agricultural policies, which until then had largely relied on land reform, and accepted an Eisenhower-backed proposal to boost agricultural production using "modern" techniques such as seed hybridization and widespread use of artificial pesticides and manures. Punjab, literally the Land of the Five Rivers and the breadbasket of the country, was designated the first state for this "scientific" transformation of agricultural production.

A central requirement of what came to be called the "Green Revolution" was the construction of three teaching and research universities in Punjab, first in Ludhiana and later in Palampur and Hissar.[1] Prakash was appointed the senior architect of these campuses. In the summer of 1963, he hurriedly handed off to Shivdatt Sharma[2] supervision of all of his Chandigarh projects and moved to Ludhiana.[3]

All three campuses were to be constructed as speedily as possible because a large staff of scientists and academics from American and Canadian universities (particularly Ohio State University) were to arrive imminently as part of the "technology transfer" agreement. Housing was urgently needed.[4] One of the first to be built was for the Prakashs, and as the families of the Western experts settled around them, the

Boys' Hostel, Ludhiana campus, photographed by Prakash from a low angle to establish a connection between the architecture and the wheat fields, c. 1965, APF

Aerial view of the hostel, photograph by Prakash, APF

neighbourhood began speaking more English than Hindi or Punjabi.[5]

Arguably, the best period of Prakash's professional life as an architect were his years in Ludhiana, from 1963 to 1968. Finally, he was the head of a significant project, equipped with a staff to execute his design ideas. Exposure to the technological impact of the Green Revolution galvanized his way of thinking about technology and urban design. And, perhaps most importantly, the opportunity to live in an old Indian city for the first time since 1947 provoked him to compare and contrast its performance and morphology to the planning ideas implemented in Chandigarh.[6]

Campus Planning and Design

Prakash's arrival in Ludhiana was not an easy one. P. N. Thapar, the erstwhile chief administrator of the Chandigarh Capital Project, had been appointed vice chancellor of this new Punjab Agricultural University (PAU) system. As Prakash later reported, Thapar was a boorish if effective administrator, and he was used to throwing his weight around to get things done.[7] The two immediately clashed. Prakash wanted to innovate on programming and forms, while Thapar insisted on simply replicating the Chandigarh designs for the sake of expediency and efficiency. A compromise was reached once Pierre Jeanneret agreed to approve all of Prakash's designs before they were executed. Eventually, however, Thapar became an ardent supporter of Prakash's ideas and, in 1969, at the end of his appointment, offered to make Prakash the head of the engineering wing of the campuses to keep him from moving back to Chandigarh, although this never came to pass.

A large parcel of agricultural land just outside the old city of Ludhiana had been taken over by the state, as at Chandigarh, via eminent domain. Here, the PAU campus developed in relative isolation within its walls. While the conceptual plan for the campus was prepared by Dr. Sutton from Ohio State University, who was the head of the technology transfer program, its specific layout, begun by M.N. Sharma and developed by Prakash, derived largely from the free-standing buildings in space institutional concepts of the modernist movement as applied at Punjab University in Chandigarh.

All the housing of PAU was based entirely on Chandigarh precedents, as required by Thapar. But the institutional buildings were designed

Entrance to the agricultural college in Ludhiana, photograph by Prakash, APF

Alternating balconies project out of the hostel complex of the Agricultural University, photograph by Prakash, APF

Hostel at the Punjab Agricultural University, Ludhiana, photograph by Prakash, APF

by Prakash in his own style. The first to be built was the Boys' Hostel, a building Prakash was clearly excited about since he photographed it extensively, including during a visit by Nehru.[8] In terms of formal elements, the Boys' Hostel was an iteration of the "Chandigarh style" elements—exposed load-bearing brick walls articulated by white-plastered panels, and held together by structurally expressive concrete columns and beams. Prakash's innovation here was ensuring that each balcony was open to the sky, an idea he had tried in the hostel for Chandigarh College of Architecture, and which later found resonance in the work of architects such as Charles Correa. A dining hall rotated 45° was connected to the hostel with a covered walkway.

The Agricultural Engineering College (AEC) was of course the main institutional building of the campus, originally intended to be modelled on the long, multi-storied block designed by Jeanneret and B. P. Mathur in the Chandigarh campus for Punjab University. Prakash sought to reinvent it, proposing a flat and wide single-story structure that built on his experience designing the Indo-Swiss Training Centre in Chandigarh. As usual, P. N. Thapar was opposed to Prakash's

The agricultural college interior court, photograph by Prakash, APF

Boys' Hostel model, photograph by Prakash, APF

Boys' Hostel, side view, photograph by Prakash, APF

reinvention, but this time Prakash got the backing of the chief agricultural scientist Dr. Sutton, which persuaded Thapar.

Prakash's design for AEC sought to modernize the concept of the open-to-sky pen accompanied with a small, covered shed that was typically built for animals adjacent to rural houses. Upgrading traditional India, rather than completely reinventing it was his "revolutionary" new idea, taken from what he believed at that time were the core principles of the Green Revolution. The resultant structure was completely self-enclosed, with no prospect towards the outside. The plan was organized around a series of alternating enclosed and open-to-sky courtyards. The exposed brick exterior walls of the AEC, like those of Tagore Theatre, were left unarticulated, except for a series of intentionally placed round openings, one per bay, created to exhaust the odours.

As with Tagore Theatre, there is an insistent functionalist rigour to Prakash's buildings at the three agricultural campuses of Punjab, an unabashed celebration of the strictly utilitarian. He paid careful attention to completely utilitarian structures like the pumping stations, which were created as perfect circles. Cost consciousness was of course a dominant concern in early postcolonial India, equally applied to Chandigarh, the agricultural universities and all the other projects of the Nehruvian era. Instead of trying to "soften" relentless elevations that resulted from utilitarian considerations (like many other Indian modernists), Prakash sought to push them as far as he could "as they were" in search of their own aesthetic sensibility.

Classroom at the Agricultural University, photograph by Prakash, APF

Agricultural Engineering College, with then recently transplanted tree, photograph by Prakash, APF

Hostel at the Punjab Agricultural University, Ludhiana, photograph by Prakash, APF

Water pumping station, Punjab Agricultural University, c. 1965, photograph by Prakash, APF

Argus C-3 and Rolleiflex T Type I cameras from the Prakash archives, photograph by author

Argus and Rolleiflex

In Ludhiana, Prakash developed a keen interest in black-and-white photography, influenced presumably by Jeanneret,[9] who regularly photographed Le Corbusier's as well as his own buildings in Chandigarh. The visiting American agricultural scientists generally sold off their imported possessions when they left, and Prakash bought quite a few pieces of equipment from them, including a wide-spool tape recorder, a Kodak slide projector, a Hoover vacuum cleaner and two cameras—an Argus C-3 and the square-format, top view Rolleiflex T Type I, which Prakash loved because of its ability to show the actual image being captured on a screen.

Almost all the images of Prakash's Ludhiana buildings published in this book are reproductions of his original photographs from the 1960s, most of which survive in the Archives. Early on weekend mornings, when the light was good and it was still not too hot, Prakash set off to capture his buildings on celluloid. The black-and-white rolls were developed locally, while the occasional, extremely expensive roll of colour

Prakash comparing photos taken with Argus and Rolleiflex cameras of the same location, APF

photographs and slides had to be sent to the United States to be developed.

Prakash's photographs seem self-consciously framed with a sense of theatricality and a disarming lack of candour.[10] In one, the raggedy outline of an extricated tree stump carefully frames the strict geometries of the buildings, providing vivid contrast. Deep shadows roll across the facades, sharply receding lines of perspective suggest drama, and high contrasts between light and dark generate exaggerated depths. One cannot also help notice the workmen and "inhabitants," carefully positioned in the picture-frame, standing motionless, waiting for the shutter, as if they were on stage.

The photographs always locate his buildings asymmetrically within the frame, as if de-centring contained a vital visual clue to their exegesis.[11] One can almost see Prakash shuffling between his two cameras, photographing the same building with both. The square shapes of the Rolleiflex negatives freeze the buildings within the frame as if to capture a core essence, while those from the Argus use the inherent directionality of the rectangle to

Rooftop photographed by Prakash with the Rolleiflex; the mess under construction in the background, APF

Prakash examining the rebars during one of his site visits, APF

shuffle the eye to a point outside the frame, as if the critical reference lay somewhere beyond.

Clearly, these are not mythical images, like those in Marcel Gautherot's *Brasilia* rising magically from a dusty Amazonian plain. Nor are these heroic images, signalling a triumphalist architecture at work, like Lewis Hine's images of the Empire State Building's construction workers taking a lunch break. They don't have the focus on plastic beauty either, like Ernst Scheidegger's, and even Jeanneret's, photos of Chandigarh.[12] Rather, Prakash's Ludhiana photos are documentary in nature but in the curated architectural photography sense, as if to explicate a sense of poiesis hidden behind the stark building forms.

To me Prakash's photographs feel like X-rays—instruments for discerning the situation in which he found himself, exact records held in

The agricultural college under construction, photograph by Prakash, APF

abeyance until the question that is to be asked of their subjects becomes clear. They project a sense of quiet anticipation. They show the ambitious worksites of a nation whose future, still unknown, is both fraught with doubt and filled with great expectation. They feel doubly framed, both self-assured and unsure, capturing the anxieties of an architect searching for meaning amongst his silent creations.

Prakash gave up his photographic habit after 1969, when he became an academic and ceased actively designing. In a carefully preserved photo album, he curated a small set of his photographs, one to a page, each precisely affixed to a particular section of the page. On one of these, of the Tagore Theatre, he meticulously drew across the page in pencil the perspective lines of the brick, as if the full story needed necessary supplementation.

Ongoing construction at the Boys' Hostel with the workers in the foreground, Agricultural University, photograph by Prakash, APF

Boys' Hostel with construction ramp, Agricultural University, photograph by Prakash, APF

Agricultural Engineering College under construction, photograph by Prakash, APF

The agricultural college with round vents, photograph by Prakash, APF

Corridor of the Agricultural University, Ludhiana, photograph by Prakash, APF

Boys' Hostel,
Agricultural University,
photograph by Prakash,
APF

View from the terrace of the Agricultural University, photograph by Prakash, APF

Boys' Hostel with mess, photographed by Prakash with his Rolleiflex camera, APF

The Agricultural University framed in a piece of deadwood, photographs by Prakash, APF

Sawtooth skylights at the Agricultural University, Ludhiana, photographs by Prakash, APF

The sculpture court at the agricultural college, Ludhiana, photograph by Prakash, APF

The Urge to Sculpture

While photography was essentially a professional interest for Prakash, the creativity engendered by his architectural design work at Ludhiana also served to rekindle his old love for art and sculpture. Later, Prakash was to remember the moment of "rekindling" as a palpably mythologized act of autogenesis:

> My dedication to the [AEC] building was no less. Living on the campus, I would stroll up to this building in my spare time and on holidays. As I did so I had an idea that this building should have a "SCULPTURE" in its courtyard to dignify it. I had, while building the TAGORE THEATRE of Chandigarh imagined myself such a sculpture and had indeed made some clay models for it. But that dream could not be realized there. Here in Ludhiana, I was living with a building under realization and the building materials were sprawled round me urging me to do something. A thought crossed my mind: Why not make a concrete sculpture from the very concrete and steel which is being used in the building! I had no experience, only the "will" but the contractor was willing to help in the experiment. With my clay figure as model, I dug the earth to make a mould and began working on a sculpture, pouring concrete, putting pieces of scrap steel bars and reinforcement, turning, twisting, breaking and remaking. In two-three months' time the sculpture—a reclining figure—was ready. When shown to Dr. Mulk Raj Anand,

Clay sculpture studies by Prakash, photograph by Prakash, APF

Sculpture at agricultural college, Ludhiana, photograph by Prakash, APF

Pour A. Prakash.

Cette sculpture n'est pas née de l'inspiration d'un Artiste. C'est un résidu des coupes d'un ouvrier du bâtiment qui a cherché à perdre le moins de métal pour les pièces d'assemblage d'une poutre.

L'Art est partout, mais il faut le découvrir. C'est la raison pour laquelle j'ai tant d'inquiétude lorsque l'on me parle d'Artiste et d'école d'Art.

Amicalement

18.5.61

Postcard from Jeanneret to Prakash recalling the foundational moment of the discovery of beauty in found objects, APF

> when he visited the university, he was full of praise for my work. For me it was a great morale booster.[13]

The extant Archives of the Aditya Prakash Foundation do not have any specific record of a proposed sculpture for Tagore Theatre, other than a photograph of some clay models. In another article where Prakash recalled his time in Ludhiana, he recorded that it was Jeanneret who opened his eyes to the possibility of seeing the beautiful in the ordinary:

> When I was building Tagore Theatre in 1960—1961, its roof trusses of steel were being assembled at the site itself. That process produced a lot of scrap which was heaped at one place for disposal. One day Pierre Jeanneret took me there—to the scrap heap. Looking we began to see (first he then I also) that there are beautiful forms lying about in the heap. We picked about 10 of them, photographed them, and then used them in the shuttering pattern of the facia, but to a casual onlooker they are only a part of the texture of the concrete. Jeanneret wrote about this discovery in his article which appeared in the *Marg* issue on Chandigarh.[14]

Jeanneret wrote his article in the 1961 *Marg* issue on Chandigarh, a single-page note titled, "Aesthetic: Reflection on Beauty of Line, Shape and Form." In it, he argued that the beautiful can be found anywhere and everywhere; one only has

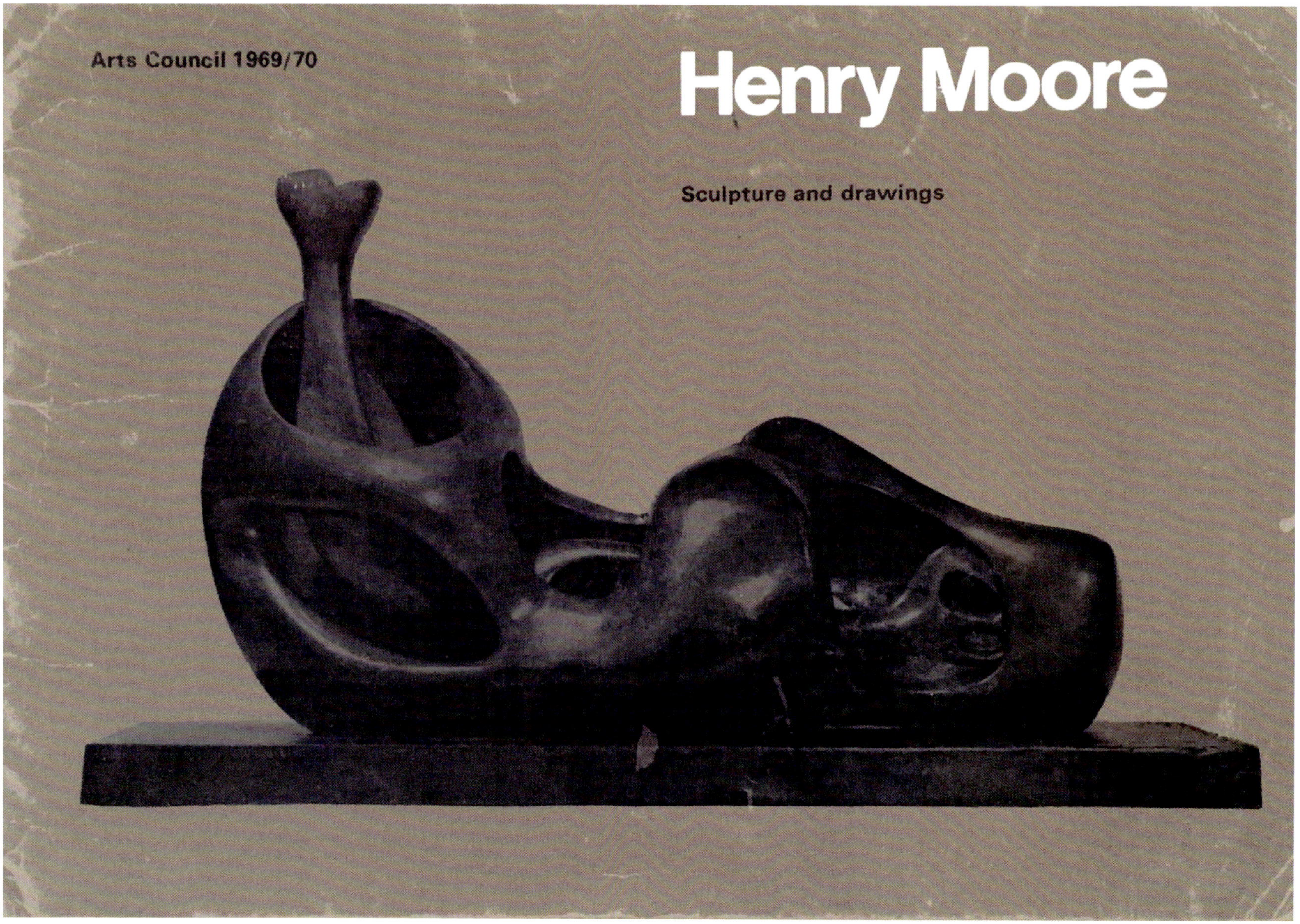

Cover of a Henry Moore exhibit catalogue in the AP Archive, APF

to have the eyes to see it and remain uncorrupted by "education." The article is illustrated with five photographs, taken by Jeanneret himself. The largest of those is of the steel cut-outs that Prakash mentions.[15]

Prakash's Agricultural College sculpture still stands in the middle of its court. There is nothing like the steel cut-outs in Jeanneret's photograph about its form. Instead, in the obvious voluptuousness of the abstracted reclining (female?) form one can discern the clear presence of his old hand-moulded sculptures from his days in the Glasgow School of Art, influenced no doubt by the work of Henry Moore. There is a clearly implied phallic quality to its "head."

Also striking is the sculpture's location, off-centre in the AEC court with pathways circling up to and around it. With its sprawling "limbs," the sculpture actively dissects and gathers the rigidly rectilinear space around it.

The Archives suggest that Prakash made four to five free-standing sculptures in wood.

Sculpture studies (by Prakash?) at the Glasgow School of Art, APF

Prakash's wood sculptures photographed with his Rolleiflex camera, APF

Only one of these, completed in Ludhiana around 1965, survives. Entrenched in the modernist style, it is intended to be a sculpture in the round, self-consciously constructed to hold its own from any point of view. Unlike the poured-in-place concrete sculpture he made for the AEC courtyard, this 27-inch hand-made wooden sculpture was created via a process of subtraction of mass, like that of the chthonic rock cut architecture of Ajanta and Ellora. One can intuit a log that has been carved out and drilled open. Even so, the expressive qualities of the sculpture mimic the plasticity of a concrete-or plaster-type sculpture with continuous lines, deep holes bored with hand augers, and a cultivated expression of the natural veins of wood.

Untitled, oil on canvas, c.1965, APF

Beginning to Paint

While photography and sculpture seemed to run their full course by the end of his tenure in Ludhiana, Prakash also took up painting during this time, and this would become a lifelong practice. In an article published in *Advance* in 1988, Prakash wrote that soon after that first sculpture in the Agricultural Engineering College, he started to paint with oils. Soon he found success, but early on he made a critical decision not to paint "professionally":

> I soon began to participate in exhibitions, receive flattering reviews, and be generally in demand for a painting. With all that I never became a professional painter and that kept me away from the rat race for patronage and selling. For me painting is an act of relaxation, of prayer, and of releasing me from the rigidity of the architectural profession. Gradually, I began to do some woodcarving, some drawings and collages and thus it goes on till today.[16]

In this sense, Prakash's vast oeuvre of paintings and drawings[17] is the work of an amateur, both in the "un-professionalized" sense of the word, and in the etymological sense as that of a lover of the arts.[18] It is difficult to know what Prakash was painting before his time in Ludhiana. In the Archives there is one surviving watercolour of the Thames with St. Paul in the background from his London days. This was one of two watercolours that he submitted to an exhibition at the Architectural Association in London in 1950. It is a beautiful work displaying great skill, but no signs of the abstract qualities of his paintings to come.

Prakash's turn to abstract modernism can be traced to diverse sources. Modern art was already institutionalized in the museums of London in the late 1940s—the Archives contain a brochure titled "60 Paintings for '51", an art exhibition curated for the Festival of Britain, with six abstract paintings and 54 more traditional figurative works. This was also the period when abstract art came into prominence globally, particularly in the United States and Western Europe. Prakash identified with these avant-garde tendencies as a young man, and felt that through them he could break free of the shackles of tradition and history. The Chandigarh experience would have reinforced the

Untitled,
oil on cardboard,
8 x 6 inches, c. 1965, APF

value of abstraction, with Le Corbusier's multi-disciplinary oeuvre as the shining example.

A more specific impetus for his turn to modern art can be traced to the contemporaneous movement in Punjab to build a broader modernist intellectual, literary, and aesthetic culture to complement the Nehruvian state's massive infrastructure investments such as the Bhakra Nangal Dam. There was a sense that Bhakra and Chandigarh should not remain isolated, and that a broader, transformative cultural makeover should be advanced emphasizing sculpture, art, poetry, and literature.

Mulk Raj Anand, the famous Indian nationalist author and editor of *Marg* magazine, was the most visible proselytizer of this enterprise.[19] Born in Amritsar, and Punjabi by culture, Anand was dedicated to the cause of art in Punjab. Drawing on his experiences with the Progressive Artists' Movement and his own literary milieu, Anand formed the Punjab Lalit Kala Akademi and took the position of the inaugural chair in Art at Panjab University in the 1950s, in the years when the entire Chandigarh Capital Project team was active, and Le Corbusier a regular visitor.[20]

In this milieu, Prakash clearly saw an opportunity to revive his old interest in art. Anand was an early supporter of Prakash's artistic work, and named the latter the secretary and then the president of the newly formed Punjab Lalit Kala Akademi. Anand connected him to

Spontaneous drawings on long narrow pieces of cartridge paper (below and facing page)**, made during the early days of painting in Ludhiana**, oil on cartridge paper, 9 x 3 inches, 1960s, APF

Indian modernists and nationalist artists, and also to their predecessors, particularly those who had been trained in Santiniketan. The work of Jamini Roy, still alive and painting in the 1950s and 1960s, became a major source of inspiration for Prakash, although the two never met.

Prakash started painting first in the studio of Hardev Singh, one of the "modern" artist-residents in Ludhiana. Prakash first exhibited in "Loose Collection," a group show of emerging artists exhibited in the gallery of Panjab University. B. N. Goswamy, who is today one of India's foremost art historians but was then only just starting out, published a review:

> The exhibition gives absolutely no evidence of any new movement in the arts being launched: fortunately, even the claim is not made. It also does not invade the viewing public with the declaration of yet another Manifesto. What it does, however, is give proof of talent and hard work, of modest ends diligently pursued.... The work of Mr. Aditya Prakash is a case in point. He is an architect by profession and is naturally deeply concerned with design and with relationship between forms. The three drawings by him, done apparently in some hurry on sheets of brown packing paper, are all in fact disciplined drawings, executed in low key and aiming at being no more than studies. They please though, and in his "Composition No. 3" it is colours that take precedence in a sense over line. In this, incidentally the dashes in red in a rectangle in the centre recalled strangely to my mind the vermillion smearings on a wayside deity.[21]

Scan image with the **BooksPlus** app

From his earliest days Prakash thought of his artworks as dispensable commodities. He was always happy to gift one or two to his Western friends and neighbours. Giving paintings to anyone who expressed appreciation for them was to remain a lifelong ethic.

Early on in Ludhiana, those paintings that did not make it to "gift-able" level, Prakash unmounted from their frames and cut up into curves, slits, and circles to make parts of new paintings and smaller works. The culture of recycling "waste" to make new art attracted him.[22] He was fond of making collages out of leftover cut pieces, along with figural forms, mostly animals, particularly the snake and the bird. Other collaged compositions consisted of cut-out squares, distributed in space in a minimalist manner.

Not many of Prakash's full-size canvases of the 1960s have survived. Three are available as slides. They show an artist abandoned to the activity of freely pulling lines across the canvas, inventing forms, and experimenting with colour and texture. One painting on a purple background (dated 22 January 1966) shows three abstract figures that appear literally to be dancing across the canvas. In another dated 15 February 1966, an explosion of circular forms in red, yellow, and black seem to reach beyond the canvas and occupy the space around them. In contrast, an acrylic-on-canvas painting that survived intact in the private collection of Dr. Edwards of Victoria, BC, shows a bull standing firm on its ground, holding fast to the canvas as if to prohibit movement. Speckled fields of blue and green, and an abstracted spinning wheel of the Gandhian-type suggest vitality, but the centrally depicted figure holds them firm in its orbit.

The Archives do contain a beautiful set of small, long and thin paintings on paper, each one something like a "free thought." Many of them are female figures, abstracted and voluptuous. Some are abstracted figural shapes, shaded to make alternating rhythms of figure and ground spaces. Most are impressionistic studies made from iterative drawing of small lines and circles, with the occasional square or scratch, as if they were intended as painting practice.

These seminal works mark the tumultuous genesis of an extensive body of work that stretched until Prakash's death in 2008. Over time, his paintings steadily gravitated in the direction of carefully composed, flat, and contained surfaces. Circles and other spiralling figures, sinuous snakes, and a plethora of gestural curves, continued to proliferate in his canvases and drawings, as if seeking an open portal to escape. Ultimately it was the search for the settled form, an architectural plan-like resolved shape, that powered the trajectory of his aesthetic desire the most.

Untitled,
oil on cardboard, 8 x 6
inches, c. 1965, APF

Untitled, oil on canvas,
c.1965, APF

Untitled, oil on canvas,
c.1965, APF

NOTES

1 A famous colonial agricultural college was located at Lyallpur (now renamed Faisalabad), but that went to Pakistan. The Ludhiana campus, which had begun before the agricultural revolution of the 1960s, was started as a replacement for the Lyallpur college.

2 Shivdatt Sharma went on to become a significant architect in his own right, with an impressive body of work both as a state architect and in private practice. See Prakash, V. (2012). *The Architecture of Shivdatt Sharma* (Modernism in India series). Ahmedabad: Mapin Publishing.

3 He took over from MN Sharma, who had already started the work on the main administration building of the PAU campus in Ludhiana.

4 The team of foreign "experts" was led by Professor T. Scott Sutton of Ohio State University. Other members of the team included Dr. Frank Parker (chief agriculturist with the Technical Cooperative Mission of India), Bob Yoder, Dean Rummel of the College of Agriculture at OSU and Dr. W. E. Krauss, associate director of the Agricultural Experiment Station, who set up the technology exchange. OSU was picked because Dr. M. S. Randhawa, an ICS officer of Punjab cadre and a botanist, had sought collaboration with botany departments all over the United States and only received a single reply, from one Dr. E. N. Transeau of OSU. So, he recommended OSU for the agricultural exchange as well. See "Interview with Professor T. Scott Sutton by Professor Robert Sutton, February 10, 1984." https://kb.osu.edu/dspace/bitstream/handle/1811/34387/Sutton%20Transcript.pdf?sequence=1, accessed 10/5/2017. Also available at *APFA*. Most of the team was from OSU, although some other agricultural scientists joined in, such as Dr. Donald Edwards, a biologist from Victoria, BC, who was working as a research scientist for the Canadian federal government. Dr. Edwards was sent to Ludhiana as part of the Colombo Plan, the international collaboration plan started in 1950 to assist Commonwealth countries in Asia. A Ph.D. from McGill University in Montreal, Edwards worked in the Department of Zoology and Entomology in the Punjab Agricultural University from 1966-68. He and his family ended up living next door to the Prakash family, and the two became close friends maintaining a relationship into the new millennium. For the new agricultural practices developed at this time see: Atwal, A., & Punjab Agricultural University. (1969). *New concepts in agricultural education in India*. Ludhiana: Punjab Agricultural University Press; exclusively distributed by Lyall Book Depot, Bhopal.

5 For a discussion of the Green Revolution and the architecture of the times see Ateya Khorakiwala's *The Well-Fed Subject: Modern Architecture in the Quantitative State, India (1943-1984)* PhD Dissertation, Harvard University, Cambridge, MA, April 2017.This dissertation includes an informative chapter on the work of Aditya Prakash.

6 Prakash recalled his time designing the campus in Palampur: "I used to go there with a couple of my colleagues, camp there for about ten days at a stretch and work out the designs in a makeshift office at the site. I used to roam about the site for long periods and come to the office brimming with ideas to be put in practice right there and tested. Thus, did the design take shape and some construction began." "My Reminiscences of the Punjab Agricultural University, Ludhiana, 1963—1967" 27 April 1988, *APFA D16*.

7 Even so, retrospectively Prakash acknowledged some value in Thapar's bullheadedness. For instance, Prakash remembered that "Thapar ordered that the Chief Engineer and I should visit Hissar every fortnight and stay there for three clear days..." Do what?' Drink brackish water and breathe sand-laden air. That is what it looked like then, but later I was to realise the value of this imposition on me. Now I believe, no architect worth his salt can design a building without intimately feeling the place he is going to design for." "My Reminiscences of the Punjab Agricultural University, Ludhiana, 1963—1967" (1988) *APFA D16*.

8 Prakash wrote, designed and published a user's manual for the students called "Your Hostel". All the key design concepts were carefully diagrammed, so that students could appreciate the innovations in design that the hostel contained. It is difficult to know what the students actually thought of the building. "Your Hostel," *APFA D15*.

9 Jeanneret was an avid photographer and the source (with Ernst Scheidegger) of most of Le Corbusier's images of Chandigarh, both those published in the *Oeuvres* and otherwise. Jeanneret was seen carrying his camera everywhere and took his photography very seriously. Jeet Malhotra, one of the Indian architects, was also a keen black and white photographer of Chandigarh. See Avermaete, T., Casciato, Maristella, Barrada, Yto, Honma, Takashi, & Centre Canadien d'Architecture, issuing body. (2014). *Casablanca Chandigarh: A report on modernization*. Montréal, Québec, Canada: Zürich, Switzerland: CCA, Canadian Centre for Architecture = Centre Canadien d'Architecture; Park Books.

10 Some of this discussion of Prakash's photography was previously published as "Double Framed: The Architectural Photography of Aditya Prakash," ARCADE Issue 31.4, November 2013, Seattle WA.

11 As Atreyee Gupta has pointed out recently, this mode of photography was made popular when images of Chandigarh's buildings taken by practitioners such as Jeet Malhotra and Le Corbusier's French accomplice Lucien Hervé were disseminated in the country via print media. Atreyee Gupta, "In a Postcolonial Diction: Postwar Abstraction and the Aesthetics of Modernization," *Art Journal* 72, 3 (2013): 30–46.

12 See Scheidegger, E., Casciato, Maristella, & Moos, Stanislaus von. (2010). *Chandigarh 1956: Le Corbusier, Pierre Jeanneret, Jane B. Drew, E. Maxwell Fry*. Zürich: Scheidegger & Spiess.

13 "My Reminiscences of the Punjab Agricultural University, Ludhiana, 1963-67" *APFA D16*.

14 "Art–As I see it" *APFA, D12_1*.

15 "Aesthetic: Reflection on beauty of line, shape and form," *Marg: A Magazine of the Arts*, Mumbai, Vol XV No 1, December 1961, pp.56—57. One of the pictures is of a rock with the caption, "Stone found in a river. I examined three thousand but finally photographed only one." Such river rock, stood up and displayed as Jeanneret does in this photograph, were the beginning of Nek Chand's famous Rock Garden in the Capitol Complex, yet to come in the 1970s. I am not aware of any direct link between Jeanneret and Nek Chand, but the connection is undeniable.

16 "Punjab Agricultural University Some Thoughts: Some Memories," *Advance: The Punjab Magazine* 37, 2 (1988): 12–15.

17 There are about 750 paintings and drawings in the Aditya Prakash Archives as of July 2017. An estimated 150–200 are in museums and private collections worldwide.

18 Late 18th century: from Italian *amatore*, from Latin *amator* "lover," from *amare* "to love."

19 Mulk Raj Anand founded *Marg* in 1946, with the support of the Parsi industrialist family of Mumbai, the Tatas. A dyed-in-the-wool modernist, Mulk Raj Anand famously proposed in his novel *Untouchable* that flush toilets could solve the problem of untouchability in India. The making of Chandigarh, with its novel buildings where "human bodies [could] breathe fresh air at various times of the day," and the agricultural revolution based on purely scientific methods was just what modern Indians needed, from Anand's point of view. See "Afterword" in SS Bhatti (2013) *Chandigarh: An Irony of History*, Rose Dog Books, Pittsburgh, PA. An avowed Marxist, Mulk Raj Anand made it his life's purpose to bring a modern Indian aesthetic into focus.

20 M. S. Randhawa, the ICS officer who became the first chief commissioner of Chandigarh, and B. N. Goswamy, Professor of Art History at Panjab University, also enthusiastically embraced this mission. Many young Punjabi artists like Sohan Qadri and Shiv Singh were cultivated by these individuals.

21 *APFA D33*. B. N. Goswamy, who received his Ph.D. in Art History from Panjab University in 1961, would have been a young critic at that time. Although Goswamy's scholarly reputation rests largely on his work on Indian Pahari miniatures and his role in identifying specific painters from the tradition, his role as a contemporary art critic in the early years—bolstered and supported by Mulk Raj Anand—is just as important.

22 It is difficult to know if the contemporary culture of "as-founds" in European and American art was an influence—there seem to be no books in the library of the Archives on these—but the ethic of recycling waste was eventually to pervade all aspects of his work.

The Chandigarh team after Pierre Jeanneret's exit, photographed at Sukhna Lake, Chandigarh. Standing (left to right): R. R. Handa, H. S. Chopra, J. L. Malhotra, A. Prakash; Sitting (left to right): B. P. Mathur, M. N. Sharma, M. S. Randhawa (Chief Commissioner), U. E. Chowdhury, A.R. Prabhawalkar, APF

PRINCIPAL, CHANDIGARH COLLEGE OF ARCHITECTURE

Prakash as part of the reception team during one of Indira Gandhi's visits to the Agricultural University. Mrs. Gandhi is escorted by Vice Chancellor Kirpal Singh, APF

Prime Minister Nehru died on 27 May 1964, and eight months later came the assassination of the chief minister of Punjab, Partap Singh Kairon, an avowed Nehruvian and steadfast supporter of Chandigarh and the agricultural revolution.[1] Trouble had been brewing in Punjab for almost a decade, as Nehruvian modernization had upset the established social order with its unequal distribution of the new wealth that was generated. There were also older simmering cultural resentments dating back to the colonial period, manifesting themselves in the call for a "Punjabi Suba," a separate Punjabi-speaking state which Nehru had staunchly opposed, citing his commitment to secularism.

Soon after Indira Gandhi became prime minister in 1966, she acceded to the agitation in Punjab and agreed to its division on the basis of language. Non-Punjabi-speaking areas became the new state of Haryana, with some areas of the old Punjab in the foothills of the Himalayas going to Himachal Pradesh. Chandigarh was designated a Union Territory, a federally administered city, capital to both the states of Punjab and Haryana. This was supposed to be a short-lived, interim solution until Haryana built its own capital city.

As support for the agricultural universities in the new Punjab waned, P. N. Thapar, a proud and uncompromising man by nature, doubled down and sought to protect and bolster "his" agricultural revolution with direct support from New Delhi. In the tumult, Prakash felt that his future in Ludhiana might be uncertain and went to speak to Thapar, who offered him a significant promotion to head both the architectural and engineering offices of the PAU system.

Meanwhile in Chandigarh, Pierre Jeanneret had fallen sick and in 1966, after a fifteen-year stint in Chandigarh, he decided to return to Geneva, Switzerland, where he died in December 1967. While there was controversy over who should succeed Jeanneret as Chief Architect of Chandigarh, M. N. Sharma was appointed to the position since he was senior-most in rank. This disgruntled Anant R. Prabhawalkar, who had been Le Corbusier and Jeanneret's preferred choice, and had for the longest time expected to succeed to the position after Jeanneret. Prabhawalkar had been Principal of the Chandigarh College of Architecture (CCA) at this time, and he decided to quit that position and sought employment outside Chandigarh.[2]

Soon after taking charge, M. N. Sharma asked Prakash to return to Chandigarh and join him as the senior architect of Chandigarh. Prakash however demurred. Since his days as the organizer of the Modern Architects Club, Prakash had nursed the dream of running CCA.

Now that Prabhawalkar had left, the position was open. Sharma was not keen on this idea, but M. S. Randhawa, Prakash's old supporter from his Ludhiana days had been appointed head of the new administration of Chandigarh, its chief commissioner, and he offered Prakash the job of the Principal.

In 1967, thus, Prakash had three choices; stay on in Ludhiana as senior architect and engineer, join Sharma as Senior Architect of Chandigarh, or take over as principal of the CCA. Prakash picked the Ludhiana position and was on his way to submit his acceptance offer when he found out that Thapar had suffered a severe stroke and would likely die from it. Prakash got cold feet and turned around, and accepted the position at CCA.

Prakash joined CCA on 13 December 1967 with an ingrained sense of idealism about the role of academics.[3] Deriving from his vision for the Modern Architects Group, Prakash argued that an architectural education was best acquired not from books, but from live projects in the city.[4] The idea was that senior CCA faculty would lead "live" projects that would be supported by junior faculty and students.

Fundamentally, his hope was that the CCA would be the place where the Chandigarh experiment would continue as a site of inquiry and applied research. The challenge was to extricate architects from the "make-believe world" of foreign influence and make them think for themselves:

> This is the challenge to the architect in India today. He has to build up a clientele for himself. He has to adapt his training to the needs of the country. He has to extricate himself from the make-believe world in which he floats under the influence of the happenings abroad. He has to evolve an indigenous system of educating himself in accordance with the resources, and requirements of the country.[5]

The problem of architectural education, as Prakash articulated in his 1972 convocation address, was the "gimmickry" that resulted from having every architect establish a "new school of thought":

> How should one learn in a college of architecture? There are so many schools of thought. Around every great architect a school of thought grows. With all its vitality and exuberance, the greatest curse of [the] modern movement in architecture has been the desire of every architect not to fall in line with any established school of thought, but to establish a school of his own... no architect wants to belong to a school of thought, and few have any of their own. This results in gimmickry—the commercial method of establishing one's own name against a product which is identical with another.

Belonging to a school of thought did not mean blindly following it. If Chandigarh was the "textbook" that the CCA should follow, Prakash viewed it a recurring research project:

> We look to Chandigarh as our Textbook. Whenever we set a design or construction or for that matter any other problem, we see how a similar problem has been solved in Chandigarh. A solution is not necessarily a right solution. We, therefore, do not start with the premise, that whatever has been done in Chandigarh is right. We want to understand the basis of what has been done, and for that we carry out a study programme of prototypes which exist, and then draw our own conclusions.[6]

It took a few years to secure approval from the administration of Chandigarh, but by the mid-1970s he had formalized this vision into a series of partially funded "Research Cells" that were invested with protocols, procedures and even basic publishing abilities. These "Research Cells" produced some of the earliest original documents on Chandigarh, such as the "Chandigarh Informograph," "Trees of Chandigarh" and "Aesthetic Legislation."[7]

In order to transform CCA into a research institution that used the Chandigarh experiment as its laboratory, Prakash had to overcome the ground realities of the institution, which were very different. Established on 7 August 1961, CCA had had a promising start. A. R. Prabhawalkar as its inaugural Principal had proved to be an enthusiastic and passionate leader, dedicated to the design principles of the "Chandigarh style." Prabhawalkar had worked closely with Le Corbusier, particularly on the Assembly building, and had a command of the metres and rhythms of the "master's" way of designing. He championed them in the college and the curriculum followed its rigours. From its infancy, the CCA had also fortunately acquired a young faculty dedicated to that cause, including Professor Surindera Singh Bhatti who would ultimately take over from Prakash as principal.

CCA's early years thus were more celebratory of the Chandigarh way of design, while Prakash wanted a more research-oriented, critical attitude. One of his first acts as Principal was to institute a thesis requirement prior to graduation, and to initiate the teaching of cross-disciplinary subjects such as Theory of Design, Urban Design, and Landscape Design. When specialized faculty was not available to teach these subjects, he encouraged the regular faculty to develop these subjects as their research specializations, and to learn by teaching. For many on the faculty, this was Prakash's most lasting contribution to their professional development.[8]

He also began the practice of inviting out-of-town jurors to evaluate and critique the work

Prakash at the oath-taking ceremony with graduates at the Chandigarh College of Architecture (CCA), Photo courtesy Balvinder Saini

of senior students. The first was Joseph Allen Stein, a California-born modernist who had settled in New Delhi, followed by Achyut Kanvinde from Delhi, a Harvard-trained architect who'd worked under Walter Gropius. Because of Prakash's openness to travelling architects, the entire spectrum of emerging Indian modernists passed through CCA in the 1970s, as did a steady stream of architects and academics from around the world. For many of them, Chandigarh was a Mecca to be visited at least once during their lifetimes.

Charles Correa and William J. R. Curtis, in particular, for whom Chandigarh was an important reference in their own work, became good friends. Both of them visited the Prakash residence repeatedly and subsequently remembered their time there fondly. Retrospectively, Correa noted:

> Of all the architects who worked in Chandigarh, Aditya was out and out the most gifted. Not only was his point of view fresh—but, more importantly, he had the design talent to back it up. Unlike the other acolytes, he did not fall into the usual "I-have-touched-the-hem-of-the-Prophet" routine to leverage his work. I think that the Tagore Theatre is probably the most surprisingly non-Corbusier building in Chandigarh—and I have in front of me that wonderfully surrealistic photograph of the model with two hands (Aditya's?) holding the elegant roof slab above it, like a benediction. It's a great photograph—mysterious and polemic at the same time.[9]

Prakash's painterly instincts helped shape a new graphic identity for CCA. On its entrance porch, he etched a mural based on the diagram of the Modulor. Initially, it was just a graphic on concrete, quite like the ones Le Corbusier put at various places on his Capitol buildings. But later it was hand-painted in primary colours picked by Prakash. Hand-painting the mural became a tradition in the college, and it is still annually repainted by the students. Prakash also used a modified version of this graphic to create a logo for the college, which became the visual identity of the institution, adorning every certificate, degree, official stationery and ceremonial scarf (though it was later changed by Prakash's successor).[10]

Prakash (holding a microphone) with students at the CCA Sports Day (on far right, V. P. Anil). They are most likely singing the national anthem, APF

Prakash, with S. S. Bhatti, awarding degrees to the CCA graduates, Photo courtesy Balvinder Saini

Prakash worked hard to institute an academic culture in the college, requiring annual study tours for the whole student body to important architectural locations around the country. He organized faculty family picnics, and instituted elaborate graduation ceremonies, complete with an academic procession, a professional oath swearing, a commencement address and a distinguished guest to hand out the degrees. Robes were specially designed for the occasion, black ones for the students, primary-coloured yellow and red ones for the faculty. There were no hoods and hats though; perhaps those he felt were not modernist enough.

Prakash also divided the student body into "Houses" and promoted a sports day, with an accompanying cultural competition amongst them.[11] *My earliest memories of my father at CCA are that of him enthusiastically cheering on the college's cricket team, the underdog team, as it battled against a superior team from out of town. It was a motley crew that, the CCA team, with students from Kashmir and Assam in the same mix as those from Punjab, Haryana, Rajasthan, and Kerala. One of the policies of the Indian government was that it reserved seats for students from states that were underserved by professional institutions. Consequently, students from all over India, and even abroad from allied Non-Aligned states like Seychelles and Iran, found themselves in schools like CCA. Diverse languages and cultures were often a barrier, and Prakash believed that physical activities would help forge a common culture.*[12] *The sports day soon became a cultural week, with skits, dramas, musical and dance performances taking over the life of the college for seven days and nights. This cultural week, now known as "Archo," still survives as one of the most cherished activities of the student body. My other early memory is going to black-and-white film screenings in the college. Once a month, a travelling-cinema man would show up at CCA with a portable projector and reels of old Bollywood films strapped to his motorcycle. The entire CCA student and faculty body would attend these screenings in the central courtyard, with the accompaniment of a bonfire during the cold winter months.*

Research Cells

Starting in the early 1970s, Prakash led the development of the culture of research at the CCA by example. Working with thesis students, he began to undertake original studies on what he considered to be urgent topics of architecture and urbanism, relevant to contemporary Chandigarh and India. Essentially, he began to craft something like an "Indian" critique of Chandigarh's Western modernism.

Prakash's "failed" experiment with the mud wall, and especially the rationale for its dismissal, dragged in Prakash's mind for a long time. In the frequency with which Prakash later recalled these incidents, one can sense an Oedipal struggle of the first generation of Indian modernists. Jeanneret, Le Corbusier, and the Nehruvian vision of modernization were the crucibles in which India's postcolonial modernism had been conceived. By the 1960s, a new modernism was beginning to find its own voice and feet.

The Ludhiana experience had cast the die for Prakash's reassessment of modernism. While designing the sprawling modernist campus of the Agricultural University, Prakash had to continually visit the old city of Ludhiana, in particular its dense and vibrant main market, the Chaura Bazaar, to meet the needs of his daily life. Almost every other day, he would hop onto his new Lambretta scooter, and with his wife and at least two or three small children in tow, weave his way through the chaotic traffic of Ludhiana to engage with the informal sector that constituted the marketplace of Chaura Bazaar. The inescapable contrast between the two, and his own sense of personal identification with both, engendered in Prakash the desire to try and make the twain meet.

Prakash's research began with his cameras. The same lenses that he used to document his spanking new modernist buildings he now trained on the chaos of Chaura Bazaar.[13] He began to make notes on how the traffic worked, how the goods were bought and sold, how the loading and unloading were done, and where the kids played and sat while the parents shopped and vended. Next to Chaura Bazaar was a train line, with a major railway crossing, and the GT Road, the historic, big highway connecting Delhi to Amritsar. The

Chaura Bazaar, Ludhiana, of the 1960s, photographed by Prakash, APF (all)

Prakash's photographs of a taxi stand in Sector 15, Chandigarh, and rickshaws, early 1970s, APF

highway, a simple two-lane road, with no curbs or breakdown lanes, was used by every mode of transport from the largest truck to the bicyclist.

As a state-appointed agent of "modernization," Prakash's first instinct was to prepare an "improvement" plan for Chaura Bazaar, to clean up the mess and make it more efficient and safer. He was particularly critical of the impact the highway had on the market and proposed that it should be elevated to keep the ground activities safe. All the major roads in the Chandigarh plan, the V2s and V3s, were after all "turned away" from the neighbourhoods, keeping the latter safe and quiet. But, later, as he warmed up to the more subtle and enriching layers of life supported by the chaos of the old city fabric, he began to question the assumptions of the Chandigarh plan through the lens of Ludhiana's chaos.

At the end of his tenure in Ludhiana, Prakash wrote a paper on his observations of Ludhiana titled "Living in Cities."[14] Dividing the city into three parts—the Industrial Zone, the GT Road and the Chaura Bazaar—Prakash argued that the job of a modernist Indian city was to find ways of introducing new technologies and urban necessities like highways into the old city, without destroying the vitality of existing urban life. If brand new cities were to be made, they would have to be built in a manner that maintains and upgrades vital existing urban networks.

Prakash had started to rethink the meaning and purpose of a modern city in India. The agricultural transformation affected by the Green Revolution had shown him the awesome power (and, later, dangers) of technology applied on a wide scale. How this could be adapted for urban planning became a quest. While the

The railway crossing through Chaura Bazaar, Ludhiana, photograph by Prakash, c. 1967, APF

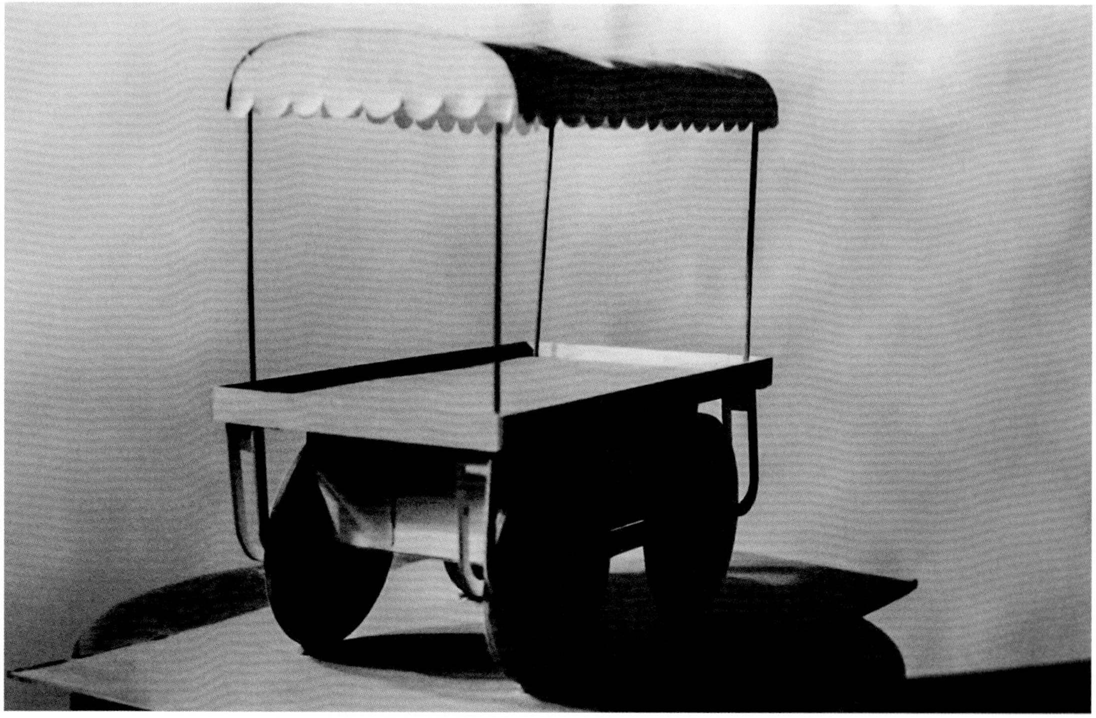

***Rehri* design study models**, early 1970s, APF

Green Revolution had focused on the agricultural economy, Prakash was interested in bringing home its lessons to the Indian city.

His very first research project after joining CCA was on the survival and significance of Chandigarh's informal markets. Although banned, like the cows, by the city's by-laws, Chandigarh from its earliest days had had a thriving *rehri* (push-cart) market system that delivered all the daily needs of the households right to their doorsteps. In Chandigarh's early days, before formal markets developed, the *rehri-wallah*s had been essential to the survival of the residents. As the "proper" markets came into their own, it was generally expected that the informal markets would disappear. But the *rehri*s remained a vital part of the new city's economy, making it impossible to ban them from the streets.

Under these circumstances, Prakash felt that the *rehri*s should not only be legalized but also modernized and made more effective. Working with two students from CCA, Pallav Mukherjee and Amar Puri, Prakash researched the *rehri*s and proposed that they be expanded in Chandigarh, with the design community taking on the challenge of designing better versions. Prakash also published a few design suggestions of his own.[15]

Prakash then turned his attention to questions of the rural-urban interface, starting with the impact of the Chandigarh experiment on its peripheral villages. In Kishangarh, one of Chandigarh's peripheral villages right next to the lake, Prakash undertook with his CCA thesis student Rakesh Sharma a study commissioned by, and done in collaboration with, Dr. P. N. Chuttani, the director of PGIMER (Post Graduate Institute of Medical Education and Research) in Chandigarh.

The Kishangarh study began with the assumption that Chandigarh's peripheral villages were endangered since their agricultural land had been taken to build the city. Some even called for the eradication of these villages since they assumed that they were parasitic on Chandigarh for all their amenities. On the contrary, the Prakash-Sharma study found that Chandigarh's peripheral villages provided essential amenities like fresh milk, vegetables, and cheap household supplies, and functioned as important staging

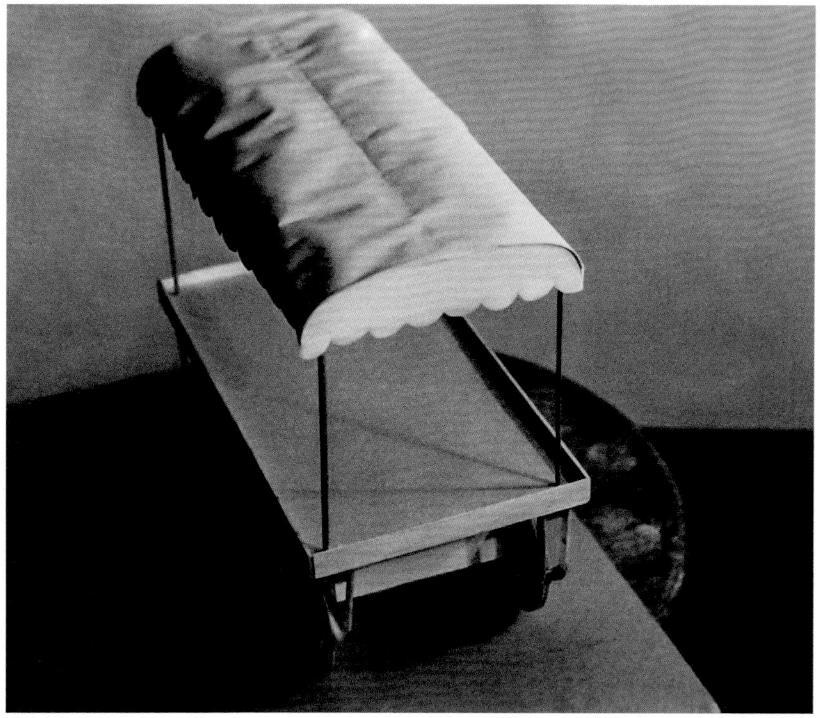

grounds for the vast informal sector that was required to support life in the city. Kishangarh was not only thriving, it was bursting at the seams. The study argued that the village should be helped to grow via sympathetic (rather than restrictive) policies that promoted its economic vitality and ensured its safety and productivity.[16]

While enhanced access was important, major roads would inevitably destroy the fragile ecology of the village. So, they proposed that growth should only be linear, and protected from the highway. Announcing a planner-like vision of architecture, the study's concluding paragraph dramatically stated:

> Although we are architects, we have kept the physical expression in the background. This is done with the clear understanding that a healthy environment, [and] good landscaping automatically results in good architecture.
> Architecture, in our vision is a not a function of cost, but of good taste. Good architecture is created by the use of local materials. Mud and thatch invariably result in good architecture. If they be well maintained it can be heavenly.[17]

Photograph from the Kishangarh study, focusing on the cows, early 1970s, APF

Images from the Kishangarh study noting texture and plastic quality of the mud (right and following page), early 1970s, APF

Images from the Kishangarh study noting texture and plastic quality of the mud, APF

Chandigarh's peripheral villages, photographed by Prakash, early 1970s, APF

In 1971, Prakash's *rehri*s research earned him an invitation to present at an academic conference in Edinburgh, organized by none other than Sir Robert Matthew, the designer of the Royal Festival Hall in London.[18] Little is known about how his presentation was received at this conference, but on his way back to India, Prakash fortuitously met Jacqueline Tyrwhitt in Athens, Greece, which became a turning point in his career.[19] Tyrwhitt had had an earlier association with Chandigarh and Nehruvian modernism in the 1950s, when she had conceptualized an exhibition on low-cost housing in New Delhi. She was at that time the editor of *Ekistics*, a journal on the "problem and science of human settlements," published by the architect and planner Constantinos Doxiadis. Although she had never met him before, Tyrwhitt welcomed Prakash to *Ekistics*, and took an immediate interest in his paper on *rehri*s. By the time he left Athens, Tyrwhitt had appointed him Corresponding Editor, India, for *Ekistics*. His association with *Ekistics*—influenced as it was by Doxiadis' systems approach—moved Prakash's interests in the direction of sustainability and the linear city.[20]

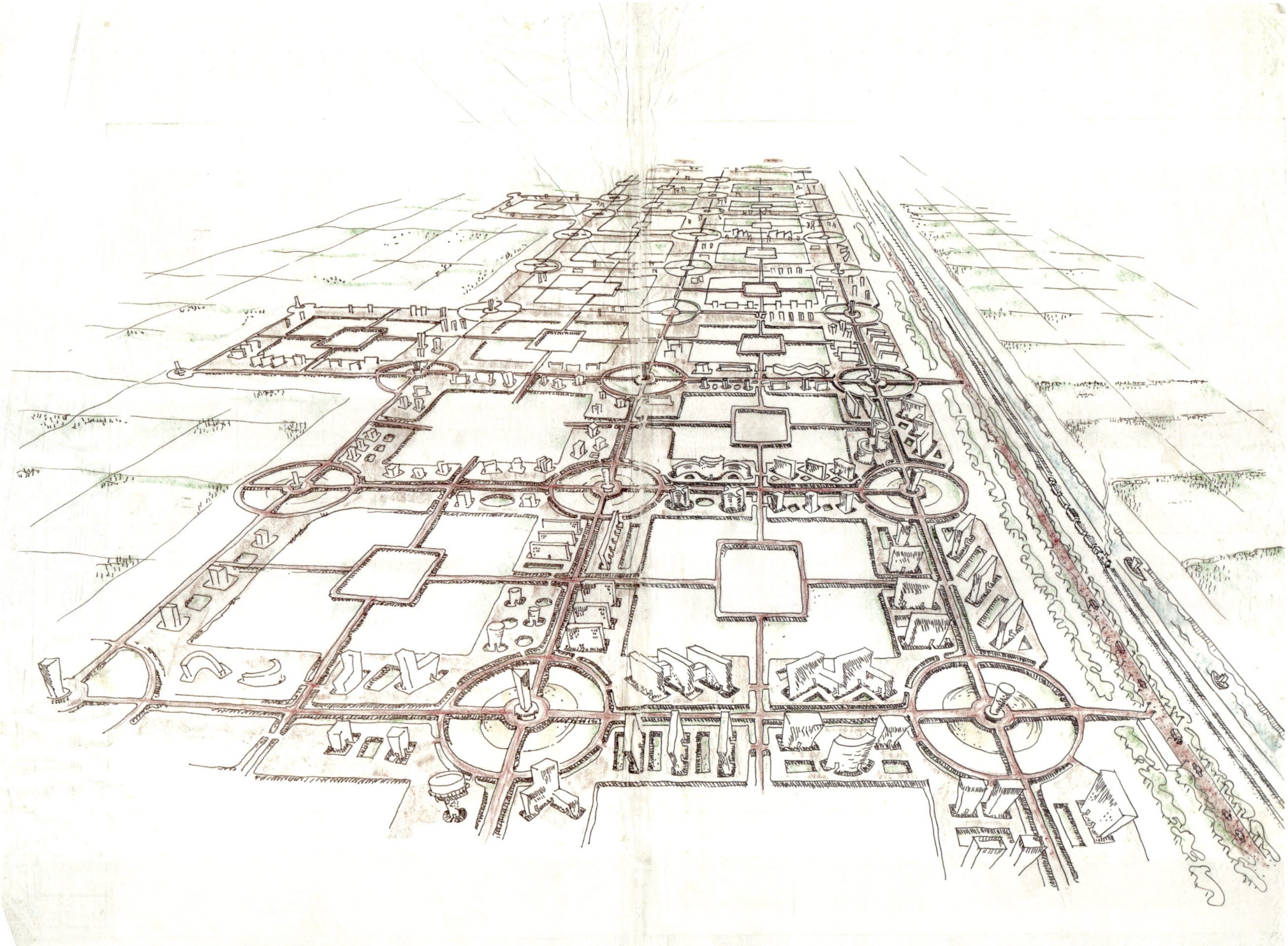

High-level perspectives of the linear city drawn by Sandeep Virmani, APF

Energy Crisis: The Self-Sustaining Linear City Vision

The 1973 oil-induced energy crises proved a watershed moment in Prakash's career as a researcher.[21] As energy costs spiralled worldwide, Prakash came to be influenced by the various alternative energy movements of the 1970s that had their roots in radical protests of the 1960s. Among these, Buckminster Fuller's solutions impressed him the most. Fuller had been visiting India since the early 1960s, and had become a close friend of Indira Gandhi, even when her father Jawaharlal Nehru was prime minister. After Indira Gandhi became prime minister herself, she actively cultivated Fuller, encouraging him to deliver his famous lectures at institutions throughout India, including at the CCA. Prakash immediately took to his wide-canvas way of thinking. Spurred by the energy crisis, his experiences in Ludhiana, and by Fuller's energetic dedication and vision, Prakash began to develop an ideal linear city plan in the early 1970s as an alternative to Chandigarh.

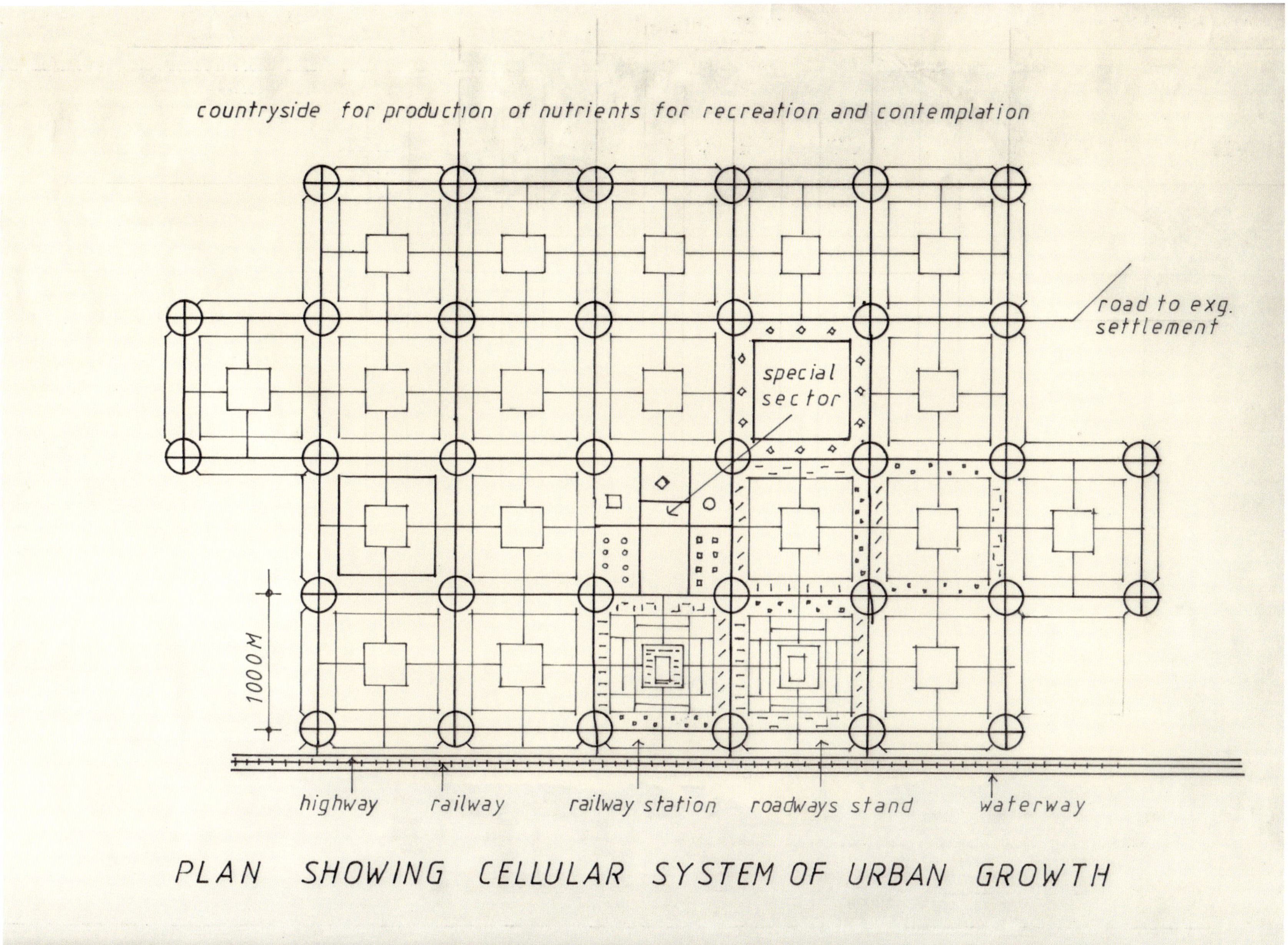

"Cellular" infinite growth plan envisaged by Prakash, APF

Prakash's interest in urban planning had its own history. As early as 1952, having only just joined the Capital Planning Office, Prakash wrote in his private journal that he dreamt of designing a city one day. The sheer and exaggerated magic of seeing Le Corbusier's pencil drawings materialize into a real city may have stirred his imagination. While he was designing Chandigarh, Le Corbusier had also published his book, *Les Trois Établissements Humains* (*The Three Human Establishments*), where he described three ideal city types, including the linear industrial city. Because it was only available in French, it is not clear if Prakash had read it, although his colleague U. E. Chowdhury was working on an English translation and may have introduced him to it.[22]

In his "Living in Cities" paper on Ludhiana, Prakash had proposed that the adjoining new highway be lifted so that its impact on the fragile systems of the local market would be minimized. Prakash argued that his simple sectional move would provide ready access to the market from the highway, while protecting

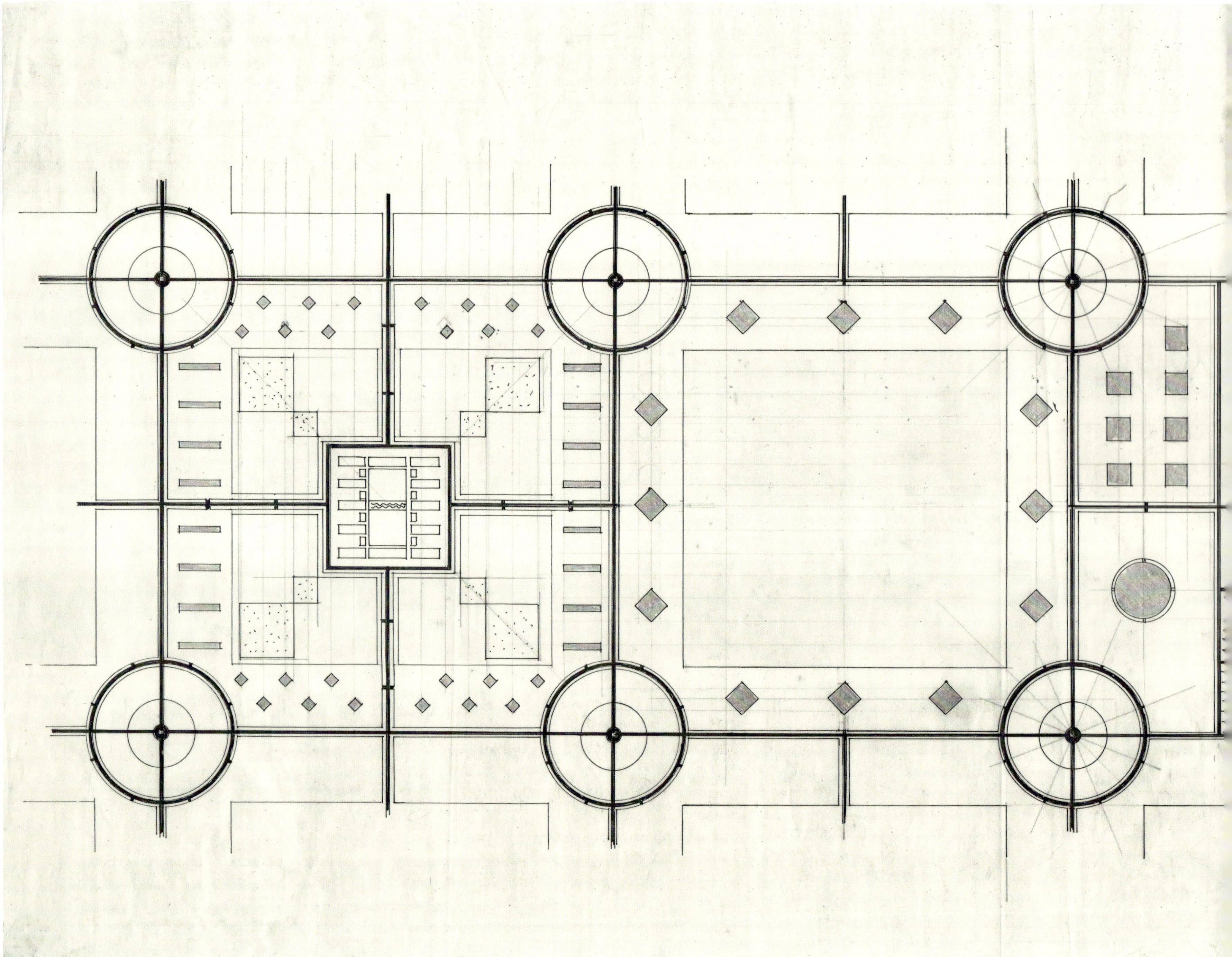

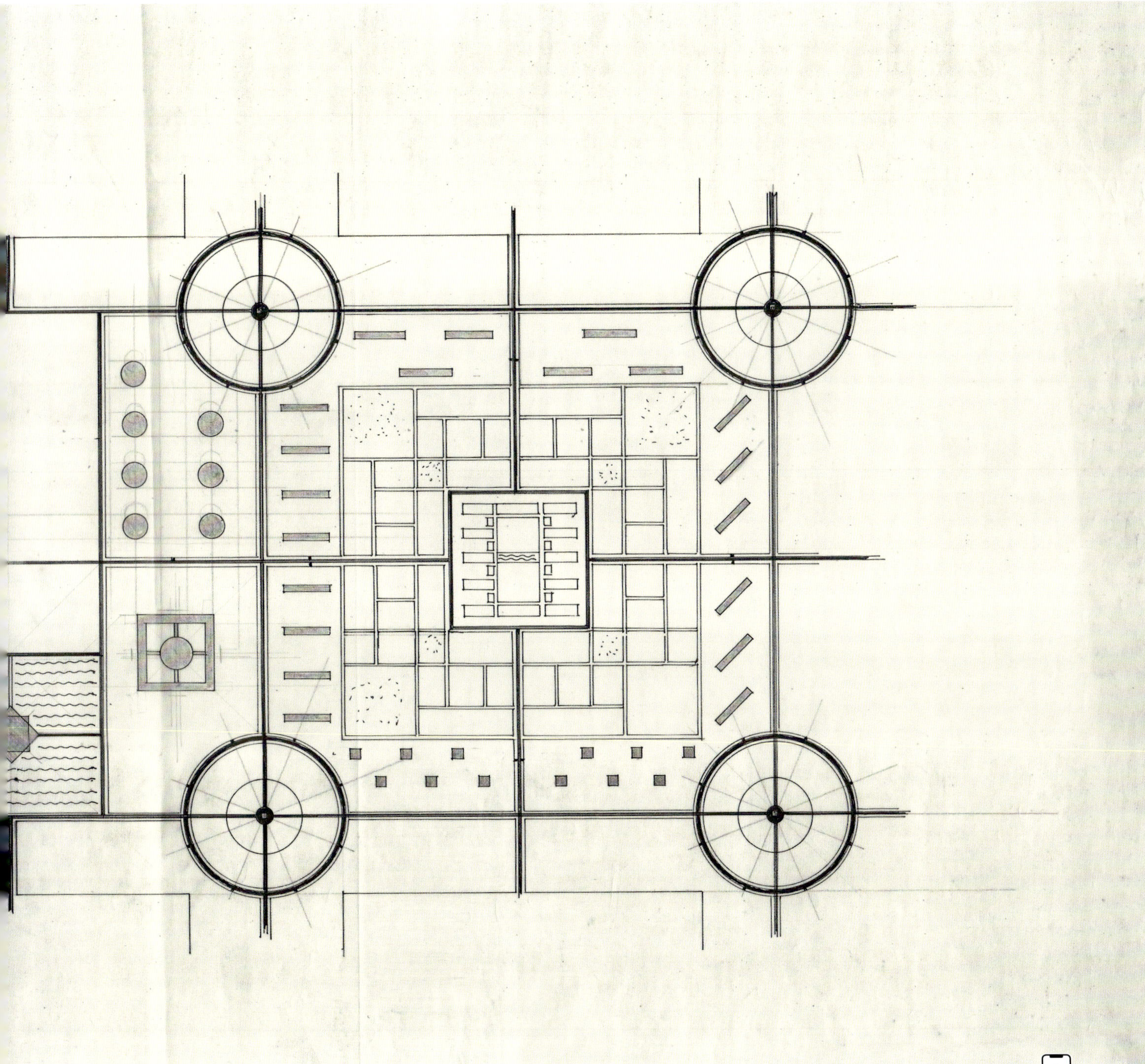

Linear city four-sector plan showing variations with use, APF

Scan image with the **BooksPlus** app

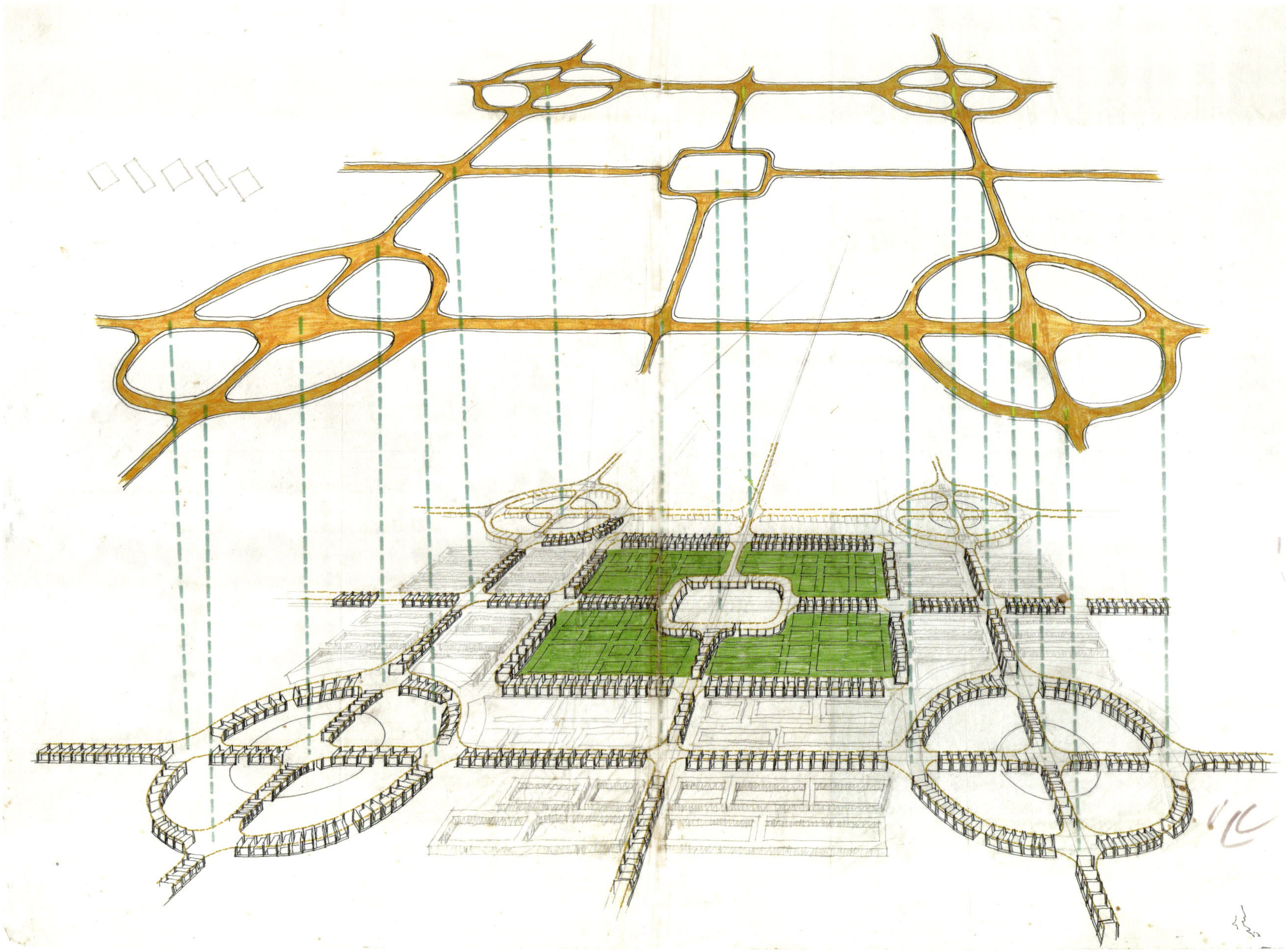

Exploded view of the linear city commercial sector drawn by Sandeep Virmani, APF

the former from the latter's invasive influences. The lifting of the highway could be paid for by selling the land beneath.[23]

The elevated highway functioned as the spine of Prakash's utopian linear city. To maintain a close connection between the urban build-up and its increasingly obscure agro-rural "hinterland," Prakash proposed that the city be no more than two to three sectors deep, but infinitely long so as to accommodate growth as needed. Remembering the beloved horse-drawn barges on Father Thames, Prakash proposed that a constant canal be engineered along the elevated highway for irrigation and transportation alike.[24]

With cars and trucks restricted to the upper levels, the continuous ground plane of Prakash's linear city was to be a haven for "non-motorized" transport and its accompanying social and economic ecologies.[25] Drawings made under Prakash's direction by another thesis student, Sandeep Virmani, show an imagined scene that could have been derived from Prakash's memory of old Ludhiana's Chaura Bazaar. *Sandeep Virmani was my "best friend" from my high-school days. He practically lived in our house. While*

Prakash demonstrates conceptually the separation of mechanized and non-mechanized transportation systems in his model of the linear city, APF

my academic and research interests went more in the direction of history and theory, Sandeep, like a surrogate son, took to my father's utopian visions of the city. The linear city became an embarrassment to me as a young adolescent in Chandigarh. Whenever an opportunity presented itself, which it did often as innumerable architects and academics were constantly funnelling through our home, my father would sit them down and regale them with the deficits of the Chandigarh plan and the virtues of his own visions. The international visitors would piously nod their heads in agreement with him (or so it seemed to me), while the local and national visitors would debate him furiously, each anxious to defend their respective mantles of inherited modernism. I hoped and prayed that the whole issue would just go away, and when it did not, turned to history and theory to understand what had happened. Sandeep, an Indian Air Force officer's son who had lived most of his life all over India, was completely unburdened by the idea of having to shoulder a legacy. He carefully listened to what my father had to say, and drew. Sandeep had a good hand; his drawings are beautiful. I could have never made them.[26]

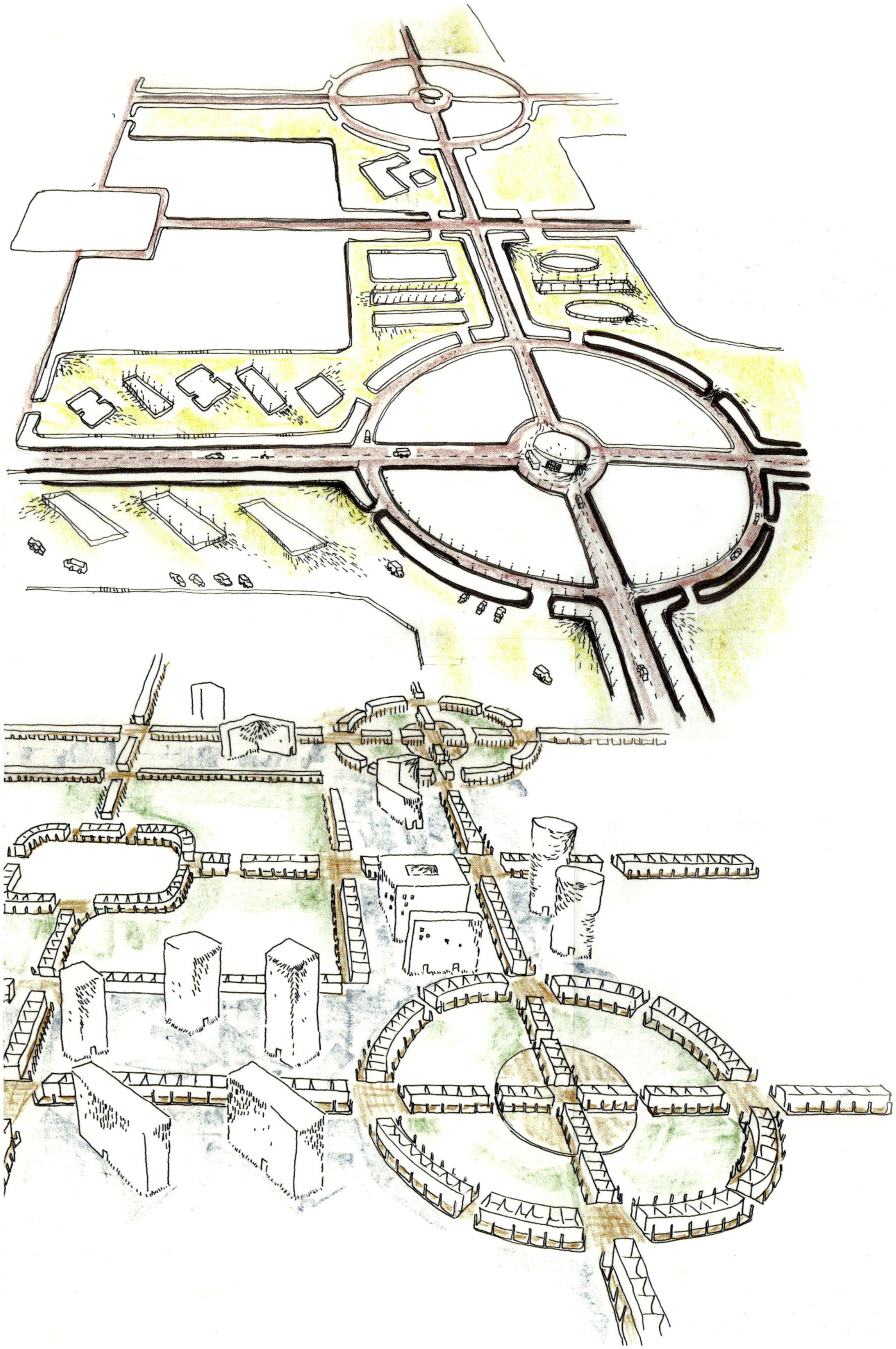

Shops below the roads were intended to pay for the elevated road system, drawn by Sandeep Virmani, APF

The perspective drawing overlaid on colouration of perspective showing separation of traffic, by Sandeep Virmani, APF

Scan image with the **BooksPlus** app

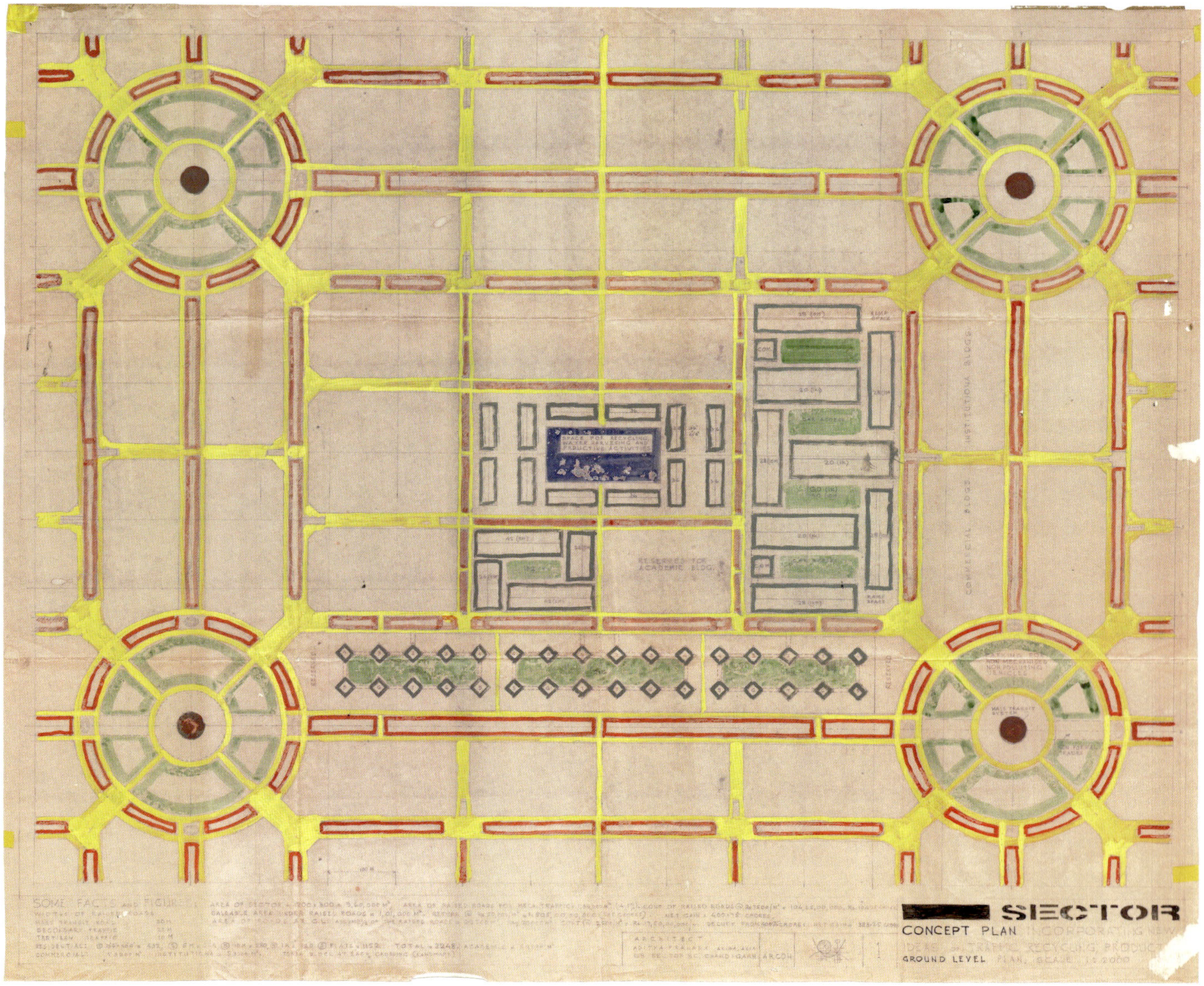

Linear city sector plan, ground level, APF

The Animal

Of course, the animal, as a productive part of the urban community, found pride of place in Prakash's conception of the new utopian city. Like the culture of "food security" and "farm-to-table" thinking of today, his rationale for animals was based on the idea of thinking of neighbourhoods as "productive" and self-sufficient entities:

> If one rears milch cattle, or draft animals in the house, if one has a smithy or a carpentry shop, or spinning spindle and weaving loom in the house, then side by side with living one is generating resources, or producing wealth. If one is training one's progeny in the family vocation in the house, then one is using the house as a school....[27]

Prakash was emotionally invested in urban communities maintaining a direct relationship with their food source and having a tangible participative role in its production. For him the specialization of function required by zoning may have been an appropriate response to the pollution and urban blight caused by the industrial revolution in 19th-century Europe, but that was not the situation of postcolonial India. As emblemized by Mahatma Gandhi's adoption of the *charkha* (spinning wheel) as the symbol

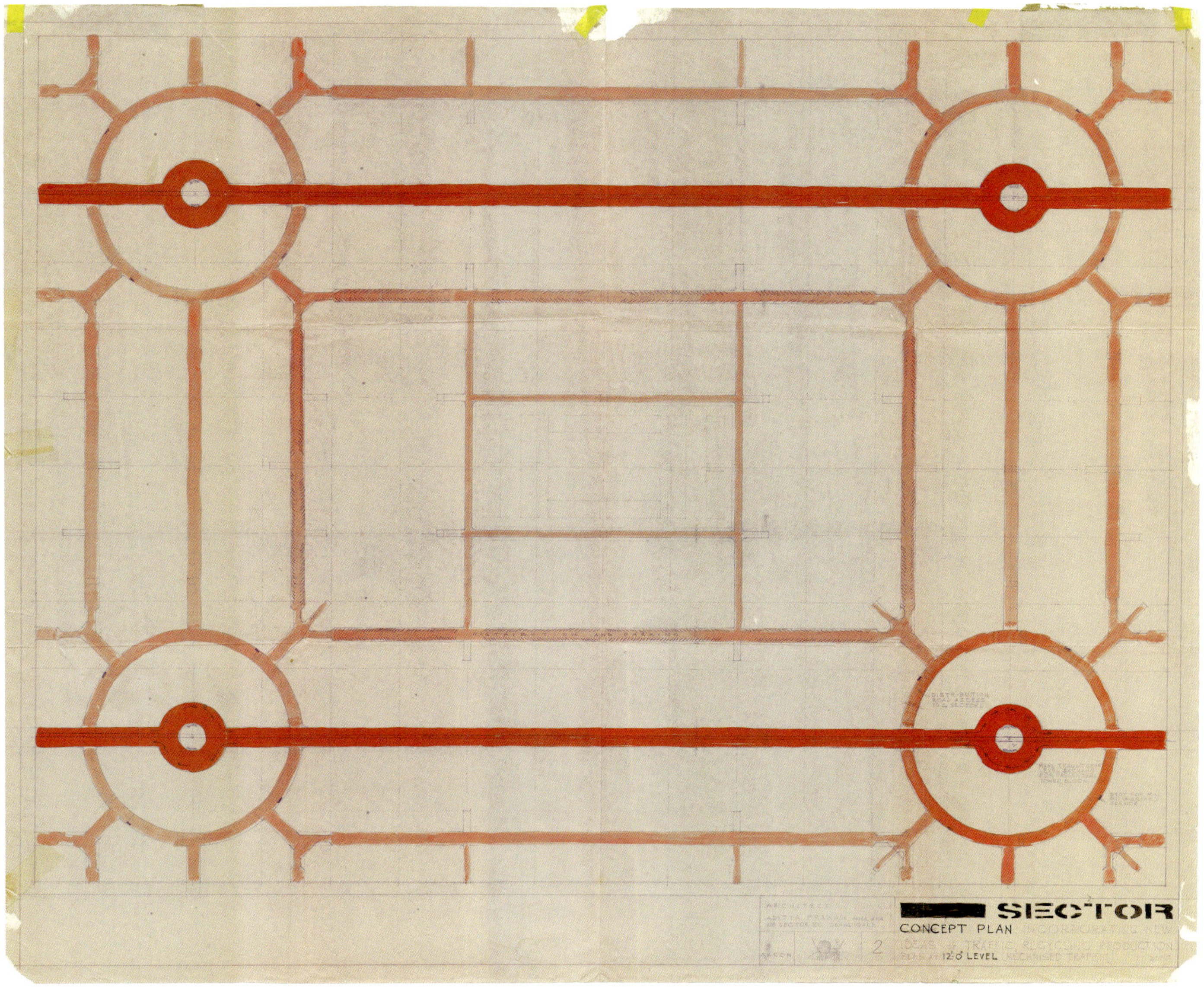

Linear city sector plan, upper road level, APF

of resistance, Prakash argued that the Indian household, and by extension the traditional Indian neighbourhood, integrated small industry into its daily rhythm—a productive ethos that was destroyed by Chandigarh's strict modernist zoning. Instead of killing cottage industries, Prakash argued, the modern Indian city should amplify them.[28]

While Gandhi celebrated the village as the ideal referential unit, Prakash argued that the animal and its attendant rural economic and social systems should be integrated into the fabric of the new cities of India as a revolutionary new concept of urbanization, rather than as the persistent remnant of an undeveloped past. The centre of each sector of his new linear city was a zone of food production, animal husbandry, and recycling. Instead of the park, Prakash wanted the green heart of the sector to be a productive zone, the site of vegetable, milk, dairy, and meat production. While the Chandigarh sector was designed to ensure that each resident could easily walk to the centre where the market was located, Prakash argued that enough food should be produced in the centre of each sector so that the basic food requirements of the entire sector were met locally. He did not imagine that the affluent urban residents would be actively involved in the growing of their own

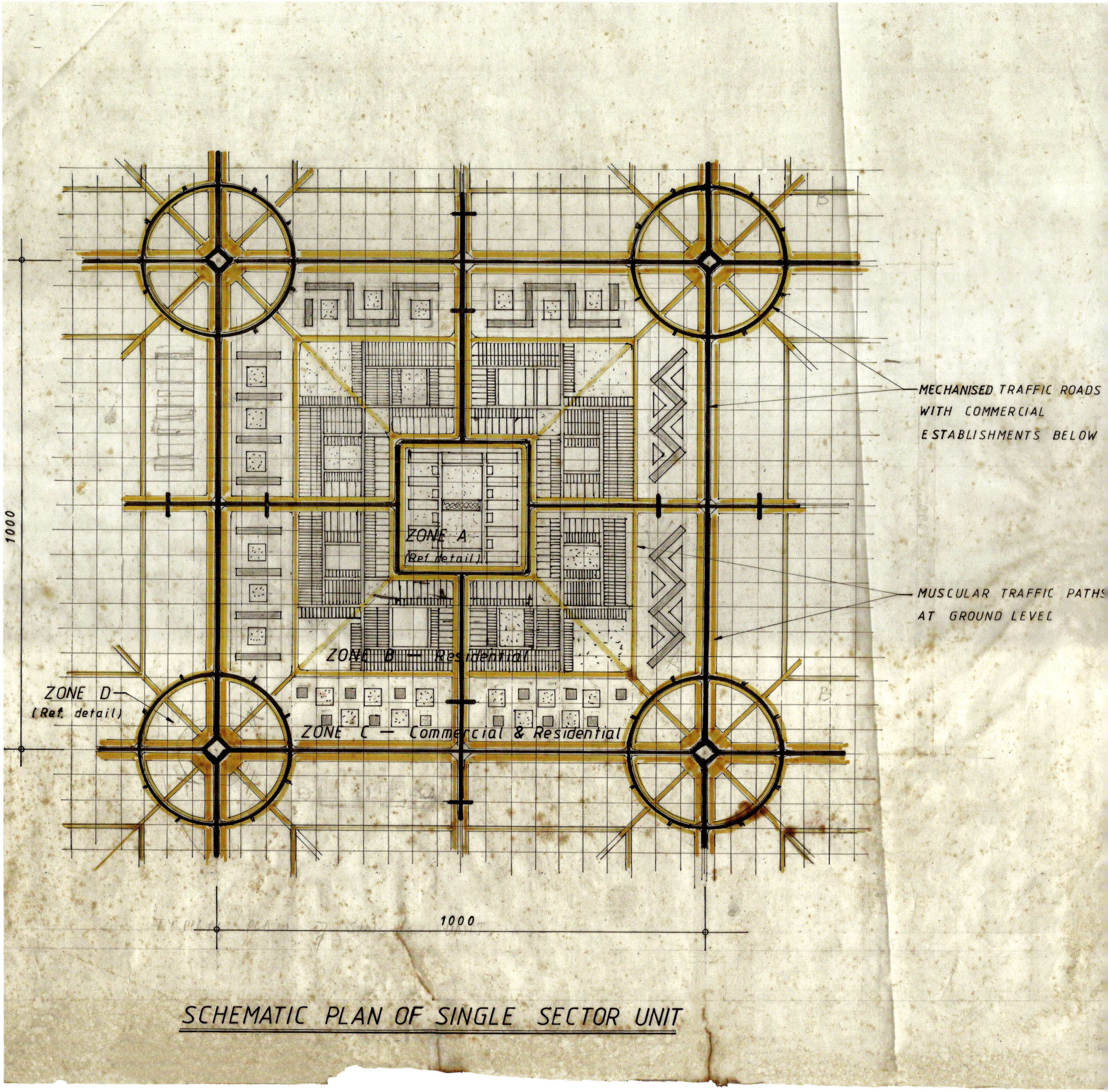
MECHANISED TRAFFIC ROADS
WITH COMMERCIAL
ESTABLISHMENTS BELOW
MUSCULAR TRAFFIC PATHS
AT GROUND LEVEL
ZONE A
(Ref detail)
ZONE B — Residential
ZONE C — Commercial & Residential
ZONE D
(Ref. detail)
1000
1000
SCHEMATIC PLAN OF SINGLE SECTOR UNIT

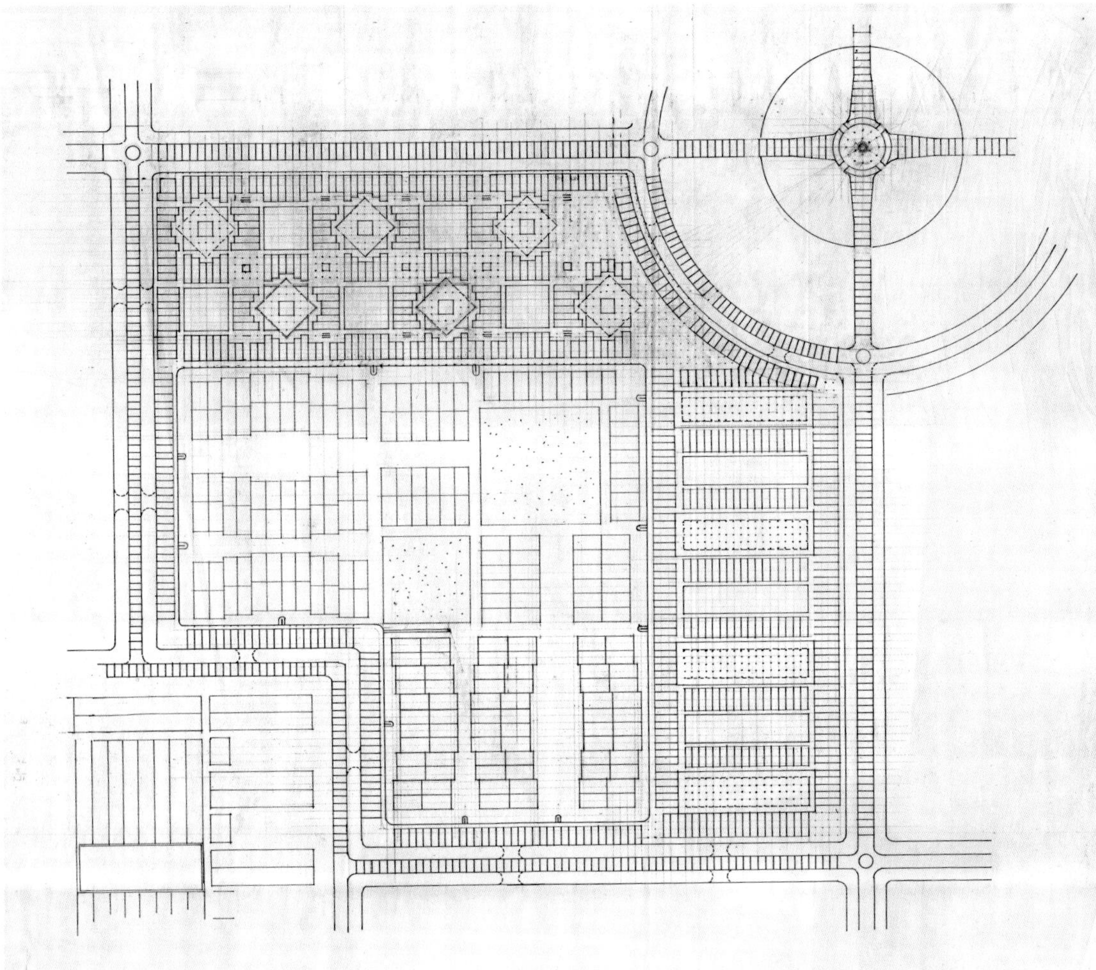

Ground-level plan of commercial area, APF

Schematic plan of single-sector unit, APF

food; he assumed that the rural sector would find employment in this productive heart of the city. The core of every sector in Prakash's city thus was a food production and recycling zone—the rural as the critical heart of the urban.

The main problem was not that the new Indian modernist urban planners did not recognize the constitute relationship and dependency between the urban and the rural, but that they were somehow ethically, or aesthetically, opposed to the very idea of the rural being a part of the urban. Again, memories from his past played a catalytic role. Prakash had grown up with milch cows and buffaloes as an integral part of his family's home in Muzaffarnagar, and living in Ludhiana he had experienced life with animals at close quarters, albeit in a "scientific" setting. He felt that an Indian family "believed that they had fallen short of what was expected of them till they had succeeded in tethering a cow to a post in the courtyard, to ensure that the family got its supply of unadulterated milk."[29] Cows, in other words, were not only of productive value but had had an identifiably affectionate relationship with his family, just as one could have with a pet dog. Given that it is commonplace to find cows on the streets in any Indian city such as Kolkata, New Delhi, or Mumbai, one day, while at the Chandigarh Capital Project Prakash asked Jeanneret why Chandigarh did not allow any cows—neither on the streets nor in homes. This is how Prakash remembered Jeanneret's response:

> Looking at the vast open spaces of the sectors I once suggested to Pierre Jeanneret, "Why may we not create spaces for keeping the cows in the some of these spaces?" Without even wanting to know my ideas about it, he cut me to size by saying, "If you think cows can be kept in the city, you leave Chandigarh." I was

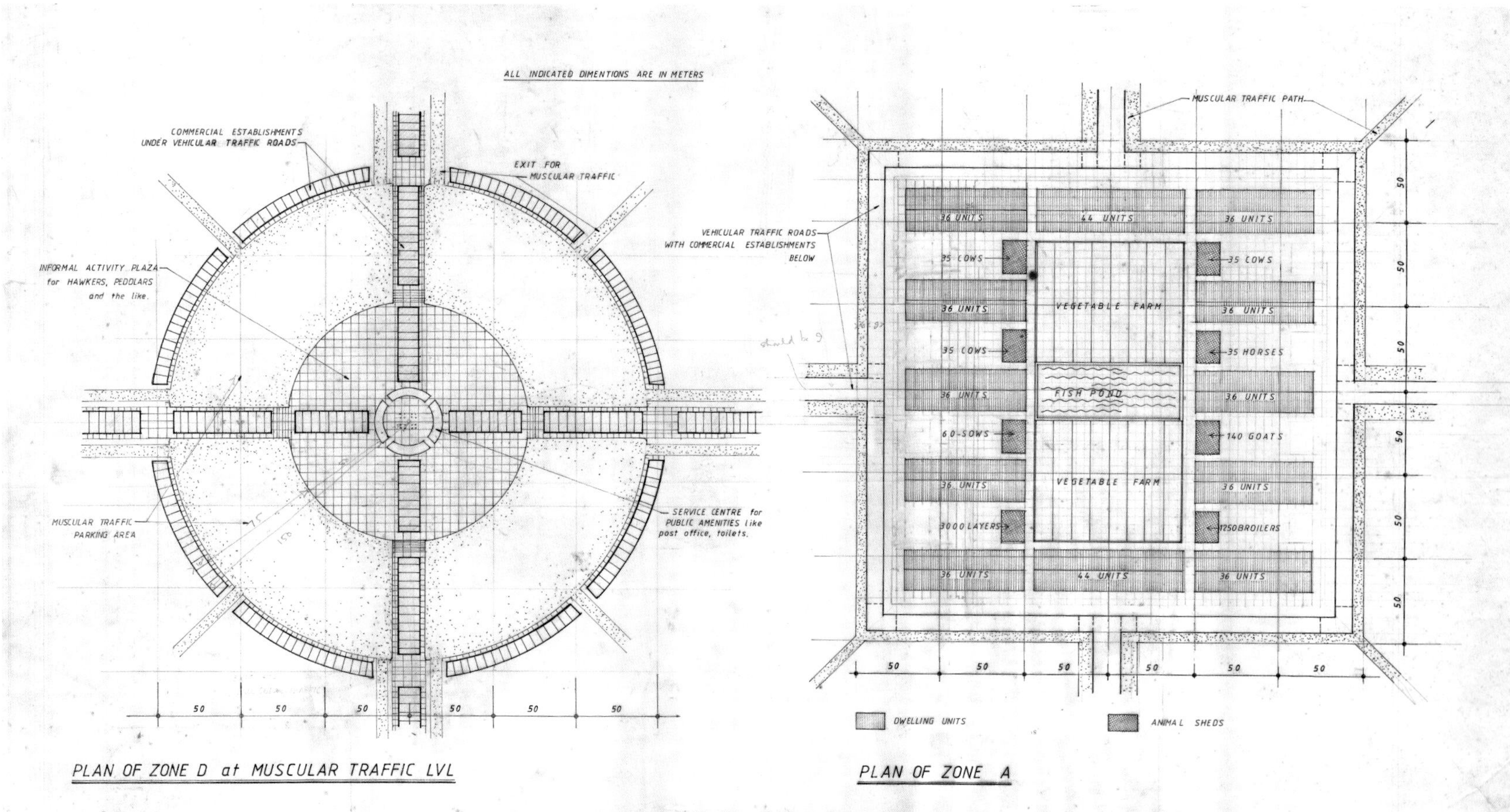

Plan at non-motorized muscular traffic level and of one of the food-producing zones, APF

silenced, but I have to this date not changed my thinking on the subject."[30]

Jeanneret's attitude, fully supported by the Indian architects and planners building Chandigarh, put Prakash's views on the animal at odds with the rest of the Chandigarh Capital Project team. This was not to change even after Jeanneret left. For Prakash, the desire to build for the modern urban "image," over thinking about the city systemically, seemed always to triumph. In a paper titled, "Why Not Ruralization?" Prakash dwelled on the false opposition between the urban and the rural in terms of their "image" and their "truth." While the urban image for Prakash was "planned, progressive, magnificent, grand, rich, sophisticated, magnetic, a provider of opportunities, clean, tidy, sanitary and educated" its truth was that it was "parasitical, consumer oriented, expensive, a waste generator." In contrast, the rural was considered to be "spontaneous, decadent, minuscule, unimpressive, poor, rustic, dull, a depriver of opportunities, dirty, untidy, insanitary, ignorant." But the village's "truth" was that it was "self-reliant, production oriented, economical, recycles all wastes, time saver, natural, considerate, nature lover"—all values that were denied to the urban because of its aesthetic hostility to the rural:

No one is allowed to keep any cows, buffaloes, goats, or sheep. Yet the cows roam the streets.

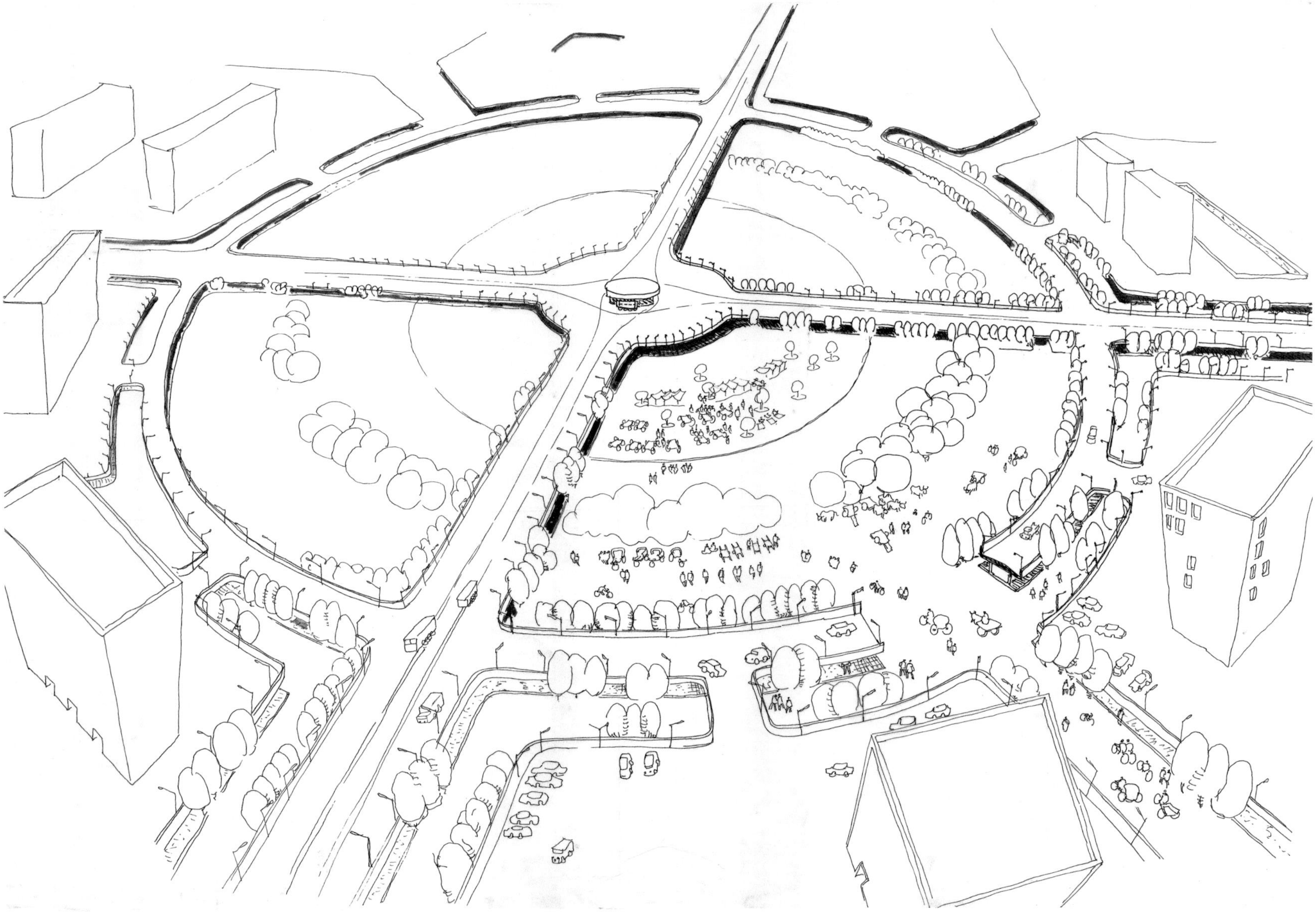

High-level perspectives of the linear city drawn by Sandeep Virmani, APF

They are frowned upon and all measures taken to extradite them. At the same time the campuses of Agricultural Universities at Ludhiana and Hissar have all these productive elements juxtaposed with the human habitation and activities... "Beauty is there in everything. It requires EYES to perceive it." Words to this effect were uttered by my friend B.P. Mathur long ago. I did not agree with him then, I do so now.[31]

Ultimately, Prakash argued that the artificial disciplinary distinction between the urban and rural should be eliminated altogether:

There is a fundamental error in our perception of the Urban and Rural activities—mainly because in our planning thought and practices, we do not include all sections of the society for equitable enjoyment of life. Our professions serve only those who can pay for our services, and since such people are few and far between, most urban sections are indeed rural in nature because the application of knowledge is piecemeal, incidental and therefore exploitative. It leads to poor quality of life for most of the sections of society. Indeed, the well-to-do also willy-nilly suffer the same fate.[32]

The Architects...have invented the term "Urban Design." "Rural Design" as a term has not found favour with the architects, possibly

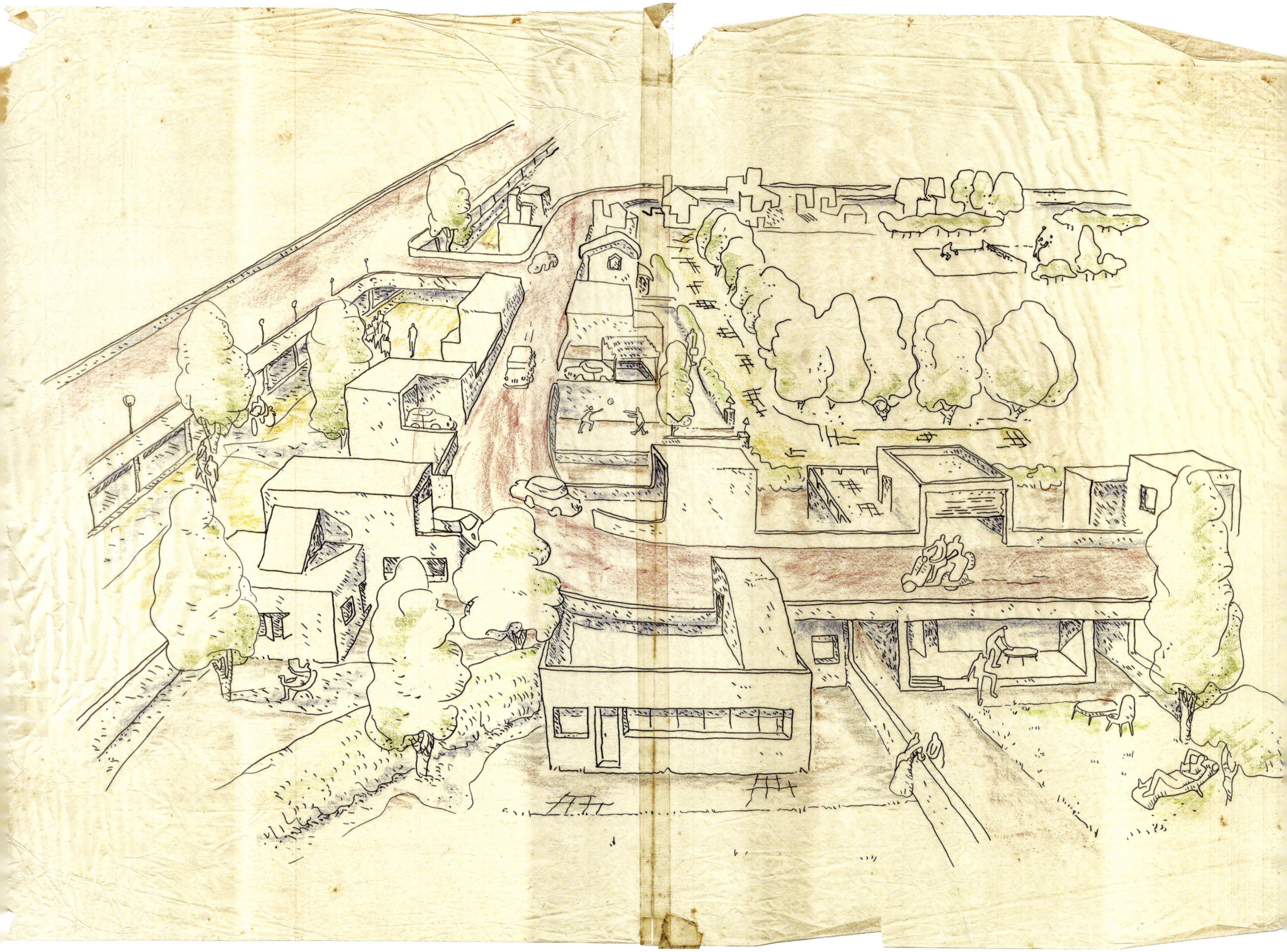

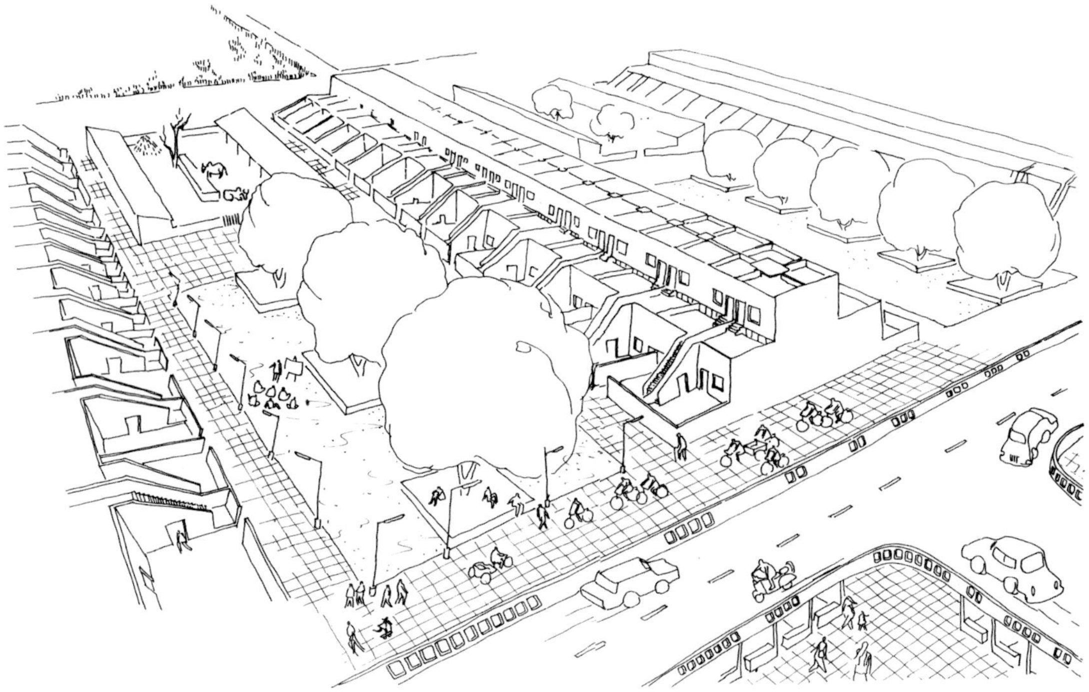

Housing block drawn by Sandeep Virmani, APF

The housing blocks, APF

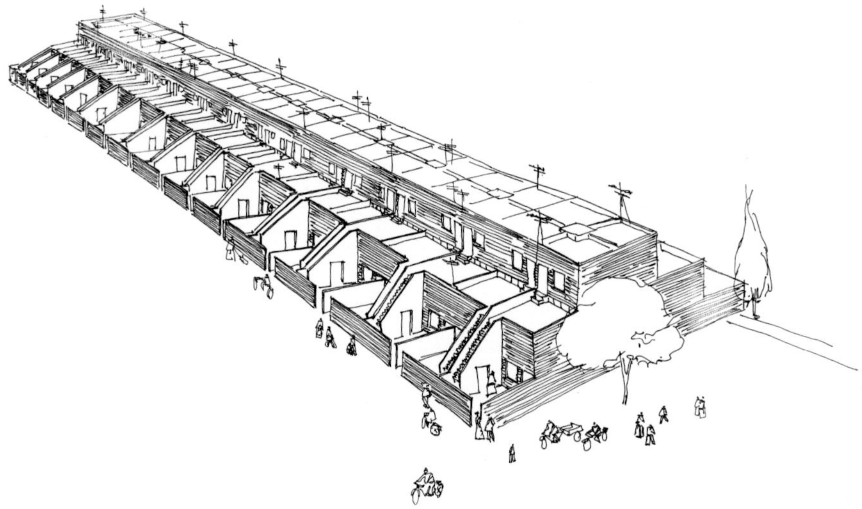

Linear city elevated highway and housing, drawn by Sandeep Virmani, APF

Shop-level perspective drawn by Sandeep Virmani, APF

Ground view of a flourishing informal sector, APF

> because there is no bread and butter in it. But Landscape Design is very much in vogue with the architects.[33]

Ultimately, Prakash's urban planning concepts did not find much purchase in the 1970s with the Chandigarh Administration, or with the design planning communities of India in general. Rather than arguing for the radical transformation of Chandigarh into a self-sufficient haven, Prakash put all his efforts into the planning of Haryana's new capital city. Per the 1966 agreement that created the new state of Haryana, its government would be housed in Chandigarh only until it had its own state capital ready. Vested political interests, however, generated a stalemate by which the state of Haryana never seriously planned its own capital because it felt it had to maintain its presence in Chandigarh to protect its interests.[34]

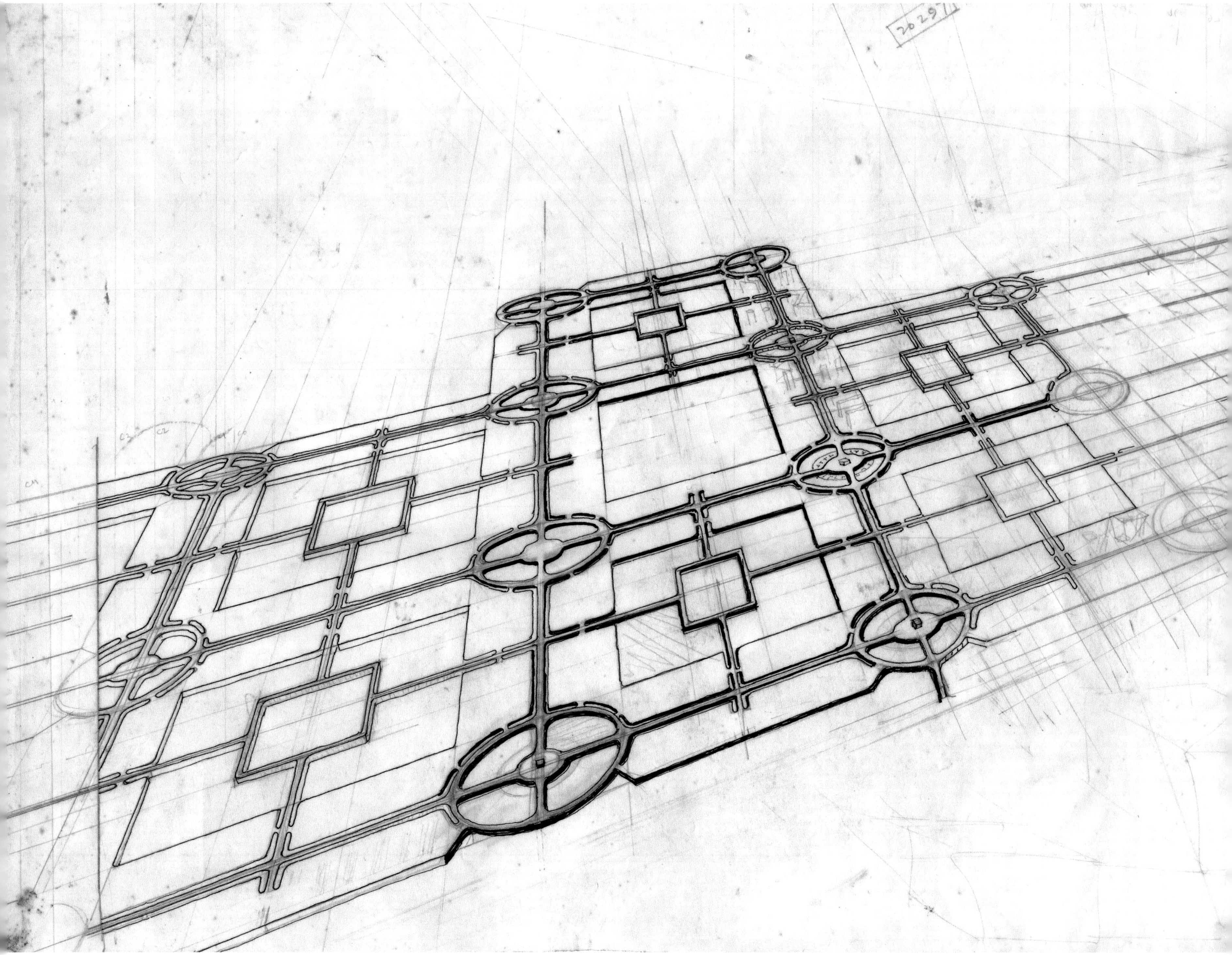

Replication of the sectors in the linear city drawn by Aditya Prakash, APF

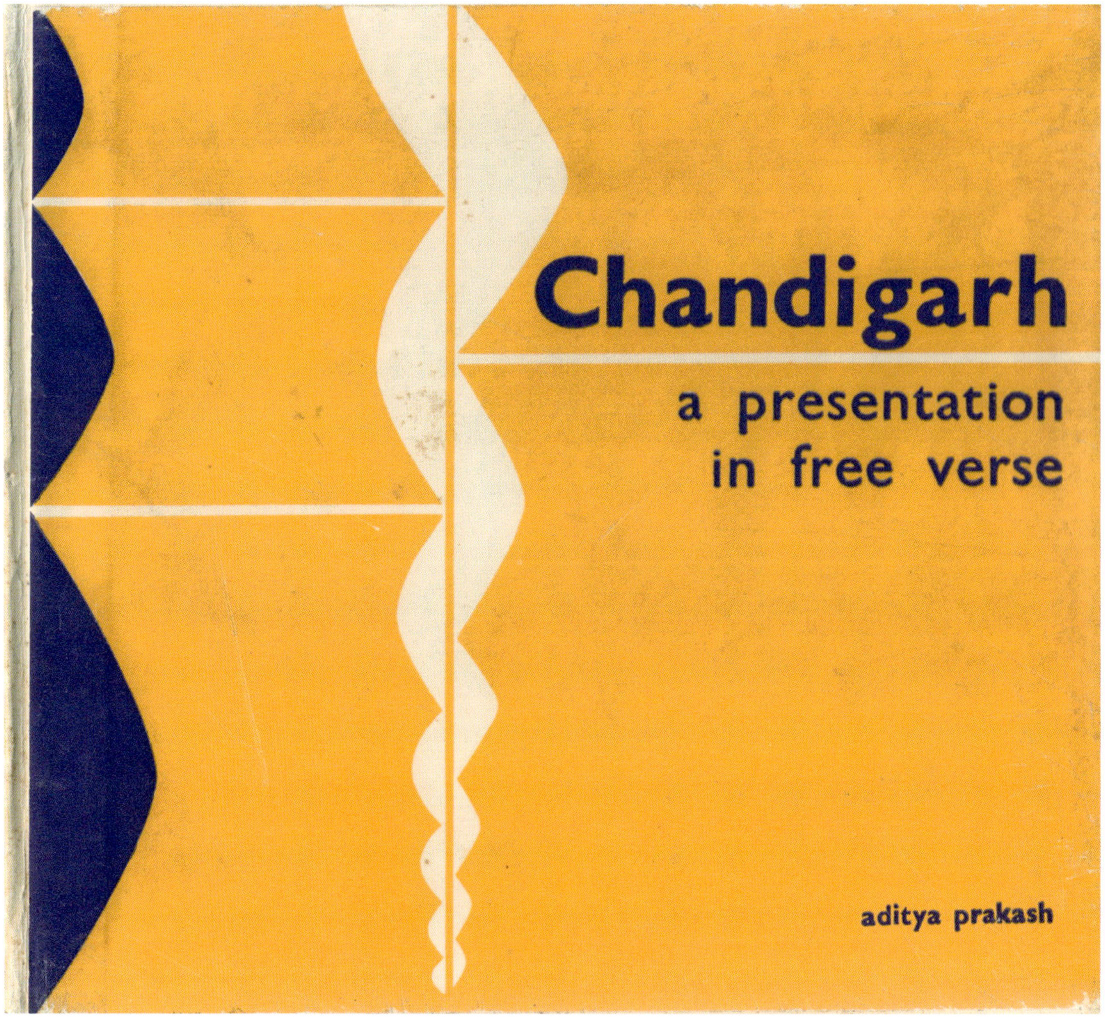

***Chandigarh: A Presentation in Free Verse* by Aditya Prakash**, 1978, APF

***Reflections on Chandigarh* by Aditya Prakash**, 1983, APF

Writing in Free Verse

In 1976 Mulk Raj Anand, on one of his innumerable visits to the city, persuaded the Chandigarh Administration to pay for a book on Chandigarh, which he felt was long overdue. In 1966, Norma Evenson had published her dissertation, an idiosyncratic aesthetic assessment of the Chandigarh experiment in its infancy, which had been poorly received in the city.[35] Madhu Sarin's research on Chandigarh was known, but still not published.[36] Prakash was the only original member of the Capital Project team who was still in Chandigarh and invested in the city, and who could write. He was of course also one of Anand's best friends.

In hindsight, it is difficult to know if the book that Prakash eventually wrote was actually the book that Anand might have wanted. A prolific novelist, with a literary descriptive style that once earned him the praise of E. M. Forster, Anand favoured books that were thick in description and plot, with a clearly outlined moral fable. The book that Prakash wrote, in contrast, was a freeform epistle, composed from epigraphic narratives. Titled *Chandigarh: A Presentation in Free Verse*, the book offers a surprisingly canonical and flattering account of Chandigarh and its design principles.[37] Little foreshadows Prakash's trenchant critiques of Chandigarh embedded in his later research, and those that appeared in future publications. But its literary mood and style are fascinating.

Chandigarh: A Presentation in Free Verse begins with a short vignette by Anand himself, describing the conditions of Chandigarh's genesis in a fast-paced dialogue style, in an imaginary scene set in a distant rest house in which Le Corbusier, Jeanneret, Drew, Fry, Thapar, Varma, Jeet Malhotra, and Anand himself discuss the city to be, while quoting Arthur Rimbaud, drinking home-made wine and passing around sketches of scenes from a local village. It is the Tower of Babel: French, English, Punjabi are spoken, nobody understands anybody, while Le Corbusier holds the pencil and draws and decides what Chandigarh is to be. "Today," Anand concludes, "that city is a lived reality, lived in, coveted, loved and sung about by Aditya Prakash, a challenge to future generations to evolve it into the finest city of humanism in the world."

As Anand's text makes clear, the book was intended as something like a citizen's guide for Chandigarh's new inhabitants, an explanation of how their new city was designed as an instrument of citizenship-making, in the modernist Nehruvian universal-nationalist mould. Prakash's narrative gives voice to that idealized subject of citizenship in the tongue of what he terms "free verse" that describes the tenets of the city, but in an oneiric tone of a chorus in a Greek tragedy. The text details simple facts and inevitabilities as if they were talismans of life.[38] Here is an example:

A sector is like a fort
Surrounded by roads instead of a moat
Entries (if not gates) at four positions located
All other areas by walls protected
The Enemy is not the Army with swords
It is the traffic which endangers life, no less.
(p.15)

The narrative is accompanied by black and white sketches by Sunirmal Chatterjee, who was the graphics instructor at the CCA, hired by Prakash. Chatterjee and Prakash were good friends. The former once tie-dyed the logo of the CCA, designed by Prakash, into a beautiful red and orange scarf. There is a fantastic free-line quality to Chatterjee's sketches which attempts to capture the essential formal and spatial characteristics of the city using the rapid movement of the hand as the instrument of capture, more so than the calculated exactness of proportion or perspective.[39] Like the text, the sketches aspire to extract the poetic from the quotidian, from the everyday syntax of the city's modernist architecture.

Immediately after the publication of *A Presentation in Free Verse*, Prakash began work on its companion volume, *Reflections on Chandigarh*, also in free verse.[40] Clearly this was the book that Prakash really wanted to write. Based on his research on the Indian city and the peripheral villages, *Reflections* was an unbridled critique of the performance of the Chandigarh plan, which he dubbed as being escapist and anti-human. Unsurprisingly, *Reflections* contains a manifesto on how to transform Chandigarh into a self-sustaining city, well-integrated with its rural periphery with a place of pride for the animal.

Unlike in his first book, this time Prakash's language is trenchant and almost acerbic, designed to catch your attention and make a point, rather than spin a dream:

> WHEN ONE CONTEMPLATES
> ON THIS STRETCH OF LAND
> AT THE FOOT OF HILLS
> WITH LAKE, MONUMENTS, FORESTS AND SPACES
> ALL AWESOME, INSPIRING, ELEVATING,
> EVEN AMIDST THE FEELING OF RESPECT
> ONE CANNOT ESCAPE ONE THOUGHT:
> IT IS ESCAPIST
> IT IS ESCAPIST IN ITS VERY CONCEPT
> IT DOES NOT BELONG TO THE PEOPLE
> INDEED IT LOOKS TOWARDS THE PEOPLE
> WITH DISDAIN IF NOT CONTEMPT...
> THE BIOLOGICAL SIMILE
> THAT THE HEAD IS AT THE TOP,
> IS, TO SAY THE LEAST, 'PATHETIC'
> (p. 39-40)

Clearly, 20 years after his involvement in building Chandigarh, Prakash was disenchanted by the city's vision, and, perhaps more importantly, by its creator. He had styled his life on Le Corbusier. To critique him so virulently testifies to the book's Oedipal character, marked in the text with a "shudder" and a "brace":

> A THINKER, A POET, A PAINTER, A SCULPTOR,
> A WRITER, A PHILOSOPHER, A CRUSADER,
> IN ONE WORD—A GENIUS.
> I SHUDDER TO THINK
> THAT I SIT TO WRITE
> A 'CRITIQUE' ON THE CITY OF HIS DREAMS.
> EVERYTIME I REACH THIS POINT, I SHUDDER,
> FOR I FEEL I AM CHALLENGING THE "OBVIOUS,"
> I AM CALLING THE "RIGHT" "THE ESCAPIST."
> BUT I MUST BRACE MYSELF TO MEET THE CHALLENGE,
> YES, I CALL THE CHANDIGARH PLAN:
> "ESCAPIST,"
> THE OTHER NAME I CAN GIVE IS:
> "DISINTEGRATED."
> (p.19)

Again, Anand wrote an Afterword to *Reflections*, but even with that endorsement Prakash was unable to find a commercial publisher for the book. Ultimately, he self-published it in 1983, with the help of his brother, Brij Nandan Prakash, who owned a small publishing house in New Delhi.

Invitation posters for plays by Abhinet theatre group, APF

Abhinet and Tagore-iterates

Even as Prakash veered towards urban planning and radical sustainability in his academic research, theatre and architectural practice continued to be significant sources of nourishment for his non-academic soul.

A chance meeting in 1973 with two faculty of Panjab University—Dr. Virendra Mehndiratta, professor of Hindi, and Dr. N. C. Thakur, professor of English literature—introduced him to a nascent theatre company called Abhinet. Champa Mangatrai, Harish Bhatia, Atul Vir Arora, Goldy Malhotra, and Prahlad Aggarwal were also early members.[41] *Abhinet* was an amateur theatre company in the best etymological sense of the term, i.e., driven by *amare*, or love of the work with no commercial interest. Starting in 1972, *Abhinet* had no plans to go professional, or work with trained actors or street performers. All of its actors, directors, make-up artists, and producers had day jobs, and a surprisingly large number of them were academics, and that too of the Nehruvian mould. They all believed in the nation-state, in its modernist aspiration, and were in Chandigarh because of its affiliation with those ideals. A part of that belief was that it was their mandate, as the first generation of postcolonial Indian academics and citizens, to produce a modernist theatre ethic in the city. There was a very reputable, very modernist Department of Indian Theatre at the University, started by Balwant Gargi, and connected to New Delhi's National School of Drama.[42] These two departments were responsible for producing some of the best actors and directors of modern India. But *Abhinet*, by contrast, revelled in its amateur status, aligning their role as citizens with unearthing new performance aesthetics.

In *Abhinet*, Prakash found a second home. Theatre served as a site where his normally reserved personality could find expression. Immersing himself into *Abhinet*'s activities, he helped create a performance stage in CCA's courtyard in the mid-1970s.

Unsurprisingly, *Abhinet* adopted Tagore Theatre as its de facto home (as did many other theatre companies of Chandigarh in time). All of *Abhinet*'s plays had an abstracted modernist look and sensibility to them that blended well with the sparse aesthetics of Tagore Theatre. Actors evoked moods and events through gestural moves and positions, their blocking was structured to optimize visual clarity, the costumes were symbolic rather than representative, and the staging of lights and background audio were choreographed to encourage active audience participation and interpretation, rather than dedicated to making immersive-realistic environments.

Of course, all of *Abhinet*'s sets also fit the minimalist-modernist mould, and Aditya Prakash was inevitably their designer. In the APF Archives, there is a typewritten Prakash manuscript titled *Stagecraft*.[43] In it, Prakash described his philosophy of theatre and set design. He begins by drawing attention to children playing the imaginary game of "Train," in which "children holding each other's garment... faithfully [follow] where the 'engine' leads." This imagination was the key to the miracle of the stage performance—staged in the following passage by the ubiquitous scare-quotes:

> A theatre "STAGE" is a similar world of imagination. A "Play" takes form in the mind of the playwright. It takes place in "Time" or sequence of "Times;" in a "Place" or sequence of "Places;" and it presents the evolution of a "Character" or a few "Characters" in "Time and Place." All this is to be presented on a "Stage" in the course of 2–3 hours. Just as a long train journey, say from Delhi to Bombay, is performed in the imaginative play "TRAIN" of children, so does a whole sequence of events present itself in the imagination of the audience while watching—nay participating in—a "Stage" performance. Audience participation is an essential component of a "PLAY" performed on a stage. Unless the "imagination" of the audience moves with the imagination of the playwright, audience participation cannot take place.

Prakash's theatre designs tried to do as much with as little as possible. A few carefully chosen props made the scene. He was fond of relocating the wings away from the edges, making implied rooms via strategic placement of individual panels. Furniture was always abstract—simple cubes and cuboids, flipped around, assembled and disassembled to cater to the needs of different scenes. One or two of his own paintings inevitably found their place somewhere on those implied walls of the scene.

Abhinet performing *The Cocktail Party* by T. S. Eliot, directed by Prakash, 1987, APF

Abhinet performance set with a painting by Prakash in the background, APF

To a significant extent, theatre buildings were also the mainstay of Prakash's architectural design practice through the 1970s. Per government rules, the faculty of the CCA were unfortunately not allowed to engage in private practice, presumably to prevent conflict of interest. Right from his first days as principal, Prakash actively lobbied against this rule, arguing that active engagement with practice was essential to ensure that the faculty was conversant with contemporary issues both at a daily design level and the larger systemic level. The Chandigarh Administration, however, was not receptive to this idea—but they allowed the faculty to engage in voluntary projects like designing their own houses or working on a project given to the institution. In other words, if the revenue accrued to the governmental coffers, they could do the work. Prakash used this sliver of opportunity to continue to design and build all the while he was in the administration.

Immediately after returning to Chandigarh, Prakash designed two houses for himself—one his own private residence in Sector 8, in 1970, and the other the official residence of the principal of the CCA in the college's campus in Sector 12, in 1971. His own house, on a standard one *kanal* (605 sq. yard) plot of the city, was essentially an argument with the Le Corbusier-Jeanneret solar analysis of the city, which presumed that the best orientation in the city faced north, or east or west if necessary, but certainly not South. Prakash disagreed. His own solar studies suggested that if protected properly, as in traditional Indian houses, a southern orientation with maximized exposure was best for designing the most effective solar protective systems, and also ideal from an architectural point of view. He argued this point in a paper titled "Solar Passive/Active Architecture" as follows:

> Functionally, South East is a very good orientation. South side gets plenty of low winter sun which is very agreeable. The summer sun attains very high altitude and thus can be easily kept out. Many people

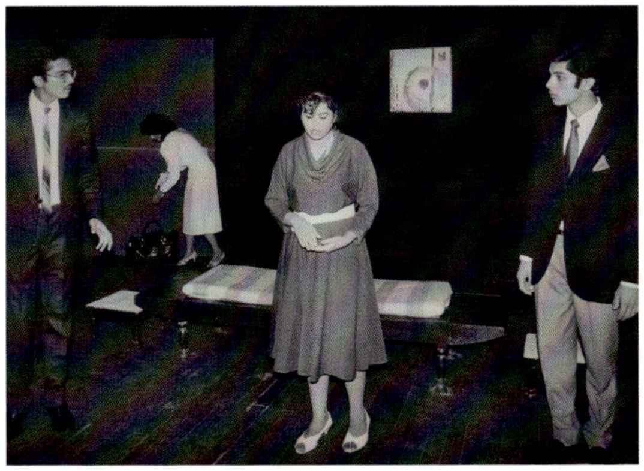

A brochure for an Abhinet play designed by Prakash, APF

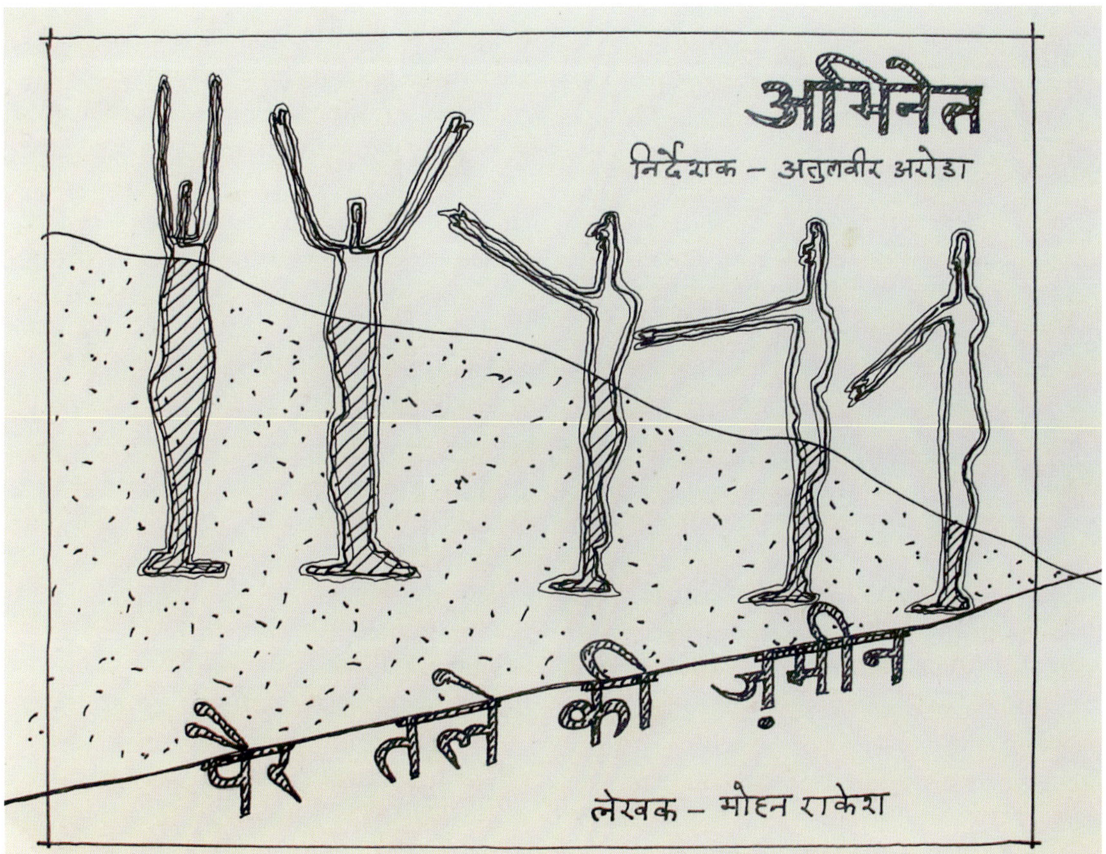

> wrongly think that South side is very hot and should be avoided. In fact, South may be called the best orientation because of sunshine in winter and shade in summer.[44]

For his own house, he picked a south-facing plot, and created a massive statement out of the solar protector that he cantilevered out and hung from the roof itself.[45] For the rest, the house followed the established vocabulary of the "Chandigarh style"—exposed load-bearing brick walls, with concrete lintels and parapets, optimized for efficiency, light and ventilation. In the mid-1970s, he also designed a beautiful house in New Delhi for the family of journalist K. K. Katyal, in much the same vocabulary—a brick-clad south-facing structure with a massive overhang and deep verandas. In 1993, after retirement, Prakash added a painting studio on top of the garage of his own house in Sector 8. A sprinkling of small glass openings, many painted onto, spread themselves across the white plastered facade. There was

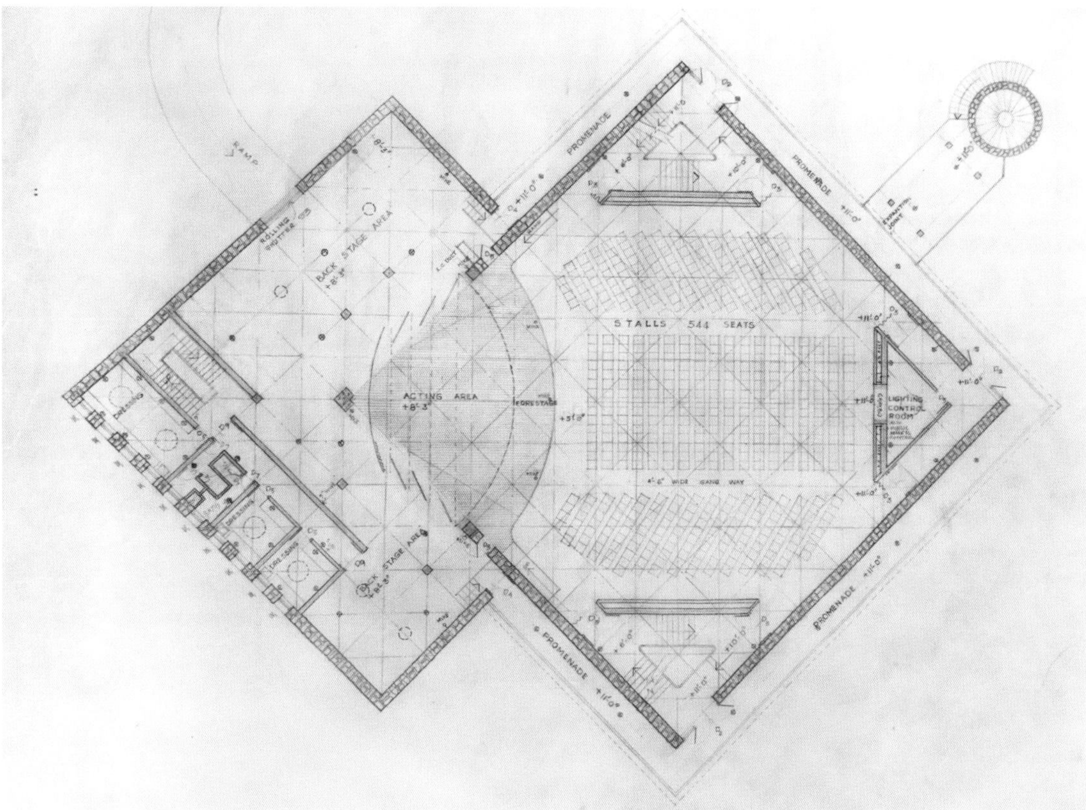

J&K Academy Plan, APF

no exposed brick, and a water tank twirled precariously over the edge like a ballerina balancing on her toes.

Unlike his own house which was semi-detached, with one shared-party wall, the principal's residence stood in the middle of a massive 16 *kanal* plot of land, an object in space in the mould of Tagore Theatre. A relentless brick box with a prominent concrete band at the top made extra-large to hide the water tanks, this residence was an expression of the "Chandigarh style" reduced to its core elements. Unlike Fry, Drew, Jeanneret, and even the Indian Chandigarh architects who sought to create a painterly poetics out of the limited palette that was available to them, Prakash in the principal's residence sought to strip the Chandigarh modernist vocabulary to its bare essentials.

Most of Prakash's emotional investment in the principal's residence went into using it as a site for sustainable urbanism. The large yard around the principal's residence was a wasted resource. It had been created by chopping down trees from the fragile ecological barrier between the city and its western intermittent river, the Patiala ki Rao. Prakash set up the yard as a productive space by building a composting pit, instructing the gardener to expend all his resources to grow vegetables for the family and not to waste any time and water on grass or ornamental plants, and by installing experimental solar water heaters and solar cookers in it, properly oriented. He even wanted a "community" of dymaxion domes built on it, but this proved too prohibitively expensive.[46]

In 1972, Prakash had an opportunity to redo Tagore Theatre, when he was invited to design a new performing arts facility in Jammu for the state of Jammu and Kashmir. Although the

J&K Academy under construction, APF

seating plan of the J&K Academy was a clone of that of Tagore Theatre, in external appearance, the two were completely different. Compared to the austere brick wrapper of Tagore Theatre that is disconnected from the internal structure, the J&K Academy's exterior is expressively structural. This time, Prakash insisted and was able to get a true space-frame roof that he cantilevered out 12 feet in every direction. From these he hung three rows of staggered promenades or verandas that make up the dramatic profile of the structure. Instead of being hidden behind an external frame, the J&K roof is exposed in a way that Kenneth Frampton would later characterize as the "tectonic" expression of structure.[47] The J&K Academy also needed a fire exit, per updated codes, and this took the form of a free-standing spiral, quite like Jeanneret's water-pumping station at Sukhna Lake in Chandigarh.

The success of the J&K Academy Theatre spurred a commission to design a theatre and performing arts academy at Srinagar. Drawings in the archives of the APF show a much more relaxed design, the audience hall and performance space formed by a complete circle. The exterior and the roof are not clear, but it seems as if Prakash had planned to use the space frame again. But this project, unfortunately, was never executed.

J&K Academy under construction, APF

Late in the 1970s, another iteration of Tagore Theatre was built in the form of an open-air theatre, in Sector 23 in Chandigarh. This time Prakash made the seating plan shallower and wider, wrapping around the stage in a more intimate manner than at Tagore. Since this theatre had no containing walls, sound could only be projected to a lesser distance without amplification. Even so, Prakash reproduced Tagore's distinctive acoustic panel, this time out of concrete with prominent inverted beams.

Through the 1970s, while he was still the principal of CCA, Prakash designed other buildings, including several residences and a massive factory for Bhushan Steel in Chandigarh's industrial area. Most of these are sparsely documented in the APF archives, though the few images that are available suggest strict iterations of the Chandigarh modernist vocabulary, with an exceptional preponderance of massive windowless load-bearing exposed brick walls.

I remember accompanying my father to the site of the Bhushan Steel Factory several times. There was re-bar everywhere, and I remember thinking that a steel factory could surely manufacture its own metal. The floors of the factory were made of poured-in-place terrazzo. My father asked the contractor on site to try and experiment. He asked him to form the terrazzo into two independent squares, three feet by three feet, as if readying them for tilt-up construction. But I soon learnt that they were meant to become table tops. Stands for these terrazzo tables were also made on site, by the steel guys, welding them together. We brought the tables back in a rented lorry, riding with the driver. They were very, very heavy. As the lorry strained, each pothole caused the terrazzo slabs to jump, ever so slightly. We forged on. One broke en route. The other, with the help of significant manpower drawn from around the neighbourhood, was placed on the terrace, outside our home, the principal's residence. That one never ever broke, and never moved. We ate dinner on it as a family, every summer night.

Open-air theatre, Chandigarh, Photo courtesy Eashan Chaufla

J&K Academy, 2010, Photos by and courtesy of Surinder Dhami

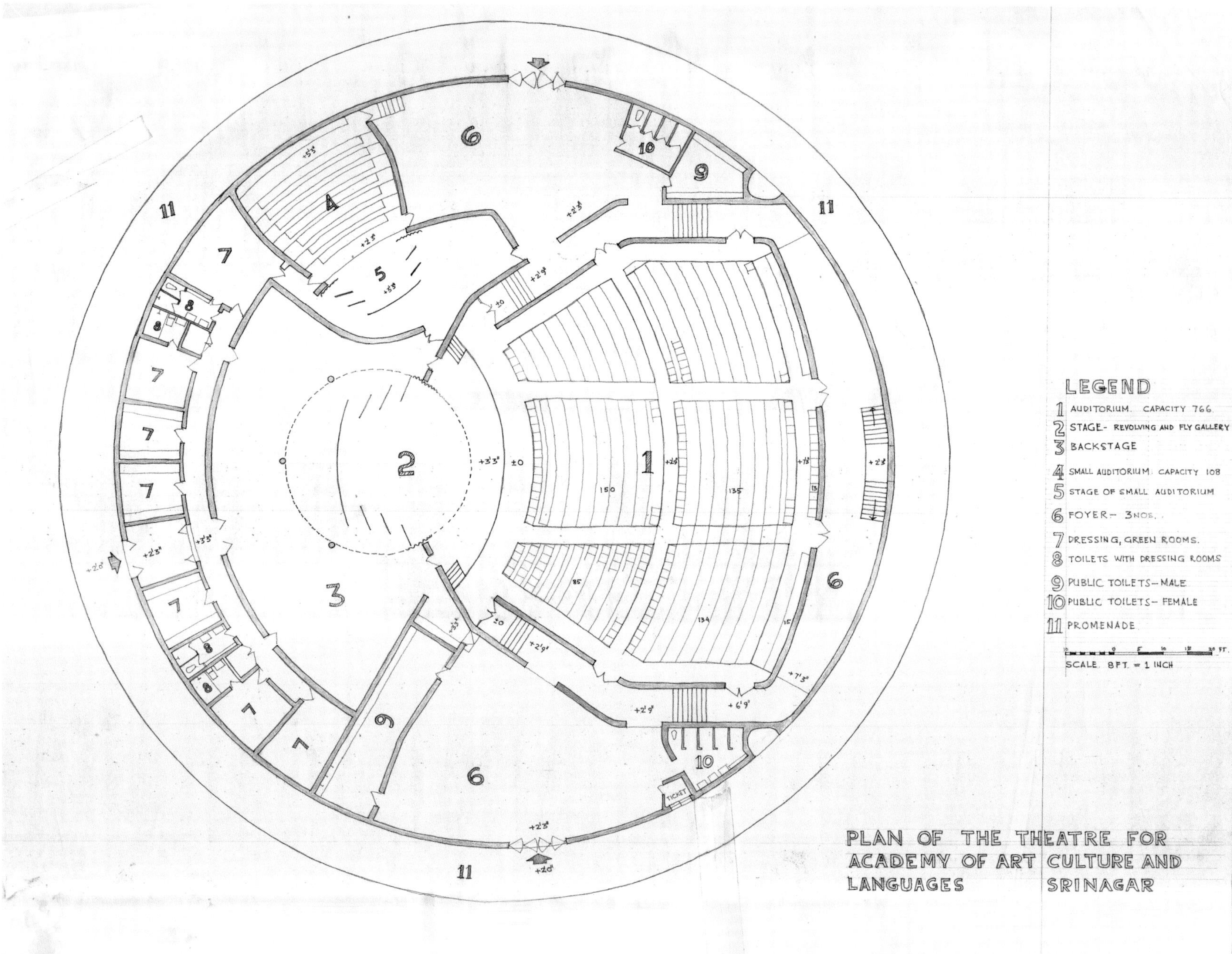

Round plan for the J&K Academy, c. 1975, APF

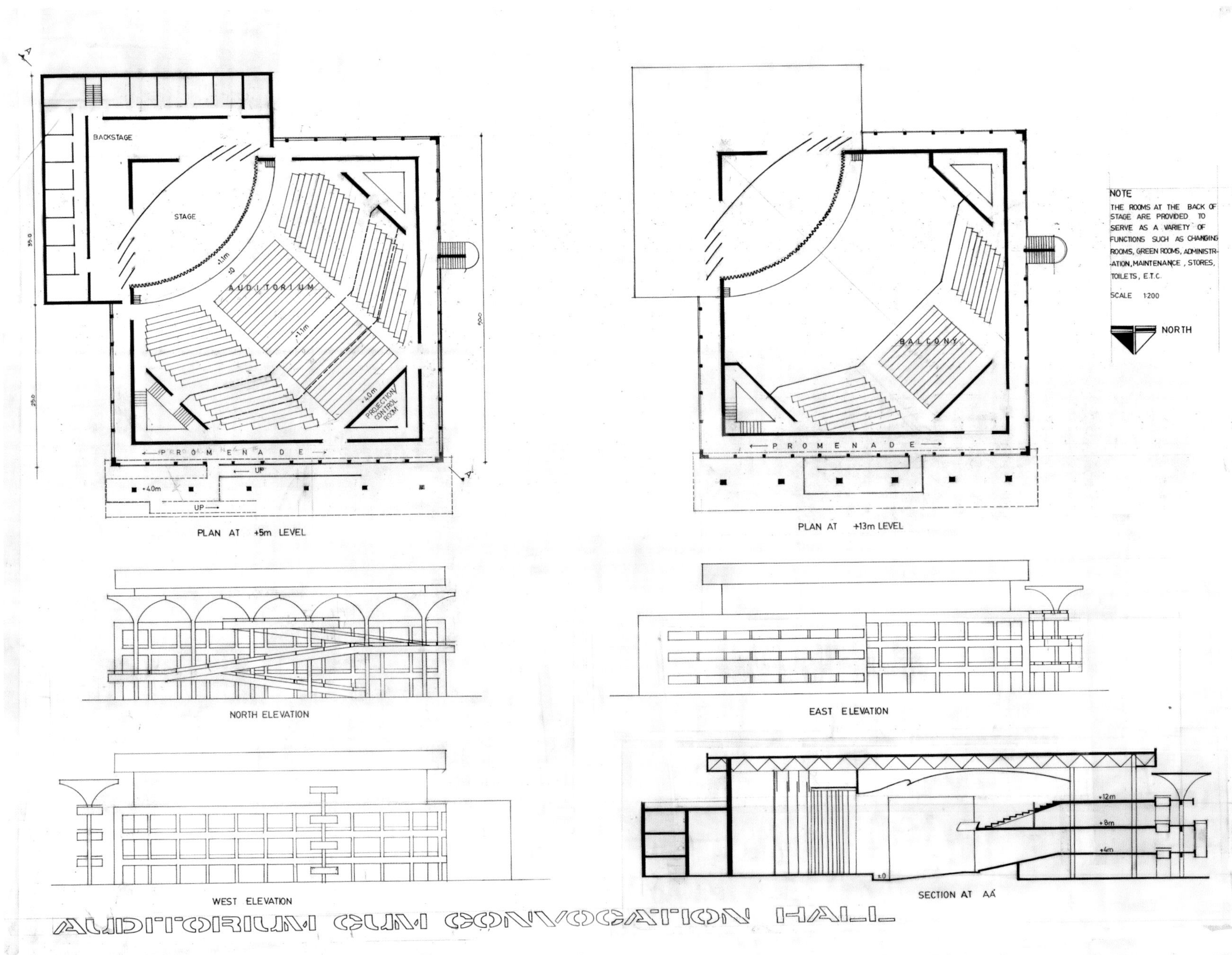

Auditorium-cum-convocation hall, APF

Untitled, paint on cartridge paper, 11 x 15 inches, 1970s, APF {3_(131)}

Untitled, ink on paper, 10 x 13.5 inches, 1980s, APF {3_(3)}

Untitled, ink on paper, 10 x 15.5 inches, 1980s, APF {3_(100)}

Scan image with the **BooksPlus** app

Untitled, ink and poster paint on cartridge paper, 1970s, APF {2_(49)}

Untitled, ink on paper, 11 x 15 inches, 1980s, APF {3_(74)}

The Painting Studio

In 1971, soon after becoming the principal of the Chandigarh College of Architecture, Prakash developed the habit of always making sure that he had a sketchbook—home-made from cut sheets of watercolour paper—sitting on his modernist desk at work. Whenever the fancy would strike him, almost daily, he would pull out a stack of sketch pens, and if needed a collection of basic poster paints, and quickly draw a "Doodle."[48]

In a review of an exhibit of some of these doodles, the art historian B. N. Goswamy wrote:

> The Doodles have the sense of a sub-conscious activity for Prakash, as if they were forms his hand outputted while his mind was with some other problem of the real world, of which one imagines there would be many and never ending given his role as the administrative head of an institution. The Doodles in this sense, most likely acted as something like an emotional "release," a stopgap activity to divert him from the exigency at hand.[49]

As "diversions," most of these "doodles " seem to be explorations of the possibilities of the continuous line, very often forming long snakes of folded arcs, contracting and expanding as they move around on the sheet. Others create geometric forms that are evenly distributed over the sheet to execute a sense of balance. Many of these were layered over with geometric shapes—squares, triangles, circles—most of them filled in, made with poster paint.

Untitled [Red green blue], oil on canvas, 24 x 24 inches, B.N. Prakash collection

Energy, oil on canvas, 25 x 25 inches, APF (17_1_1)

Sometime in the mid-1970s, he also set up a painting corner in his office by simply propping up his canvas on a table. The entire faculty and staff of the CCA became familiar with the figure of Prakash, brush in hand, leaning into the canvas, applying paint, and then standing back, waiting and pausing, to study his work, and to decide where to paint next—all this while continuing a conversation with a colleague. He never learnt to, and never liked to, paint on an easel.

In contrast to the free-flowing character of the doodles, Prakash's CCA canvases of the early 1970s have a studied spatiality about them. Their basic visual organization, their parti, appears planimetric with the space of the canvas treated as a site that is carefully partitioned and then filled with distinct shapes that sometimes interlock. Thus, the small canvas in red, blue, and green is divided into two golden section ratio-ed zones, within which two main forms—that look like sections of a hand and one of the Sukhna Lake lights—jostle around a central red square. Four squares hold down the corners.

A second canvas in yellow, cream and purple from the early 1970s is also divided into two, though a secondary yellow and purple strip shows up at the edge to balance the composition. A set of concentric circles straddles the two sections of the painting as if affecting a circulation system connecting them. Finally, in a third iteration of the same elements also from the early 1970s, the dividing line is angled and the forms—a snake and a square with two circles on one side, and two galaxy-like "cosmic" spirals on the other—stay firmly lodged in their respective zones. These last two paintings, made with painting chisels, were somehow special to Prakash, and they remained a treasured part of his personal collection, a permanent fixture in his drawing room.

Studied architectural plans could easily be developed out of these paintings, and they could

Untitled, poster paint on paper, 11 x 15 inches, 1970s, APF {2_(15)}

Untitled, ink and poster paint on white cartridge paper, 7.5 x 11 inches, 1976, APF {2_(19)}

Untitled, acrylic on packing paper, 27 x 38 inches, 2000s, APF

Untitled, acrylic on canvas, 28 x 28 inches, 1971, APF (17_1_6)

not contrast more with the spontaneous world of the doodles. It is clear that these two worlds for Prakash at this time were distinct. Paintings had to be carefully studied, while small drawings were allowed to emerge spontaneously. This is a distinction he both continually maintained and eroded throughout his practice as a painter.

One of ways in which he merged these two worlds was by making "by-product" paintings. While painting in the 1970s, he often kept a square wooden board at hand, with the mandate that any paint remaining on his chisels or brushes had to be applied to that board. The paint was already in the hand and had to be used and so he let it go, relying on over-painting to continually remake the composition. Collagist and dense, these boards are literally an archive of his other paintings. Only two of these boards have survived in the Archives, which Prakash had made into side tables.

In Prakash's later abstract canvases from the late 1970s onwards, the upward facing arc recurs again and again, dominating everything else that follows. Though usually solo, it could often be found in convoluted clusters of arcs, swirling together to form a jumble in the middle of the canvas. With no discernible figural representation, the arcs appear lost within their own dance, unmindful of anything beyond the frame.

Every now and then, all the lines seem to dance separately, and yet harmonize. One of the last paintings that he did, a large acrylic on packing paper in orange, white, yellow, and black, is one such work. Five sets of curves spin in from different edges of the frame and complete a simple curve of two, then disappear. Unlike the excess of energy that seems to dominate most of his abstract works, this acrylic in orange, white, yellow, and black has an unusual sense of reserve and silence to it.

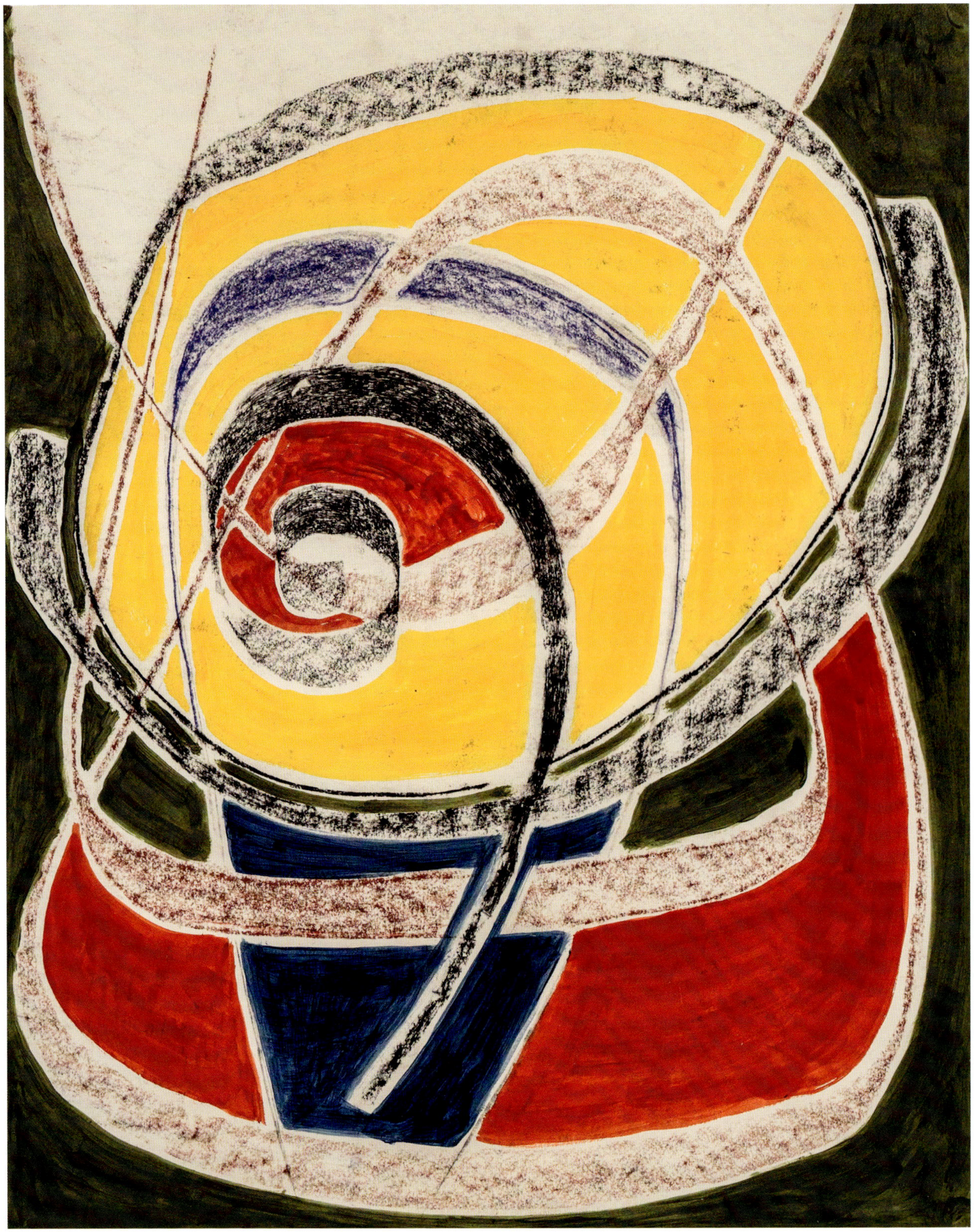

Untitled,
acrylic on packing paper,
22.25 x 28 inches, 2000s,
APF {11.12(25)}

Untitled, acrylic on canvas, 23 x 35 inches, 1990s, APF (17_4_13)

Untitled, acrylic on canvas, 23 x 30 inches, 2000, APF {16_(39)}

In St. John's High School, the private school run by Irish Catholic Brothers in Chandigarh where I studied from grades one to ten, there was an annual art competition. In 4th grade, I won first prize for a drawing of a "rock-band" roughly imitated from my memory of Archie comics. The prize was a big book titled Arthur Singer's Book of Birds.[50] *I was disappointed. Compared to my American pop-culture oriented young adult fantasy world, Arthur Singer's meticulous documentation of the birds of the United States, famously used to make postage stamps, was both boring and uninspiring. Not so for my father. He picked up the book that I had unceremoniously discarded and pored over it. Almost immediately he began to draw them. What was it about those birds? I never could understand.*

In December 1974, Prakash acquired a copy of *Arthur Singer's Book of Birds*, a painstaking compendium of birds of the world, drawn in immaculate detail. Obsessed with the forms of the birds, he began to draw them, not realistically a la Arthur Singer, but in one long continuous line. From this point on, he painted and drew birds repeatedly, not only as figural elements in innumerable paintings and murals but also on small drawings, on the backs of postcards, inside book covers, as motifs for letterheads as well as at the bottom of letters as part of his signature. There are hundreds of ink and pen, acrylic and poster paint drawings and paintings of birds in the APF Archives. Many of them depict seated birds, always proud and still. But most of them show them in flight, as if ready to burst out of their frames.

Untitled, acrylic on canvas, 8 x 10 inches, 2000s, APF {16_(80)}

Untitled, poster paint on cartridge paper, 10 x 13.25 inches, 1970s, APF {6_(22)}

Untitled, ink on paper, 10 x 8 inches, 1970s, APF

Untitled, ink on paper, 12 x 8 inches, 1970s, APF

While most of Prakash's paintings and drawings remained untitled, a few of the continuous line bird drawings in the Archives do have titles inscribed right across them. All of these: "Why not Fly," "Takeoff Tension," "Flight to Freedom," and "Sighting the Destination," offer flight as a metaphor for freedom and escape. This should not be particularly surprising. The flying bird, after all, is an ancient motif of the very human desire to escape, carried by the metaphor "wings of desire." Even so Prakash's obsession with birds invites interpretation as symbolic of a sense of being weighed down by the exigencies of life.[51]

If the bird was Prakash's favourite form to draw, a close second was its formal cousin, the free-form arc. We have already discussed the arcs as a part of his interest in the continuous line. But, the free form arcs, when facing upward reached up to the sky and, like the bird, can also be read as signifying the desire for liberation and freedom.[52]

The arcs also have a mooring in the Urdu script. Many of his paintings feel like abstractions of written Urdu or Arabic. In this sense, they have a 'scripted' feel to them. Prakash grew up reading, writing and speaking Urdu, the official language of the Mughal court and the primary tongue of Muslim India. In colonial India, even in English-medium schools, Urdu was a required subject and Prakash immediately took to it. In particular, he loved Urdu poetry which enjoys legendary status even to this day in the cultural memory of South Asia. Prakash memorized famous Urdu couplets, and he would quote them on demand, suited to the occasion, with drama and flair.

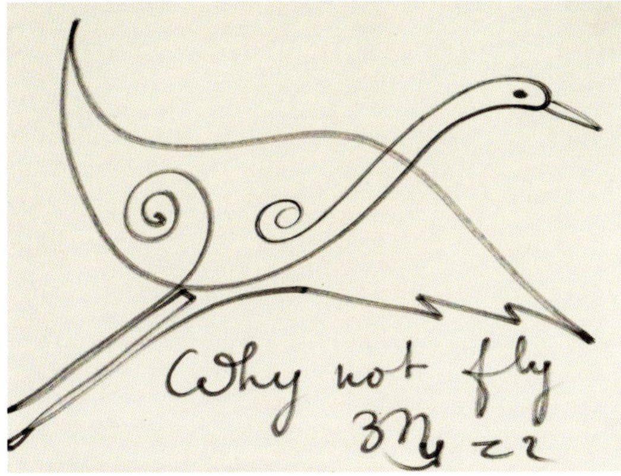

Untitled, ink on paper,
11 x 15 inches, 1980s, APF
{3_(49)}

Untitled, poster paint
on cartridge paper,
7.5 x 11 inches, 1970s,
APF {4_(30)}

Untitled,
colour photograph print,
20 x 16 inches, 1980s,
APF {2_(109)}

Untitled,
acrylic on board,
15.5 x 15.5 inches, 1990s,
APF {2_(37)}

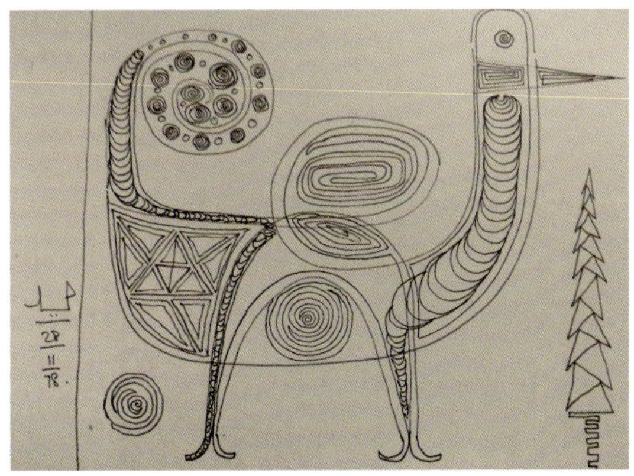

Untitled, ink on paper,
10 x 8 inches, 1970s, APF

Untitled,
acrylic on canvas,
40 x 30 inches, 2007,
APF

The famous Urdu poetry of South Asia, such as that of Zafar, Ghalib and Faiz, is more often than not laced with desire and the pathos of loss and longing. Urdu was Prakash's preferred written language of choice whenever he wanted to express himself emotionally. It was as if the child in him actually spoke Urdu, rather than Hindi, his daily language, or English, his professional tongue, right until the end of his life. Thus, for example, we find him commiserating with the bird in winter, writing the following with a pencil in Urdu, on the wall of his painting studio:

In front of me, on a tree of a branch, some birds are sitting.
It is morning. Did they spend the whole night on that branch?
In winter, in frost, in cold winds, did they in their hearts
Ever think, that everyone snuggled in their bed
Spent the whole night sleeping; did it occur to them, that we birds
Are sitting outside in the cold, on the branch of this tree...
(English translation by me.) [53]

A core part of understanding and even reading Urdu lies in engaging its calligraphic qualities.[54] Like the Arabic script from which it is derived, Urdu is written from right to left, and although it is phonetic in form, it has an embedded pictographic and spatial character owning to its origins in the hieroglyphic languages of Pharaonic Egypt and the cuneiforms of Ugaritic culture. The characters' *harakat* (movement) across the page and their accenting by various marks carries significant potential to supplement their content via visual character. Calligraphic art is a well-developed artform, particularly as ornament on the facades of Islamic buildings including those in India.

The swirling arc, as hybridized abstractions of the form of the bird and of the Urdu script, suggests simultaneously the pathos of longing and also the desire to escape. To be sure, Prakash himself never ascribed specific meaning to his abstract works, but described them simply as formal constructs, studies in visual composition, essays in search of visual beauty in the mode of Le Corbusier's Modulor. Most catalogues of his exhibitions simply listed the paintings as "Composition 1," "Composition 2," and so on, or by their content, which at times made for a risible catalogue, such as "Horse 1," "Horse 2," "Two Horses," "Horse and Donkey," "Two Camels 1," "Two Camels 2," "Camel," "Tethered Camel," "Camel Sitting," and so on. These interpretations are designed simply to suggest some context, the play of forces in his life. Others may be able to furnish more considered readings.

An undated felt pen on paper drawing contains the caption "WHY IS THIS BIRD

Scan image with the **BooksPlus** app

Untitled,
pen on cartridge paper,
8 x 12 inches, 1990s,
APF {10_(2)}

BEAUTIFUL"? The drawing of a simple flamingo is unadorned, made from a single continuous line, except for its feet.

The search for *what* makes things beautiful, rather than expressing the beautiful per se, was an abiding question in Prakash's painting and to a lesser extent in his architecture. He was focused on somehow extracting and depicting what made things beautiful as a core part of his composition. Le Corbusier's Modulor was the key visual tool in this quest. Originally, Prakash had learnt the Modulor as part of his design work on the building of Chandigarh College of Architecture. He transformed its dimensions to suit the Indian brick size, in all his architecture both in Ludhiana and in back in Chandigarh. He also used the Modulor to design the mural for the porch of CCA, where of course it was integrally connected to the architecture and its architectural thinking.

Starting in the early 1980s, soon after his retirement, the Modulor resurfaced as a major element in his paintings, sometimes in disguised form, but often quite explicitly as the framework of the art. The Modulor diagram was a special kind of work that could be repeatedly deployed in various forms in a painting to call out, measure and calibrate the free form that is its main formal subject. The Modulor as a diagram, in other words, functioned both as the underlying graph-paper of the formal composition and a necessary part of the composition in his paintings and drawings.[55]

For Le Corbusier, the Modulor was akin to a musical scale, critical as a reference for visual notes, but not a work of art in and of itself. For Prakash, in contrast, the Modulor diagram itself was a work of art that could be expressed as such—which he did in many a painting—and used as an integrated underlying graph for the formal composition of a painting. Repeatedly, in various forms and sizes, he started a painting by partitioning it along Modulor lines, and then inserted a figural shape across it. Like Le Corbusier's plan, both the Modulor graph and the figure always functioned as integrated parts of the composition.

At the same time, however, Prakash often also started with a figural shape, and then subsequently laid the Modulor graph around it, measuring and calibrating the dimensions that made that form beautiful. This mode became more and more his norm in later works—the Modulor as an instrument of measuring the beautiful, whose role as a graphic measure was part of the composition itself.

The Modulor diagram in this sense can also be understood as playing the same role as the Urdu script does in the writing of poetry in that language—the *harakat* of the Modulor diagram supports the message of the figural form.

Untitled,
acrylic on canvas,
13 x 37 inches, 1990s,
APF (17_4_22)

Untitled,
acrylic on packing paper,
40 x 28 inches, 2007,
APF {11.12(23)}

Untitled,
acrylic on packing paper,
38 x 27 inches, 2000s,
APF (17_6_4)

Scan image with the **BooksPlus** app

Untitled,
acrylic on packing paper,
27 x 38 inches, 2000s,
APF (17_6_7)

The cover of Le Corbusier's book on the Modulor depicts the figure of the six-foot man, inscribed into the frame. The various dimensions of the Modulor emanate from points in his body, but the Modulor Man himself appears gaunt and thin, abstracted and quite lifeless. By contrast, the multitudes of Prakash's figures that are inscribed into the same Modulor are determinedly lively, vivifying the Modulor even as they draw their life from it. Significantly, most of them are women.

The Undoing of Postmodernism

By the mid-1970s it was amply clear that the Nehruvian nation-state was not only in decline, but in crisis. As Indira Gandhi's socialist policies failed to generate wealth and employment, the energy problems became an opportunity for the opposition to radicalize protest against the government and its policies. Urban students, who faced unemployment and a corrupt administrative machinery, became the centre of the protests, organizing successive strikes around the country, including many at the CCA. Facing widespread unemployment, with no access to government

Untitled,
acrylic on canvas,
27.5 x 47.5 inches, 1980s,
APF (17_2_2)

Untitled,
acrylic on packing paper,
27 x 38 inches, 2000s,
APF (17_6_6)

Untitled,
acrylic on packing paper,
28 x 41.5 inches, 2000s,
APF (17_6_20)

sector jobs, the disaffected urban youth emerged as a widespread social phenomenon in India at this time.[56]

In 1975, Indira Gandhi as prime minister used her executive powers to declare a national state of Emergency, suspending the Parliament and centralizing all authority. While the reasons behind these drastic steps are still hotly contested, the fact that she had violated the institution of democracy, the Nehruvian pillar of pride, sent shock waves through the Indian modernist communities of all colour and political affiliation.

The two years of the Emergency brought a heightened sense of order in civic life (the trains ran on time), but investment in the desultory public sector enterprises and corruption across the ranks of government were sustained, and even strengthened as access to power became all important. The Emergency, under the cover of law and order, suppressed a lot of angry energy, which again burst onto the streets right after elections in 1977—which Indira Gandhi lost handily—in the form of demonstrations, strikes, shut-downs, and sit-ins. Chaos unfolded as the hapless new Janata Party government struggled to reform policy and take control. By 1979, the new government was also voted out of power, and Indira Gandhi returned as prime minister, but without any mandate other than to restore law and order.

The political chaos of the late 1970s significantly affected the academic culture of the CCA. As student morale deteriorated, strikes, sit-ins, and demonstrations became routine. At one of these events the Buckminster Fuller Dymaxion domes, so lovingly built by Prakash in the early 1970s, were burnt to the ground.

The political crisis dovetailed with Western critiques of modern architecture and urbanism. Le Corbusier came to be identified as a lynchpin of modernism, and with the rise of attacks on him, the Chandigarh star also began to fade in the global architectural imagination. The new generation of architects and critics that now visited Chandigarh did so to bear witness to the presumed failure of Le Corbusier's creation. Prakash was ready for them, with his radical critiques of Chandigarh's unsustainability, but quickly found that their interests were "merely" aesthetic and cultural, seeking "ethos" and "identity" rather than animal husbandry.

Prakash was particularly disappointed by the response of the Indian professional community when many architects, who had earlier identified themselves as dyed-in-the-wool modernists, started happily catering to new Western expectations that they rediscover their local aesthetic roots.[57] In spite of his critiques of the modernist city, Prakash was too steeped in the modernist idiom to ever embrace the aesthetics of 1980s postmodernism in India, or the West. One could argue that he embraced the modernist view of the world to a fault. He never designed a building that deviated far from the "Chandigarh style," which for him was a question of ethics.

Combining with the decline of the Nehruvian nation-state, student unrest and the rise of aesthetic postmodernism was the entrenchment of Chandigarh's bureaucratic administration. By the late 1970s, as Chandigarh became successful and wealthy, the pre-eminence of founding architects and engineers visibly began to fade. As power naturally yielded to new administrators like Finance Secretaries and Home Secretaries, and as new wealthy classes wielded greater influence in the affairs of the city, Prakash and others of his ilk began to feel more marginalized.[58]

There were at least two occasions when Prakash actively considered leaving CCA. In 1970, he entered the competition for designing the Jawaharlal Nehru University campus in New Delhi; if he had won he would have quit as principal and set up his own private practice.[59] Prakash's proposal was built rigorously on the tenets of Chandigarh modernism, while the winning entry created a series of courts and plaza, reminiscent of the work of Louis Kahn and a nascent postmodernism to come.

In 1974, Prakash was offered the position of chief architect of the ITDC (Indian Tourism Development Corporation), which he eventually declined. The ITDC was embarking on an ambitious project of hotel construction and needed a suitable professional to head their design staff. Prakash passed up this opportunity to focus on research and education, which, given the decline in the academic culture at CCA in the late 1970s, burnt a hole in his mind as a significant lost opportunity.

In 1982, after 14 years at its helm, Prakash retired as principal of the Chandigarh College of Architecture. It is difficult to objectively assess his legacy as an educator. (I have provided a more subjective assessment at the end of this book.) In 1995, the Indian Institute of Architects awarded him its Gold Medal for contributions as an architect and an educator. The citation reads:

> Not only did Dr. Aditya Prakash lead the way by being one of the founding fathers of the Chandigarh College of Architecture, he could be said to be one of the "Architects" of Architectural Education in Northern India.[60]

With the advent of social media, I have maintained a Facebook page for my father, which I started essentially as a means of posting interesting bits of information and evocative images that I have encountered of him while researching the APF Archives. Without any advertisement, that Facebook page has acquired an organic following, with 732 page "likes" as of February 2019. Most Followers are silent; I do not know them. But there is a small, self-selected coterie of about 30 of them, all former students from the early and mid-1970s, who regularly comment and exchange notes. Unsolicited, they routinely make it a special point to note the significant impact Aditya Prakash had on their lives, not just professional.

NOTES

1 Kairon was dogged by corruption charges and had just stepped down as Chief Minister. He apparently had been offered the position of Defense Minister in the central government and was on his way back from New Delhi to Amritsar when he was assassinated on the highway. See https://www.hindustantimes.com/punjab/builder-of-punjab-the-lost-legacy-of-sardar-partap-singh-kairon/story-LgBkUbottLrpMYISj2o9zH.html, accessed Monday, March 19, 2018.

2 Early in the 1970s, Prabhawalkar was selected as the architectural advisor to the Government of Mauritius by Prime Minister Seewoosagur Ramgoolam, a part of the transnational sharing of expertise amongst non-aligned nations. This was a prestigious appointment, modelled on Le Corbusier's appointment in Chandigarh. Unfortunately, Prabhwalkar died young in Mauritius in 1974.

3 He may have subconsciously sought to emulate his father, who had been the headmaster of a school.

4 Prakash published extensively on his views regarding architectural education, making the case that it must move beyond training architects for a paying clientele, and instead focus on the larger needs of life, which for him essentially meant the problem of urbanization and its relationship to the rural. For most of this discussion, see "Education of an Architect Bearing in Mind the Economic, Cultural, and Technical Needs of the Country," *APFA D8_5*. Even in a convocation address delivered on 24 April 1970, he called for "unlearning" what you have learned in the College of Architecture. See "Convocation Address, CCA, 24 April 1970," *APFA D8_6*. In 1986 for CCA's 25th anniversary, Prakash wrote a reflection on architectural education and his role in shaping it at CCA, arguing that architectural education should be essentially based on technical problem-solving. See "Random Thoughts on Architectural Education," *APFA D6b*. See also a simultaneous interview with B. V. Doshi and Aditya Prakash in *Science Today* May 1973: 38—41.

5 "Architecture as a Career," *APFA D3*.

6 "Address by Principal Aditya Prakash on the occasion of the College Convocation and Annual Prize Distribution on 12 April 1973" *APFA D17*.

7 All these are in-house publications available at the Chandigarh College of Architecture, Panjab University, Chandigarh.

8 See for instance Mukul Bansal "Architect who did more than make a livelihood," *The Tribune*, Friday 7 September 2017; and Rajnish Wattas "Goodbye Guru." http://irtsaforums.net/blog/?p=8243, accessed 10/13/2017 9:52 AM.

9 In email to the author, dated September 3, 2008.

10 Apparently, there was even a "dress-code" for the workshops—khaki pants! Thanks to Balwinder Saini for this insight.

11 The Houses were named after significant destinations from the history of the architecture of India, namely Nalanda, Sanchi, Sikri, and Bijapur.

12 The act of dividing the college into Houses, and the belief that sports can unify people of different backgrounds, of course are derived from colonial ideologies.

13 There is a complete set of black-and-white photographs in the Archives of Ludhiana from the 1960s. Unlike the "artistic" framing of the architectural images, most of these are taken from a high vantage point, as if to capture a situation. They are clearly documentary, though it is unclear what they are precisely trying to document. It does not seem that these photographs are trying to convey a message; rather, it seems that their purpose is to simply document the facts, like a scientist, for later evaluation.

In the photos, the punched-out square openings are echoed in Tagore Theatre.

14 "Living in Cities" *APFA D8_3*

15 The *rehri* research was done with the help of students Pallav Mukherjee (who later joined the faculty of CCA) and Amar Puri. It was published "Mobile Shops in Chandigarh" in the *Architects' Year Book* Vol 14, 1974, pp. 78–84. Prakash also conducted a study on Labour Housing in Chandigarh, see *APFA D88*.

16 Earlier in his article "Planning of Office Buildings" published January 1959 in *Indian Construction News*, Prakash argued that cities should be built vertically to conserve agricultural land "in view of the food shortage and rising population of the country..., agricultural land should not be encroached upon more than what is absolutely essential." When Prakash wrote this, he was still a Junior Architect in Chandigarh in the Capital Planning office. Similar ideas are echoed in his unpublished paper from the same time period "Future Urbanization and Human Habitations" *APFA D8*.

17 "Kishangarh" APFA D17.

18 Robert Matthew returned to Edinburgh in 1953 and established the Department of Architecture there, from which he ultimately retired in 1968. However, I have been unable to determine the title or program of this conference.

19 Jacqueline Tyrwhitt of course had had a long association with India. She had visited Chandigarh during the 1950s and had authored an exhibition on the "model village" in New Delhi in 1954. See: Shoshkes, Ellen. "Mid-Century Modernism: Jaqueline Tyrwhitt and

the Village Center at the 1954 International Exhibition of Low-Cost Housing in New Delhi." *Traditional Dwellings and Settlements Review* 24 (2012): 14.

20 It is important, in this sense, to locate Aditya Prakash's interests in developing rigorously "local" solutions as modern knowledge, using direct observation in the context of such modernist thinking that was proliferating around the world, spread in particular by institutions such as Ekistics and the United Nations. See M. Ijlal Muzaffar *The periphery within: modern architecture and the making of the Third World* Ph. D. dissertation, MIT, 2007

21 "Energy Crisis and Future Pattern of Human Settlements in Developing Countries," *APFA D21*.

22 Published as Le Corbusier. (1979). *The three human establishments*. Chandigarh: Punjab Govt., Dept. of Town & Country Planning. Translated by Eulie Chowdhury.

23 That elevated highways could kill urban life, as they did in US cities amid "urban renewal", does not seem to have even occurred to Aditya Prakash. In the density of the Asian and African city, this still holds true. Life gravitated to the highway in the Indian context, Prakash observed.

24 Canal building was of course a major preoccupation in both colonial and postcolonial India, especially in Punjab after the construction of the big hydroelectric dams such as Bhakra. See also Acciavatti, A., Bierig, Aleksandr, & Corrigall, Duncan. (2015). *Ganges Water Machine: Designing New India's Ancient River*. San Francisco: Applied Research Design Publishing.

25 By submerging roads, Le Corbusier also separated the vehicular traffic system from the pedestrian in the Capitol Complex in Chandigarh.

26 The following is Sandeep Virmani's testament to Aditya Prakash, written in 2014:

"Aditya Prakash was my best friend's father. However, over the years he became my mentor, guide and friend. Once as a young teenager, I mustered the guts to ask him what was the meaning of an abstract painting that hung in his drawing room, that he had recently painted. He put the book down, and explained at length what it meant to him, and asked me to decide what it might mean to me! I believe, in retrospect, that that embodied the essence of his approach to education. A teacher must share his/her own struggle and beliefs with all its beauty and sometimes gruesome detail, leaving the student to learn from this honest inquiry.

I do not know if he was aware of how he taught, or if he theorised on this approach in college; but I think he was a less understood man, his genius exposed to few. And perhaps he himself was responsible for this in many ways— he was awkward socially, reticent and inept at "marketing"/communicating his ideas, which the world had a lot to gain from.

I came into the Chandigarh College of Architecture the year he left, so I did not see him as a formal teacher or administrator; but he did admit to me once that he should not have spent so many years in education. He did not explain, but his ideas in urbanism or education were always flowing against the mainstream, way ahead of their times. And he did not care to explain if not asked. If I am not mistaken, it was he who told me that Le Corbusier designed the studios and library of CCA, but refused to design the classrooms, saying that architecture cannot be taught, but must be learnt! Ironically, he himself designed the classrooms later and attached them to the Le Corbusier building, but I believe he did not subscribe to classroom teaching. In a world so strongly driven by a belief in the "Banking" concept of education, he had little chance of establishing his pedagogy in a government college like CCA.

My classroom was his garage, which was converted to be his "Studio", leaving his car to stand outside under a porch. I spent the critical three years here with him when his ideas on urbanism were given form and content. Here is where I learnt my architecture... and much more from him.

Sometimes he hosted friends and socialists like writer Mulk Raj Anand, film maker Zul Vellani and other artists and thinkers who would come together from different parts of the country. As the drinks went around, there was a cocktail of poetry, insights into "real" India, ideas on nation building, disagreements on Gandhi and Nehru's ideology. When the music and drinks had sufficiently eased the mood, we as "young India" were encouraged to share our views on the conversations. We were taken seriously. Once I shared a drawing of a female figure I had sketched with a renowned artist in the gathering, who went on to prescribe how I should draw it; and Aditya Prakash defended and encouraged my exploration into *my* style. I was inducted into a prestigious dramatics group in the city by him and very quickly, I was playing lead roles in his plays and even providing inputs on set design. He listened carefully to a young mind's ideas, even on subjects he was proficient in. His qualities as a teacher were the attributes of a parent who is rarely judgmental, who shares as an equal and encourages you to be daring in your explorations.

But to be accurate, he was all this to me as I espoused and was inclined to be "Gandhian" in my values and motivations. I have also seen him be harsh on... everything else.

He was influenced strongly by Gandhi, Le Corbusier, and the idea of Nehruvian India. The idea of serving independent India brought him back from the UK, when Nehru appealed to professionals to return. Though he built Chandigarh with Le Corbusier, a critique of Corb's

Chandigarh convinced him this was not an Indian city. He asked us students to go and identify and interview those for whom the "symbol of independent India", "a city unfettered by the past", did not work! Pavement dwellers, milkmen cycling into town from neighbouring villages, the cobbler and the *rehri-wallah* formed the kernels of his ideas on urbanism. Gandhi's beliefs that India resides in our villages, in communities, in frugality, made him realize that Indian modernism will have to learn equally from the west as from our villages. Simultaneously, that the idea of "genius" as Le Corbusier and capitalism propounded will find solutions for the future was evident in his swagger and style as well. He would often be thrilled by an idea he himself propounded and say, "That is genius!"

Even though the Urban Affairs Ministry dropped the idea of building the new capital for the State of Haryana for which they had requested Aditya Prakash; he continued to explore the possibility of some of these ideas being implemented through a series of competitions that we worked on, including IGNOU and a street improvement project for Rohtak. The ideas were appreciated, won competitions but unfortunately never built. I doubt the full import and significance of these ideas was even realised by the proponents and jury.

These seeds remained dormant in me through the next decade as I grew in my endeavours in development; and quite naturally sprouted when we were designing a large rehabilitation project in my city of Bhuj post the 2001 earthquake. Some of these ideas of the recycling zone are taking shape here. I cannot forget the emotional surge of the couple of days Aditya Prakash spent with me in the year 2000, when he came to see me and my work. With the pride of a son and student I introduced him to the people I worked with. He blessed me and graced the foundation stone ceremony for my new home, and

departed." Sandeep Virmani in *Aditya Prakash, Architect, Urbanist, Artist, Dramatist, Educationist, Mentor, Guide, Friend*. Prepared in response to Lakshmi Krishnaswamy's M. S. Thesis Questionnaire, April 2014. Krishnaswamy, L., (2014). *Garbage Dump Expertise: Tracing the 'Common Man' Project in the Works of Aditya Prakash*, ProQuest Dissertations and Theses.

27 "Design for Human Settlements" *APFA D21, p. 2. (1979)*

28 E. F. Schumacher's *Small is Beautiful: Economics as if People Mattered* (Harper, 1975), which had an image of Gandhi on its cover, was a major reference text for Aditya Prakash. His own writings on self-sufficiency, the value of cottage industries and rural-urban integration, or what he liked to called "ruralization" are of course vast and diverse. See in particular "Human settlements: a self-sustaining approach," *Ekistics* 278 (Sept/Oct 1979): 305–313, and "A self-sustaining approach," *Seminar* August 1985: 31—39.

29 "Chandigarh—Capital of Two States" *APFA D21*.

30 "Le Corbusier's Chandigarh, Architecture and the Cultural Context" presentation made at Symposium held at the College of Art, Architecture and Planning, Cornell University, 1990. *APFA D16*.

31 "Why Not Ruralization", *APFA D3c*. Prakash's note on how he retrospectively came to agree with Mathur's comment on how 'Beauty is there in everything', can also be understood as a retrospective critique of the foundational concept of the Modulor that beauty must have an underlying order, which for Le Corbusier came from the golden ratio and the right angle.

32 *APFA D3b* Memo Pad.

33 "The Role of Architects in Urban and Rural Design," *APFA D3c*.

34 Through the 1970s, Haryana in fact built up a new city, Panchkula, just beyond the border of Chandigarh, rather than invest in its own distinct capital.

35 Evenson, N., & University of California, Berkeley. College of Environmental Design. (1966). *Chandigarh*. (Environmental design and development series). Berkeley: University of California Press.

36 Which was ultimately published as Sarin, M. (1982). *Urban Planning in the Third World: The Chandigarh Experience*. London: Bronx, N.Y.: Mansell Pub.; Distributed in the U.S. and Canada by H.W. Wilson.

37 Prakash, A. (1980). *Chandigarh: A Presentation in Free Verse*. Chandigarh: A. Prakash. Produced by Marg Publications, Bombay.

38 In a sense, Prakash's writing has something like Vikram Seth's *Golden Gate*-like quality, which attempts to sublimate the rigorously quotidian into the poetic.

39 The opposite of a Sunirmal Chatterjee drawing would be the equally amazing, precise drawings of someone like Francis D.K. Ching.

40 Prakash, A. (1983). *Reflections on Chandigarh*. New Delhi: B.N. Prakash.

41 Other members in the records, but unknown to me are, Mrs. Roy and Surinderpal Kaur. Source: email correspondence with Saumya Sharma dated March 2018.

42 Balwant Gargi, the renowned modernist Punjabi language dramatist, novelist, and short story writer from Bhatinda, taught at the University of Washington in Seattle from 1966–1967, after which he moved to Chandigarh as founder-director of the department of Indian Theatre. Gargi was a colourful man who exerted a strong presence in the city and its modernist milieu. *Abhinet* can be a seen as a culturist response to the intellectual and aesthetic revolution fomented by Gargi in Chandigarh. Gargi's unceremonious departure from Chandigarh and his subsequent autobiographical novel of 1979 sent shock waves through the city's urban elite. See http://www.tribuneindia.com/news/sunday-special/people/love-loss-and-drama-in-balwant-gargi-s-days/181594.html, accessed Thursday, October 19 2017, and Gāragī, B. (1979). *The Naked Triangle: An autobiographical novel*. Sahibabad, Distt. Ghaziabad: Vikas.

43 "Stagecraft" *APFA D3c*.

44 "Solar Passive/Active Architecture" *APFA D12_6*

45 With two levels added after Prakash's death in 2008, this where the Archives of The Aditya Prakash Foundation are located.

46 Several dymaxion domes were, however, built at the Chandigarh College of Architecture, some of which still stand.

47 B.V. Doshi also designed one of the Tagore Theatres in the mid-1960s. Initially, he too conceived a structure in which the massive trusses were exposed. A later note on one of the drawings suggests that he perhaps received instruction from Le Corbusier that the interior must in no way be expressed on the exterior. Le Corbusier proselytized the "free-façade," and the Miracle Box, was a tight external wrapper.

48 A collection of these "Doodle" albums is in the APFA, though uncatalogued.

49 APFA_D33

50 *Arthur Singer's Book of Birds in Colour*. Adapted for Younger Readers from *Birds of the World* Publisher: Paul Hamlyn, 1970.

51 Le Corbusier's form of the Open Hand also of course resembles the profile of a bird, and raised as it is in the sky, it clearly carries connotations of flight. Prakash frequently drew the Open Hand, and he had several models of the Hand in his collection. But all of his references to the Hand in Prakash's drawings seem to be as an autobiographical metonym for Le Corbusier, rather than a bird of flight.

52 Again, the arc occurs in Le Corbusier's paintings and architecture as well, as for instance in the *Porte Émail*, or the Enamel Door, marking the ceremonial entrance of the Assembly building in Chandigarh, as also in the profiles of the Secretariat, the unbuilt Governor's House and the portico of the Assembly.

53 Written in pencil on the wall of Aditya Prakash's studio in Sector 8, Chandigarh. Its transliteration into Devanagari script was done by Professor Jameel Ahmad, Senior Lecturer, Asian Languages and Literature, University of Washington, 11/11/08.

54 The following discussion of Urdu is based on an unpublished essay by Michelle Rostami titled "Aditya Prakash: Painting and Space Making" presented as part of the work of the Chandigarh Urban Lab 2014.

55 One way to grasp his use of the Modulor is to compare it to the column grids in Le Corbusier's plans. While it is the free-form walls of his plans, which sometimes align with the columns but more often strikingly do not, that are responsible for generating the poesies of the plan, there can be no doubt that the a priori columnar grid much celebrated in the annals of modernism not only serves a structural purpose, but is also an integral part of the plan's composition.

56 The 1975 blockbuster *Deewar*, which established Amitabh Bachchan's iconic identity as the "angry young man," can be seen as emblematic of the times, particularly given that the filial conflict at the heart of the film's narrative is set up by inability of one of the two brothers to secure a job because of nepotism and corruption.

57 A key "culprit" in this regard, for Prakash, was the trilogy of the Festivals of India that were held in Paris, Washington DC and Moscow in the mid-1980s that actively cultivated the selling of the "Indian" image to the West. See Aditya Prakash's response to one of these festivals in "The Aftermath of Vistara" *APFA D6b*. For a discussion of the festivals see Brown, R. (2017). *Displaying Time: The many temporalities of the Festival of India* (Global South Asia). Seattle: University of Washington Press.

58 The relationship between M. N. Sharma and Prakash soured significantly through the 1970s. When Sharma retired as chief architect in 1979 (and left to become a consultant in East Africa), he specifically recommended against appointing Prakash as his successor.

59 This competition was done with Vijay Malik, a CCA grad, who went on to found Planners Group, a very successful Chandigarh-based architectural design practice.

60 "Citation, IIA Mahdav Achwal Gold Medal 1995" *APFA D37*.

Scan image with the **BooksPlus** app

ON HIS OWN

Prakash on the roof of RBI Housing

Prakash at the Chandigarh Lalit Kala Akademi workshop, APF

Prakash's retirement as Principal of the Chandigarh College of Architecture on 31 March 1982 was not voluntary. It was required per the mandatory rules of the Government of India. Like most senior government officers in India, he felt he was in the middle of his career with several incomplete projects, when it was time for him to leave. Prakash felt bereft. In order to keep his mind occupied, he took on new activities like becoming a book critic for a local newspaper. He also agreed to write an introductory coffee table book on Chandigarh for Abhinav Publications, a local publisher. But Prakash's strongest response was to try and stay committed to his academic concepts, in particular, his urban vision, to doggedly try and pursue it, regardless of the challenges of the times.

The 1980s were, relatively speaking, turbulent times both in India and for Prakash. Indira Gandhi was embattled as a prime minister, barely able to hold her socialist interpretation of the Nehruvian state together. India was in crisis, with massive unemployment, industrial stagnation, and widespread corruption resulting in the infamous "Hindu rate of growth" that was stuck at a lethargic two per cent. In Punjab and Chandigarh, terrorism was widespread, and in 1984, Indira Gandhi was assassinated by her bodyguards, an act of reprisal for the Indian army's assault on the Golden Temple at Amritsar.

Through the 1980s, Prakash nevertheless continued to believe in a modified version of the developmentalist vision of the Nehruvian nation-state. He repeatedly and unsuccessfully made the case for his self-sustaining city, which ran him afoul with the urban elite of Chandigarh which was beginning to enjoy the high real-estate values of their properties. He also fell out of favour with the architectural establishment of the country which was focused on the aesthetic contentions of postmodernism. Prakash hoped that the administration of Indira Gandhi's son and successor Rajiv Gandhi would usher in a new way to galvanize state-sponsored, integrated urban, and economic development in a self-sustaining mould. There was a brief window of opportunity in 1985. Rajiv Gandhi, who had just succeeded his mother Indira as prime minister, signed an accord with Sant Harchand Singh Longowal, the president of the Akali Dal of Punjab, promising that Chandigarh would be handed over to Punjab as a part of a multilateral agreement. This would require building a new capital for Haryana. Prakash saw an opportunity and immediately published a series of opinion pieces in the local newspapers, arguing that Haryana should be as forward-thinking as Punjab had been in the 1950s when it decided to make Chandigarh as a bold new experiment under the leadership of Partap Singh Kairon and Jawaharlal Nehru.[3] Prakash argued that his linear city

Upturned curve as water tank of a house in Jagadhri, APF

proposal was a kind of "Chandigarh 2.0" thinking, ripe for a forward-thinking leadership of Haryana.

It is difficult to know what kind of traction Prakash's self-sustaining linear city might have had with the government of Haryana. Sant Longowal was assassinated on 20 August 1985, which effectively voided the accord that he had signed. After that, Rajiv Gandhi's interests turned mostly towards the newly globalizing and digitizing world, and until he too was assassinated in 1991, he determinedly moved the Indian economy towards privatization and economic liberalization.

The only form in which his urban ideas were partially realized was in the consulting that Prakash did with the National Thermal Power Corporation (NTPC) and the coal mines of India. In a series of detailed reports on mitigating the environmental impact of these polluting industries, Prakash insisted that their "remedial" work go beyond cleaning the soil and water to include developing self-sustaining neighbourhoods for the workers.[4] It is unclear how far Prakash's recommendations were implemented by NTPC on the ground, though by the lack of follow-up correspondence in the Archives, and the general culture of apathy that prevailed in public sector undertakings of the Government of India at that time, one assumes that Prakash's report was never implemented systematically.

In 1991, then Finance Minister (and later Prime Minister) Manmohan Singh began the so-called liberalization of the Indian economy, devaluing the currency, slashing duties and tariffs, and announcing the intended closure of public sector industries. As the new neo-liberal order began to settle in under Prime Ministers Narasimha Rao and Manmohan Singh, Prakash found himself increasingly distanced from its quick-wheeling, consumerist orientation, and in particular from its real estate–driven vision of urban planning. Nonetheless, he repeatedly published op-eds in the local newspapers, trying to proselytize for self-sustainable development as a model for the new era of urban growth that was being ushered in by neo-liberalism. But then, as is now, sustainable urban design and development were only of interest to non-governmental organizations and Western academics, neither of whom had much impact

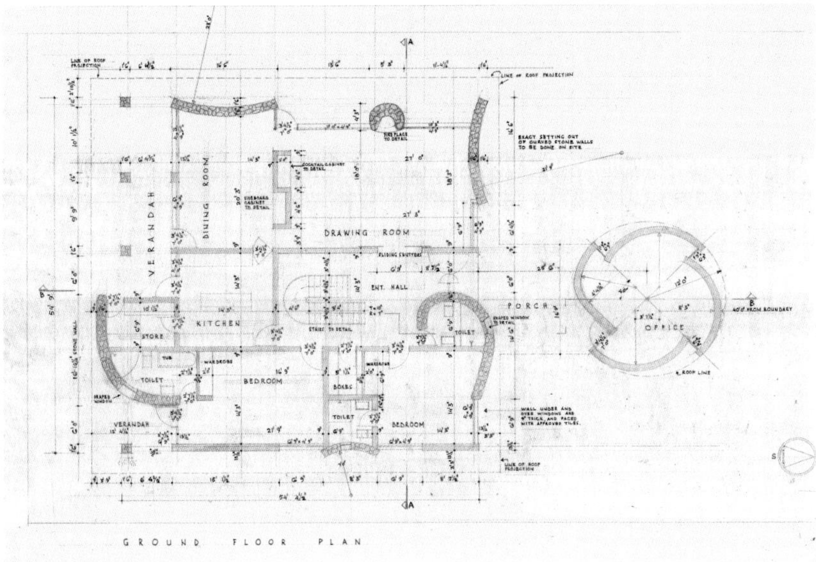

Proposed house for unknown client, APF

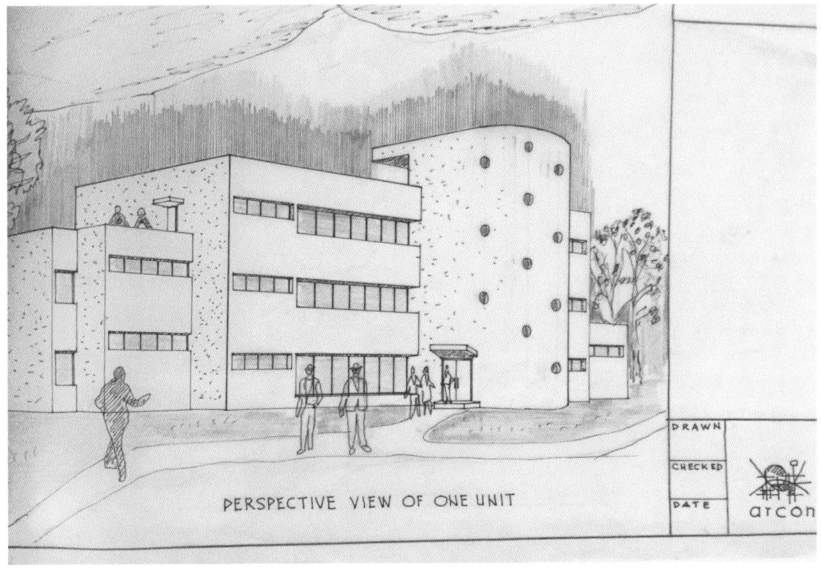

Hand-drawn perspective of an Arcon project. APF

on growth in Chandigarh or its peripheries. Nonetheless he kept publishing his thoughts on urbanization and growth, even though each time he had to put his "head on the chopping block and await the punch of the blow that is to come."[5]

Terrorism was a frightening spectre in the 1980s. Living in Chandigarh we would routinely hear reports of gunmen pulling passengers out of buses, separating them by religion, and gunning down all the non-Sikhs. As usual it was the rural communities that paid the highest price. Chandigarh, where two state administrations were housed, was heavily fortified. Everywhere we went, there were paramilitary to be found, usually heavily sand-bagged. Everyone lived under a pall of fear and intimidation. The paramilitary routinely stopped residents to check them, and set up frequent check posts to question and search all who passed through them. My father resented these checks viscerally. He clearly felt violated, threatened in the city he had helped build from scratch. His voice would tremble as he answered the paramilitary, audibly struggling to keep his composure. Operation Bluestar and Indira Gandhi's assassination shook us to the core. Rajiv Gandhi, and his accord with Longowal, felt like a godsend, a fleeting beacon of hope. When it ended, and later when Rajiv Gandhi was assassinated in 1991, all seemed lost. So, in 1986, I moved to the United States to go to graduate school and get out of India.

In October 1990, during my tenure as the president of Exedra, Cornell University's student chapter of the Society of Architectural Historians, we organized a symposium on Chandigarh reconsidered, titled Le Corbusier's Chandigarh: Architecture as Cultural Text.[6] *I got my father invited as the opening keynote speaker. One imagines he could have used the platform to promote his thoughts on a self-sustaining city, but, at my behest, he chose to deliver a scripted eulogy to the Chandigarh experiment. National pride and the defence of the Le Corbusier mantle trumped critique. Later, the planning faculty led by Porus Olpadwala invited him for a brown bag discussion, where he unleashed his real urban vision for Chandigarh. They loved it. In the wake of postmodernism, the international movements towards sustainability and ecological design were just beginning to gather steam; but none of us knew that then.*

RBI housing just after construction, APF

Back elevation, night perspective drawing, RBI housing, APF

Arcon Architects

To continue to "earn his keep", Prakash hung out his shingle, and started a private practice. Founded with his daughter, Chetna Purnami, in 1982, Arcon Architects enjoyed some success with its steadfastness to the studied palette of Chandigarh modernism. For a small practice, Arcon Architects was exceptionally productive. The APF Archives contain more than 700 original drawings of a wide range of projects ranging from small murals and furnishings to competition entries for entire campuses. Broadly speaking, the work begins with a sense of uncertainty about its character in the early 1980s, with some postmodernist touches creeping into the elevational details, as if Prakash felt he had to somehow ingratiate himself with the times. These are mostly competition entries, trying to jump-start his practice. Through the 1990s, the work returns to more rigorous modernist roots, until it finally yields to a painterly aesthetic in the 2000s.

None of Arcon's "postmodernist" competition entries were built. One of Arcon's earliest built works is the Sandhu Residence in Sector 27, Chandigarh, designed primarily by Chetna Purnami. Based on the push and pull of white cubes, with strong subtracted volumes, this is a decidedly modernist work, but with Chetna leading the project, its formal vocabulary is less in the "Chandigarh style," and more in the idiom of the 1930s international "white" modernism.

Any postmodernist hesitation quickly disappeared as soon as some of the bigger projects materialized in the mid-1980s, beginning with a large Milkfed plant in Jalandhar, and Reserve Bank Housing in Chandigarh. The Milkfed plant for the National Dairy Development Board (NDDB) picked up on themes from Prakash's Agricultural College from his Ludhiana days.

RBI housing stair perspective, APF

A series of massive brick bays separated by structural concrete piers are punctured only occasionally by carefully placed vents and openings. The staff quarters for the Reserve Bank of India had to fit into the strict building by-laws regulating the walk-up apartments built in Chandigarh's newer sectors. But here again, Prakash returned to his Boys' Hostel scheme from Ludhiana and set up an alternating rhythm of balconies so that each apartment had a space that looked up to the sky.

Prakash's old interest in the expressive curve shows up in his design for the "Duty Rooms" of the Milkfed plant. A small structure, it starts out as a rigorous rectilinear box, like the principal's residence. But then, its roofline becomes a powerful swooping curve, something like the bow of the barges used to pull ships through ports. In the same way, a house Prakash designed in Jagadhri also terminates in a curve, except this

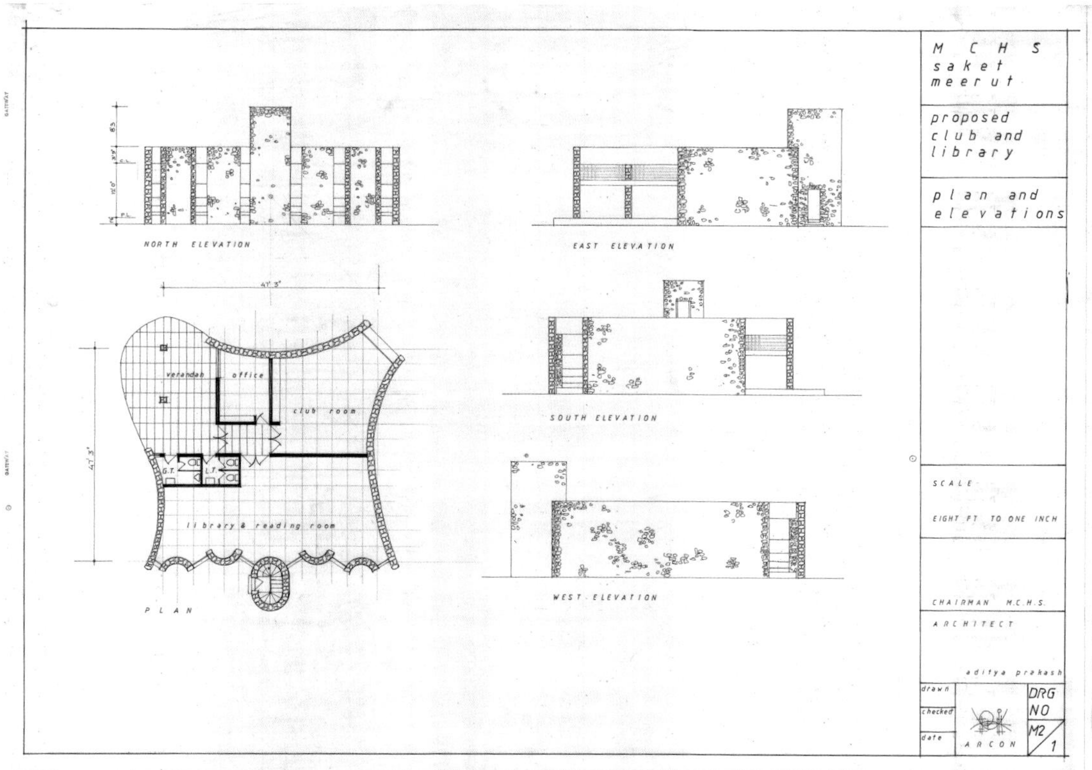

Random rubble design of Jeanneret vintage by Prakash, c.1982, APF

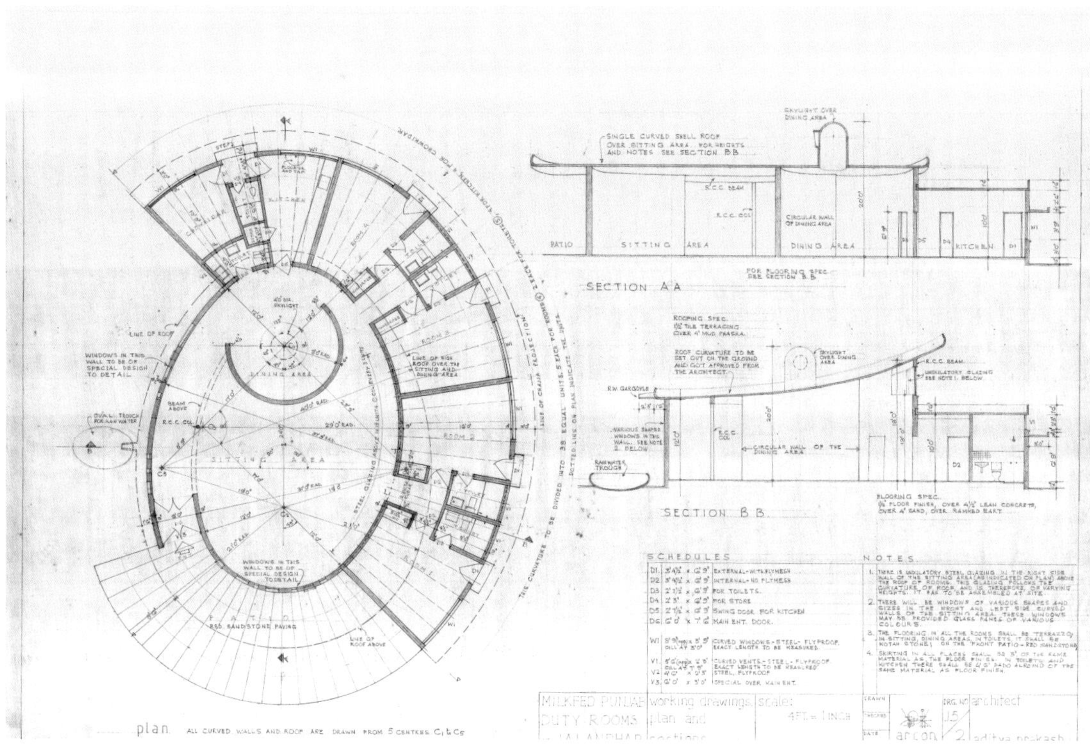

time, it is a dramatic upward-turning crescent, which holds the water tank.[7]

A unique structure with a hyper-modernist section is the clubhouse for a Football Club for the Municipal Corporation of Saket, Meerut, that Prakash designed in 1984. In this Prakash used the roof as the seating, harking back to his old interest in making the roof productive. This seems to have been a redesign of an earlier proposal, in which he had picked up on the random rubble masonry of Jeanneret vintage, combined with investment in the gentle curve derived from one of his paintings.

Educational campuses were to remain a staple of Prakash's Arcon practice, including significant work for the Thapar Institute of Engineering and Technology (TIET) in Patiala, Maharaja Aggarsain Public School in Kurukshetra, and DAV College Jalandhar. In an ironic twist of fate, Prakash returned to design in the campus of the Punjab Agricultural University in Hissar late

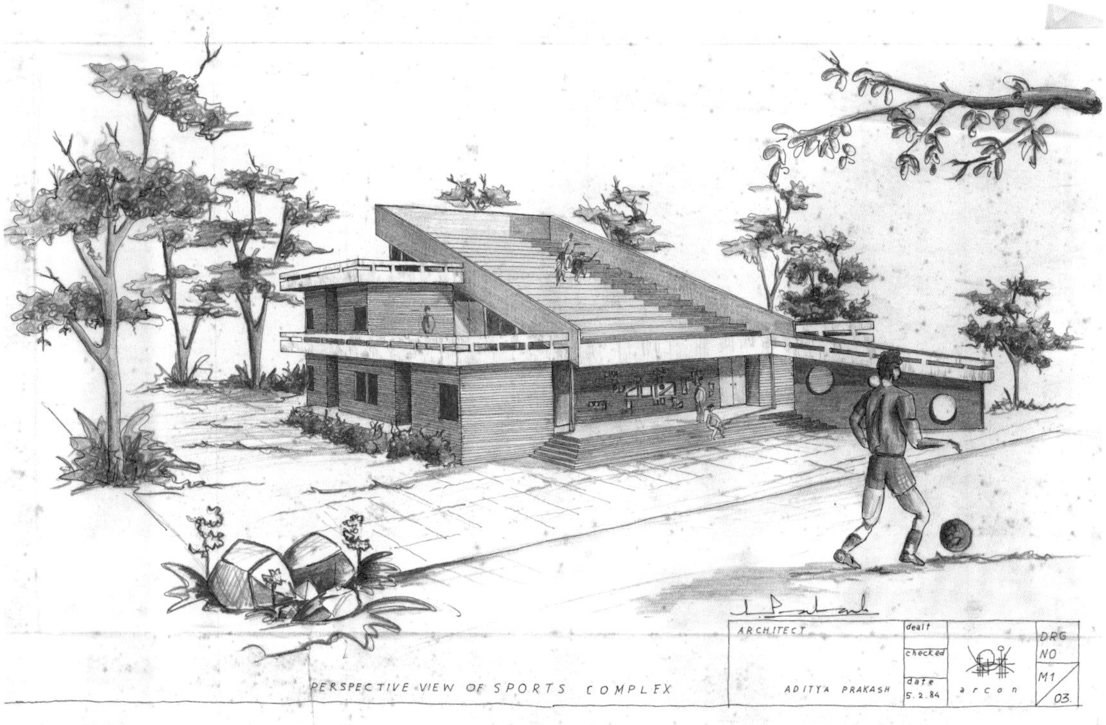

Hand-drawn perspective of Football Club, Meerut, 1984, APF

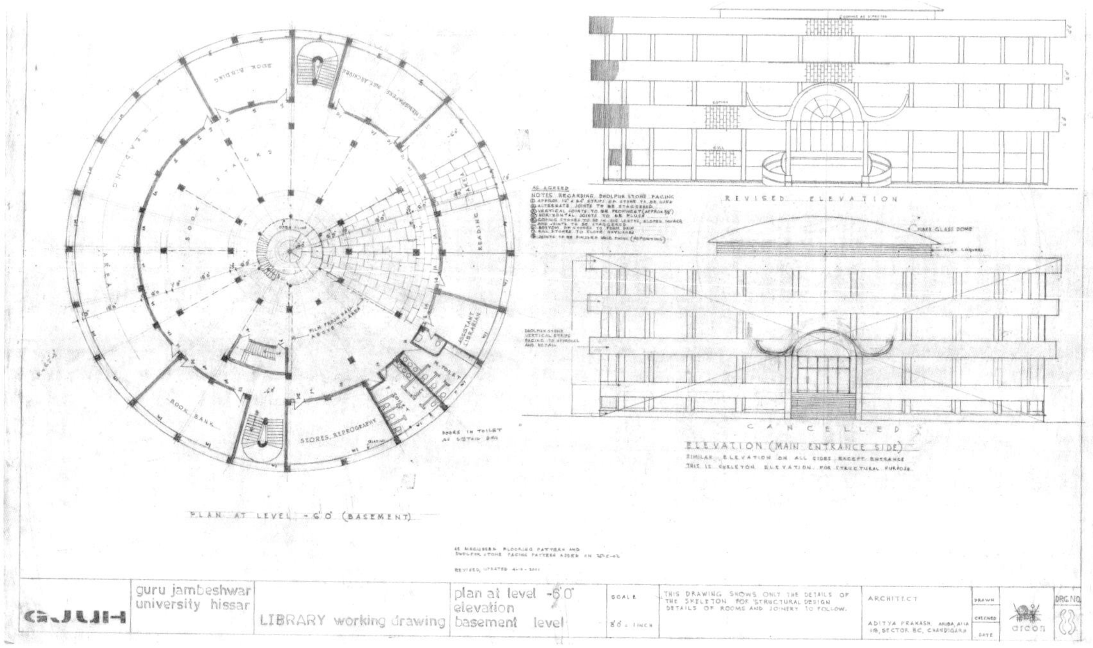

Elevation of the library at TIET, Hissar, APF

in the 1990s, now called the Guru Jambheshwar University. But here, at the very site of some of his oldest modernist works, Prakash chose not to stay steadfast to his old tried and true vocabulary. Instead, in the design of a new library for the University, he broke completely free of the Le Corbusier-Pierre Jeanneret 1950s modernist sensibility. Massive concrete walls, with full circle openings reminiscent of Louis Kahn's IIM Ahmedabad, set up an assemblage that is surmounted by the most unlikely of domes—a free-form shape derived not from any kind of structural logic but, it seems, from one of Prakash's late paintings.

For the most, Prakash functioned as a sole practitioner, though he had a single employee for several stretches.[8] The office was located in the converted garage of his residence in Sector 8, Chandigarh. The walls were panelled with soft-wood (chinar) boards, layered with drawings, sketches, notices, calendars, and blueprints.

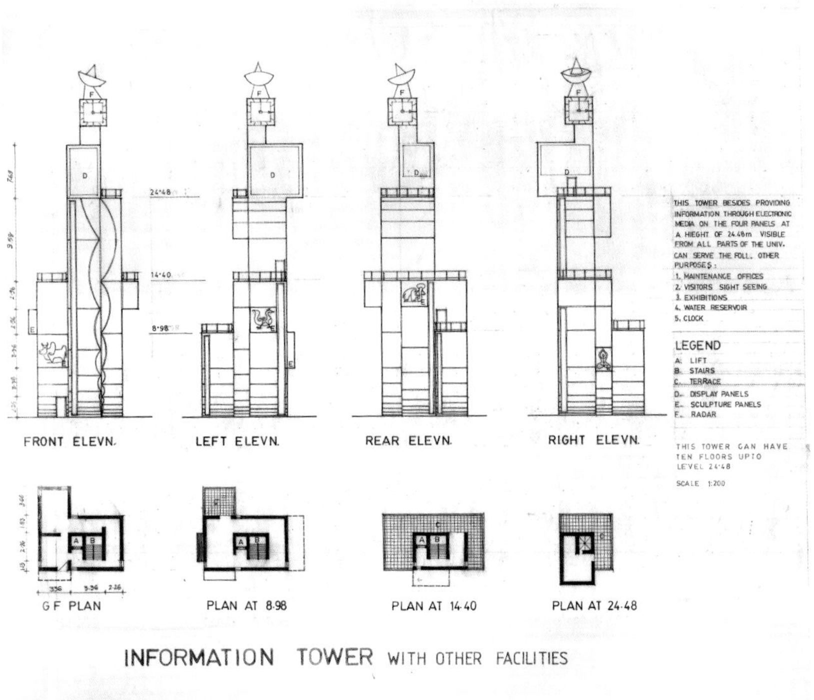

Communications Tower, Thapar Institute of Engineering and Technology (TIET), Hissar, APF

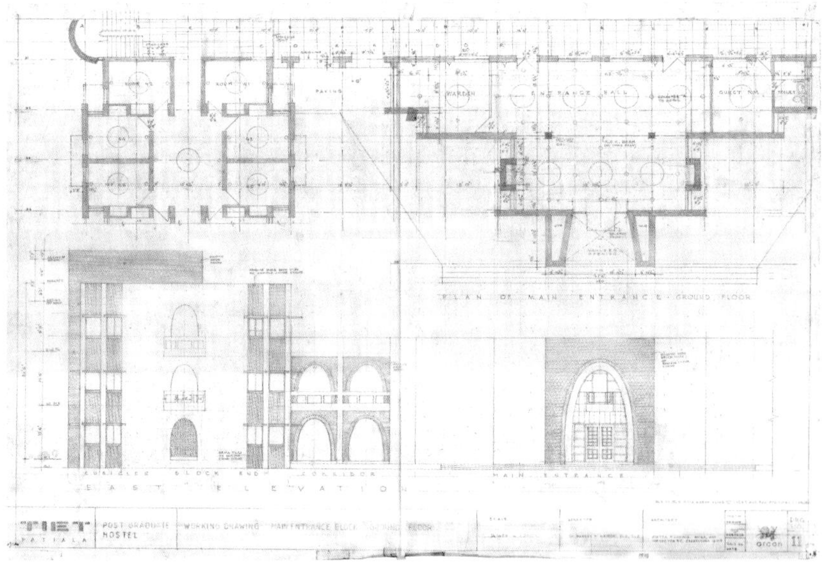

TIET postgraduate hostel, Hissar, APF

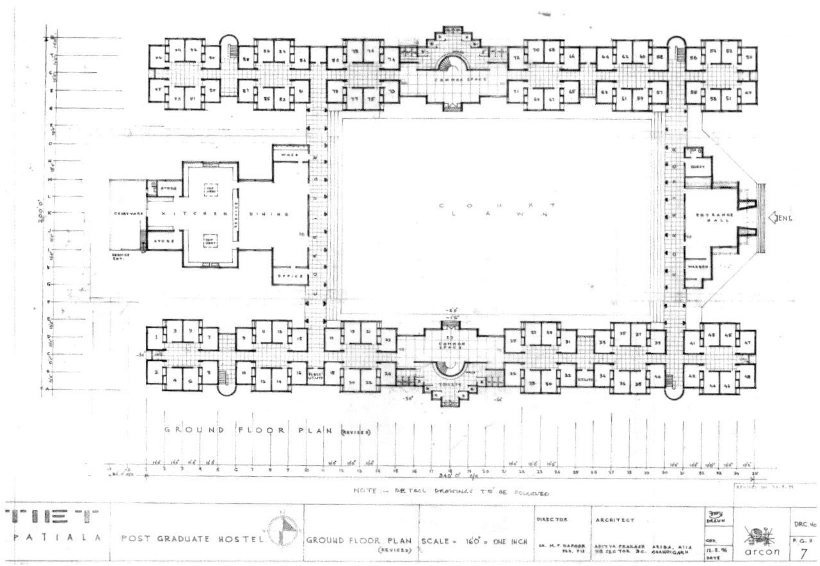

TIET staff housing, Hissar, APF

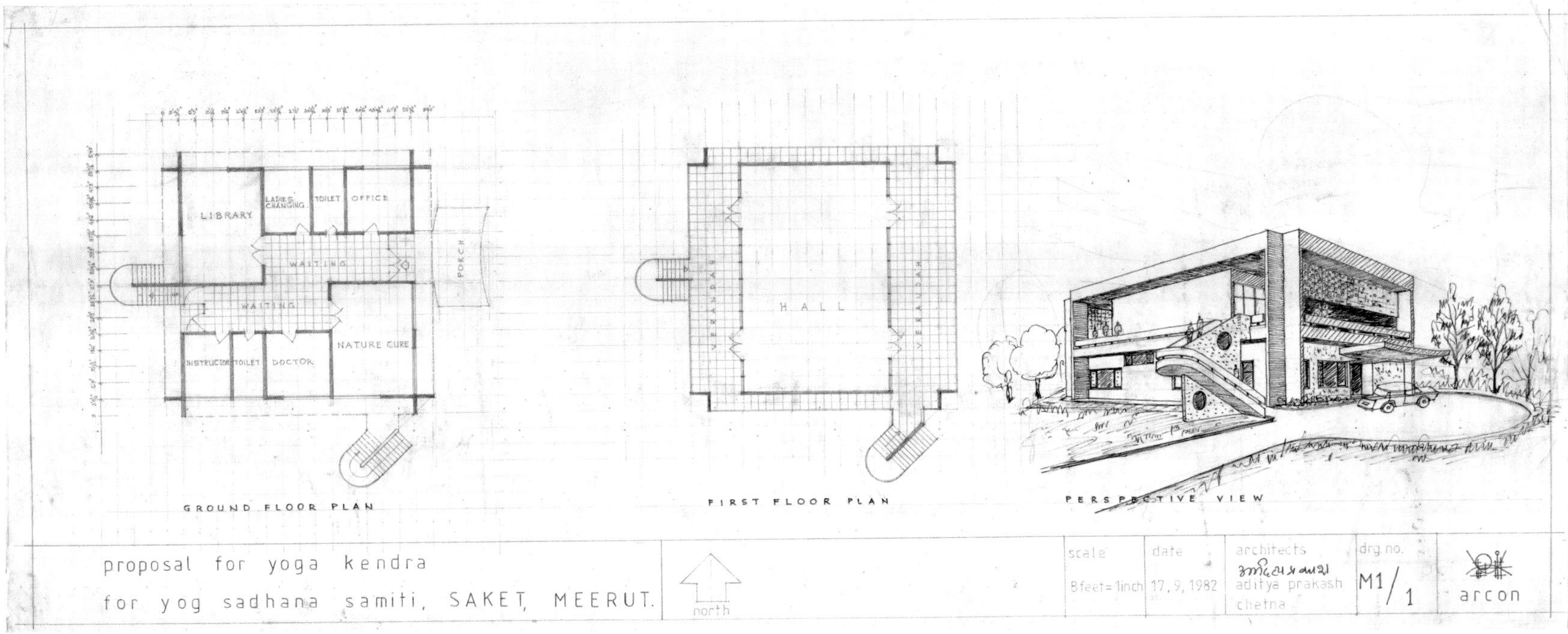

Proposed yoga centre,
Meerut, APF

Old saw-horses, drafting boards, T-squares, and flexible nib ink pens from his days in London and Ludhiana shared space with later generation German Rotring rapidographs, stencils, and parallel bars. An old English portable typewriter stood (mostly shelved) next to a bulky workhorse by Godrej. There weren't many books; just one long shelf.

Arcon Architects powered all my projects through architecture school. I rarely, if ever, consulted with my father on my school projects. They had to be "my own." But I did all my work in the space of Arcon Architects, liberally plundering all its resources, not just the paper and the pencils, but the ideas and concepts I "discovered" on the walls and in the journals. This was in the 1980s. Once I left for the United States in 1986, I lost touch with what was done under the aegis of Arcon. It was only when I began to organize the Archives to write this book that I discovered the astonishing output that came after.

Hand-drawn perspective of Prakash's painting-studio addition to his residence, APF

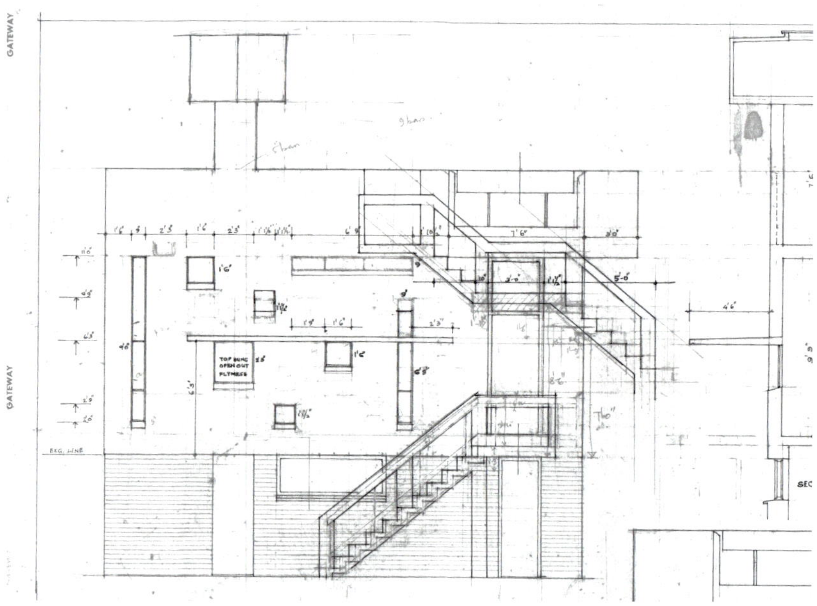

Studio addition to Prakash residence, 1992, APF

The Animal, Again

While professional work with Arcon Architects waxed and waned, Prakash's commitment to his painting studio, located above the architecture office in the garage, was steadfast and long-lasting. He added the painting studio in 1992, with an iconic wall with random punched out openings that he fitted with coloured glass. Unlike the professional studio below, the art studio's interior was devoid of infrastructure—no phones, no instruments, no desks, drawing boards or filing cabinets occupied the space. Just a set of tables lining one of the walls that doubled as painting easels, and a plethora of paints, brushes, mixing palettes, scalpels, charcoals, and straight edges. In the corner was

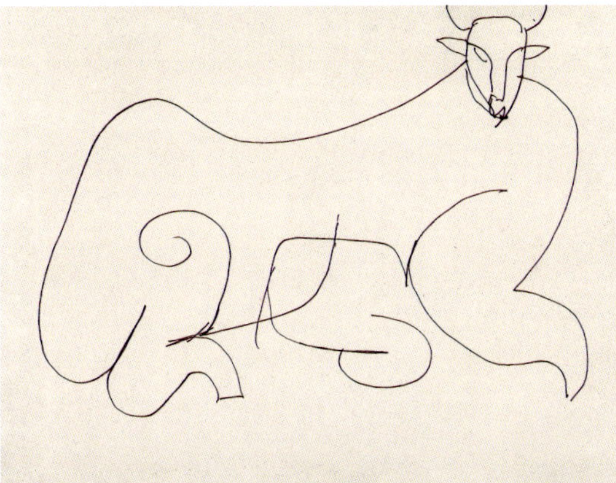

Bull, acrylic on canvas, 16 x 16 inches, 1980s, APF (17_3_2)

Formal studies by Prakash, before the final painting (above-right), ink on paper, 15 x 11 inches, 1999, APF

a large sink, connected directly to a special tank overhead which ensured a constant supply of water to clean the brushes. His trusty Swiss knife along with a bunch of other blades, scalpels, cutting and sharpening instruments were also bunched together, always at hand.

In this way, the amateur work begun in the 1960s eventually blossomed into his primary passion, particularly after retirement. Rather than a supplement to the professional work of architecture and urbanism, painting was a release for Prakash, a way to escape from the daily trials and disappointments of life. "For me 'ART' is relaxation, contemplation, and prayer," he wrote in 1994 in an introductory note to one of his exhibitions, outlining painting as an antidote to the more goal-oriented, and more frustrating, work of academic administration, practice, and research.[9]

The painting work that Prakash began in the 1960s, exploring the formal possibilities of the free-flowing line in abstract form, was to continue throughout his painting career. The sense of freedom associated with the idea of free form, like his books in "free verse," attracted him. It was a liberating concept, the idea that he could approach art without any training or expectation. Almost all of his paintings from the 1960s and the 1970s are abstract free forms and even after he had invested significantly in the figural form starting in the late 1970s, abstract art, with the free-flowing line, continued to be a staple of his output.

Untitled, acrylic on canvas, 16 x 16 inches, 1990s, APF (17_6_23)

Scan image with the **BooksPlus** app

Untitled, acrylic on canvas, 16 x 16 inches, 1990s, APF (17_3_1)

In general, his free-form works are animated by a strong kinetic energy, driven by the movement of the line. Acrylics were his preferred media, packing paper his base layer of choice along with the canvas. Every morning, after making his tea and doing his yoga, Prakash painted in his art studio. For the most, he painted "for himself." If the work was a drawing on paper, it simply went into a drawer. If it was a canvas, he would drill another screw into an empty spot in the walls of his own house and hang it up. When that was not feasible, he would simply take down an old canvas and replace it. Other than a couple of paintings from the early 1970s in his Drawing Room, which held onto their location steadfastly, all others were subject to summary removal. If a guest walking through the house admired a painting, it was hers/his.[10]

At the same time, he slowly acceded into the culture of exhibiting. Through the 1970s, he exhibited mostly as part of group shows of local artists. After his retirement, he also began putting up one-man shows in local art galleries in Chandigarh, usually for a period of a week or two. Finally, the Taj Art Gallery in Mumbai (then Bombay), invited him to a solo show in 1989, followed by a reprise in 1991. Both shows received favourable reviews and many works were sold. His third, and last, Mumbai exhibition, at the Bajaj Art Gallery in Nariman Point, came

Bull, acrylic on canvas, 36 x 24 inches, 1980s, APF (17_3_3)

Untitled, acrylic on canvas, 16 x 16 inches, 1990s, APF {16_(28)}

in 1993. After that he held bi-annual solo shows in various galleries in Chandigarh through the 1990s. He stopped exhibiting and signing his paintings somewhere in the early 2000s.

After retirement, Prakash's obsession with the bird form morphed into a complete menagerie of animal forms. A multitude of beasts of the jungle, and a few beasts of burden, suddenly began to settle into the Modulor divisions of his frames. Bulls posed majestically, commanding the canvas; camels struck a pose, both sitting and standing, trying to occupy all sectors of the frame; snakes, single and in multitudes, began slithering across the canvas, making every sort of swirl and whirl they could with their long, trailing bodies; every now and then a horse or two would gallop into the frame; the occasional gazelle could be seen standing at attention astride a Modulor rectangle or two; and then of course the elephant, always majestic and triumphant, showed up repeatedly to occupy the full frame of the painting in a show of power.

One of the reasons that animals would have attracted him was that their non-human shapes more readily lent themselves to the formal possibility of occupying as many of the Modulor squares and rectangles as possible. The continuous line that makes the profile of a pink, yellow, and black camel from the 1980s, for instance, makes its way through six of the eight

Untitled, acrylic on canvas, 16 x 16 inches, 1990s, APF (17_3_10)

Untitled, acrylic on canvas, 16 x 16 inches, 1990s, APF {11.12(5)}

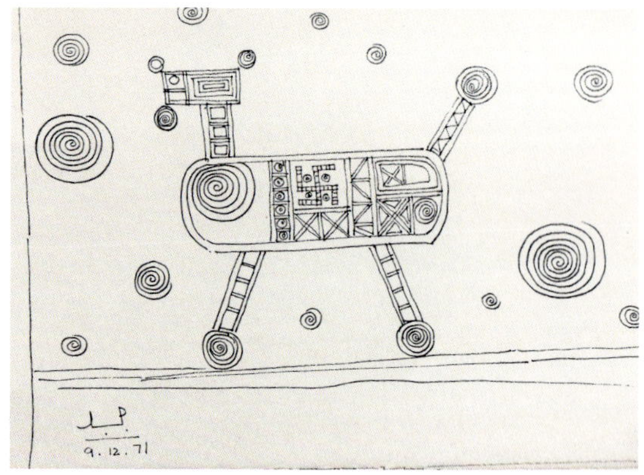

Untitled doodles (second row), ink on paper, 10 x 8 inches each, 1970s, APF

Modulor divisions of the canvas, as if to claim those territories. In a painting of a small brown-and-grey elephant and her calf from the 1990s, the mother pushes through all six of her framing Modulor divisions, while the baby works hard to assert itself into three of them.

Beyond the formal, his interest in the animal also connected with his urban planning visions. We can recall his early affection for the resident animals of his childhood home, and their subsequent mistreatment by the Chandigarh plan. The question of what he hoped to achieve by foregrounding animals in his paintings must remain speculative and conjectural, but their preponderance suggests a kind of ethical imperative.

Prakash's interest in animals could also be traced to Le Corbusier, who famously and obsessively drew the bull and the occasional donkey in his sketchbooks while in India. These morphed into his *Taureaux* series of paintings and gouaches made while Chandigarh was being built, which in turn were represented in the profiles of the Assembly and the Governor's Palace—abstracted bull forms, one standing, and the other rampant on its hind legs. Unlike the main fabric of the city which was hostile to animals, Le Corbusier's own Capitol was self-consciously constructed as part of an agro-rural landscape. Le Corbusier wrote about this, and published Lucien Hervé and Ernst Scheidegger's

Untitled, acrylic on canvas, 16 x 16 inches, 1990s, APF (17_3_5)

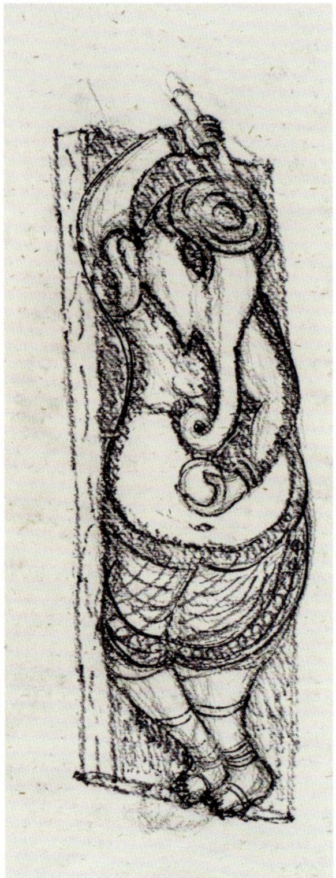

Ganesha, charcoal on tracing paper, size unknown, 1990s, APF

Reclining Ganesha, charcoal on paper, 20 x 12 inches, 1990s, APF {2_(20)}

photographs that showed the Capitol buildings from the vantage of the rural landscape, often with a cow or a bull in the foreground.

Nowhere in his writings, however, does Prakash credit Le Corbusier as being sympathetic to the animal or the rural. For him, the Chandigarh Plan was rigorously anti-rural and anti-animal, and he sought to reform that. For Le Corbusier the bull was of interest for its figural and symbolic qualities—as a muscular form attractively open to abstraction, and as a symbol of masculinity, somewhat autobiographical if only via projection. The agro-rural landscape was an idealized site that he took as his mandate to sublimate into modernity. For Prakash, the animal was an affectionate and productive beast that deserved to be intimately integrated into the daily life of a city. He even once postulated that animals responded to art, citing sporadic examples of dogs responding to the sight of their master and cows giving more milk if exposed to classical music.[11]

The animal, in other words, occupied Prakash's imagination in an intimate way. For Le Corbusier, certain animals—in particular the bull and the crow—essentially functioned as displaced autobiographical signatures. For

A formal study by Prakash, ink on paper, 15 x 11 inches, 1999, APF

Untitled, acrylic on canvas, 16 x 16 inches, 1980s, APF {17_3_6}

Ganesha, acrylic on canvas, 21 x 17 inches, 1990s, APF {16_(14)}

Prakash, based on his intimate life experiences with them, the animal was an integral part of the continuum of life that was not totally centred on the human. The animal shapes in his art were not cold abstraction, but about a kind of love, a multi-species entanglement. In Indian aesthetics, the experience of the beautiful—the task of the artist—is described as being the production of "*rasa*". *Rasa* is not abstraction in the Platonic sense. It is more tangible and corporeal; it refers to experiencing the "mood" or "flavour" or the more fluid and intimate form of something that is ordinarily more frozen, congealed or solidified.

There is also the question of why animals took over his frames only after he retired from public service. He saw his life after retirement as a liberation, freedom from the yoke of government service, and also from his "responsibilities" in life, particularly those that required subservience to authority. After retirement, he could perhaps express himself more freely, in terms of his own loves, in particular his affinity for animals, traceable back to his youth.[12]

Untitled,
acrylic on canvas,
24 x 24 inches,
1990s, APF {16_(04)}

Untitled,
acrylic and charcoal on
canvas, 16 x 16 inches,
1990s, APF {2_(93)}

Indic motifs

On 6 December 1992, communal forces led by the then relatively weak BJP (Bharatiya Janata Party) demolished Babri Masjid, a 16th-century mosque that they claimed stood on the birth site of the Hindu god Rama. Babri Masjid's demolition, and subsequent rise of the BJP as a political force announced the arrival of the challenge to another pillar of the Nehruvian state, the resolute investment in secularism. Around this time, in the early 1990s, Prakash also began to experiment with Indic forms in his paintings. This may have been a delayed response to the culturalist critiques of postmodernism, and/or it may have been prompted by India's embrace of globalization. It may also have been intended as a critique of communalism.

Retrospectively, Prakash would originate his turn to Indic art to a specific event in the late 1970s, when he says his thinking "underwent a somersault":

> There was also the time when I was an admirer of modern art, modern architecture, and also an ardent follower of Le Corbusier (I still am but with some reservations). I happened to visit Mahabalipuram and chanced to discover a "School of Architecture" there. It took me by surprise, so I walked in. It was not the usual school as I had known. I met the Principal and he informed me that they teach everything according to the tenets of the ancient scriptures of India. They basically taught sculpture and forms of South Indian temples. I asked to see how they go about it. I saw the form of "Dancing Ganesha" drawn on the chalk board. I was immediately impressed. My thinking in architectural education underwent a somersault. I felt that education in architecture,

Untitled,
acrylic and charcoal on canvas, 28 x 28 inches, 1990s, APF (17_4_6)

Untitled,
acrylic on canvas, 13.25 x 13.25 inches, 1990s, APF {2_(90)}

> and for that matter in all arts can only be the teaching of all inherited crafts. Namely how to achieve the results our ancients achieved, or the Greeks, Romans, Egyptians achieved. Then to imbibe their aesthetic value according to one's own sensibility.[13]

While his turn to the Indic can be seen as a reassessment of the value of "inherited" crafts, Prakash's interpretation of "one's own sensibility" was derived from his training in modernism. In an interview with Nonika Singh, a journalist reporting on his 2006 exhibition in the IndusInd Gallery in Chandigarh, he asserted, "[s]ince times immemorial, Indian art has been rooted in abstraction."[14] Dating back to his days in the Delhi Polytechnic in the mid-1940s, he was always inspired by the staid and studied compositions of Jamini Roy.[15] Like Prakash's, Jamini Roy's paintings are flat, figural compositions, carefully constructed and very respectful of the frame. They are also bright, multi-coloured and full of animals. While Roy's forms actively reference tribal and folk art, particularly the Kalighat tradition, Prakash's paintings are rigorously modernist and devoted to abstraction. Unlike Roy's, Prakash's paintings do not explicitly seek to carry narrative; they are still-lifes, interested only in their own formal construction.

One could trace a parallel between his graphing of Indic forms with the Modulor, and the intellectual Indian systems of temple design and sculpture. Hindu temple geometries and sculptural forms both derive from a series of complex geometric and arithmetical operations, all of which originate in astrological graphs called *mandalas*. While the body of the temple retains active traces of its geometrical origins, the figural

sculpture is represented as an independent form. By this differentiation, the "message" of the temple as a whole is to underscore the "cosmic" connectivity between the world of the temple and that of the human and divine forms.

In this way, the Modulor divisions with their graphing of Indic forms in his paintings can be read as a modernization of the relationship between the complex geometries of a Hindu temple and the figural sculpture to which they are the background. Both seek to plumb the "truth" of the beautiful, as a pipeline to the underlying "truth" of the cosmos. The "cosmos" in fact was a significant obsession in Prakash's paintings. He constantly wrote about it, the titles of many of his paintings carried the word in it, and at least one of his solo exhibitions was assembled under its banner.

The form of the spiral galaxy recurs in many of his paintings, drawings and murals. Some paintings have figures inscribed on them, which can be read as reinterpretations of the Indic *vastupurushamandala* diagram of the cosmic man. In one of his late works, the cosmos is depicted in alternating yellow and black spirals, which focus in on a red circle centred on a man's navel, as in the *vastupurushamandala*. In one exceptional painting, we see something like the cosmos emerging from within a woman's legs.[16]

Even so, it seems clear that the cosmos for Prakash was as much the phenomenon of deep space, billions of light years across that was advanced by modern astrophysics, as it was short-hand for respect for the larger orders of life. The invocation to the cosmos was an invocation

Vastupurushamandala, 34 x 34 inches, 1990s, APF (17_4_24)

Untitled, acrylic and charcoal on canvas, 30 x 47 inches, 1990s, APF (17_4_7)

Scan image with the **BooksPlus** app

ı began only about half a century ago,
like a renaissance.
ıscent-effort' is an apt phrase
than such a comprehensive term as the 'renaissance'.

ıis ancient dance-art survives,
and atomic age,
·,
lure in the shape and form
› but may flourish in its purer aspect.
no mechanical method
ther, or in what form,

ıt of beliefs and doctrines,
urther period.
ɔne age
he iron age.
›eautiful crafts of Byzantium,
›late early medieval sculpture,
ve of form.
eason to believe that
to promote Bharata Natyam will prolong themselves
ıt during our own generation.

however,
e have, on the one hand,
ıi Devi and Ramachandra Rao
t this dance
kground entire;
other hand,
ial European-educated middle class men and women,

Pages from the December 1979 issue of *Marg* magazine titled "In Praise of Bharata Natyam" with Prakash's analytic lines drawn on them (above and facing page, right)

Untitled, acrylic on canvas, 26 x 42.5 inches, 1990s, APF (17_4_12)

Untitled, acrylic on canvas, 27.75 x 40.5 inches, 2000s, APF {11.12(2)}

of the ecological, the larger systems that support and have long supported life here on earth. In an unpublished paper found in the APF Archives titled, "Energy and Pollution," he tabulated the kinds of "Waste," to make the argument that polluting activities must be given up. "All wa[s]tes are not pollutants," he noted. "Some are, some are cleansing." In the paper he then proceeded to tabulate Wastes. The first column lists "Pollutant" systems such as "Chemical," "Mechanical," and "Atomic." The second column lists "Non Pollutant" systems such as "Animal/ Muscular Power," "Solar," and "Wind"; and then, there is a third column with the heading "Cleansing" under which he lists "Cosmic/Spiritual" and "Earth."[17]

Cleansing one's body with water as the rite of ritual purification is an ancient act, with multiple cultural and religious codings. In Hinduism it occupies a special place as the rite of bathing in the flowing waters of a river, for all rivers and particularly the Ganges, are considered sacred. Even in the Arya Samaj's simplified Hindu practices that Prakash's father followed, ritual cleansing with water at the beginning of every fire ceremony was rigorously practised.

Prakash was not actively religious, but he maintained a broad undefined notion of the "spiritual," which he repeatedly invoked in his writings, usually in connection with cultivating the ethic of responsibility to the larger

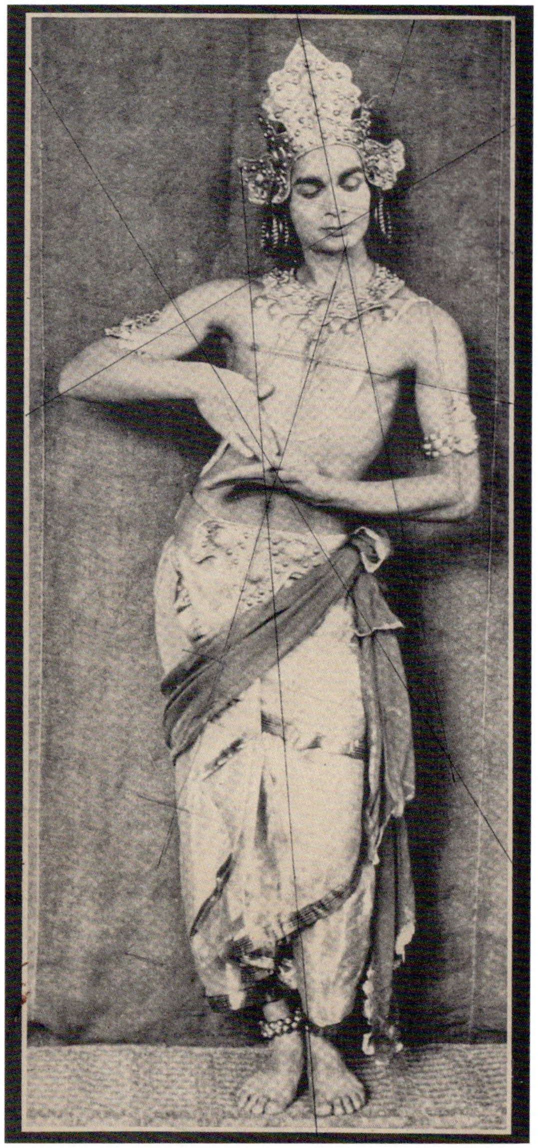

Overlaying the Modulor on photographs of figures in Prakash's quest for the beautiful, APF

Bronze figure of Uma, from *Marg* magazine, December 1979, APF

equilibrium of nature/cosmos as something like an act of faith. If we offer devotion to the cosmos—by not polluting, cultivating a relationship with animals, growing and consuming wisely, and so on—then, the cosmos will offer its benevolence in return.[18] In this way, one could construe the "beautiful" for Prakash as the natural consequence of the benevolence of the cosmos, which required the devotion of a life lived responsibly and self-sustainably. In this sense, then, in the absence of being able to build his sustainable city, Prakash's daily practice, or *puja*, of painting was a substitutive act of sustainable living, sublimated via devotion to the beautiful in the "works of God".[19]

There are many study drawings in the APF Archives with axial lines drawn over photographs of historic Indian art and sculpture.[20] Rather than the communicative function of idioms such as folk art traditions, what interested Prakash more was the Modulor-inspired search for the underlying orders of the beautiful in Indian art. He used these to make paintings, usually inscribed with the Modulor graph, of iconic Indic figures such as Ganesh, Rama, Shiva-Parvati (deities of the Hindu pantheon), the meditating yogi and the dancing female. Ganesh was a favourite. As a cross between the animal and the human, it is easy to see why Ganesh would be attractive to Prakash's non-anthropocentric proclivities.

Untitled (facing page, right), acrylic and charcoal on canvas, 17 x 21 inches, 1990s, APF (17_4_36)

Untitled, acrylic on canvas, 23 x 33 inches, 2000s, APF {16_(17)}

Untitled,
acrylic on packing paper,
28 x 41.5 inches, 2000s,
APF (17_6_20)

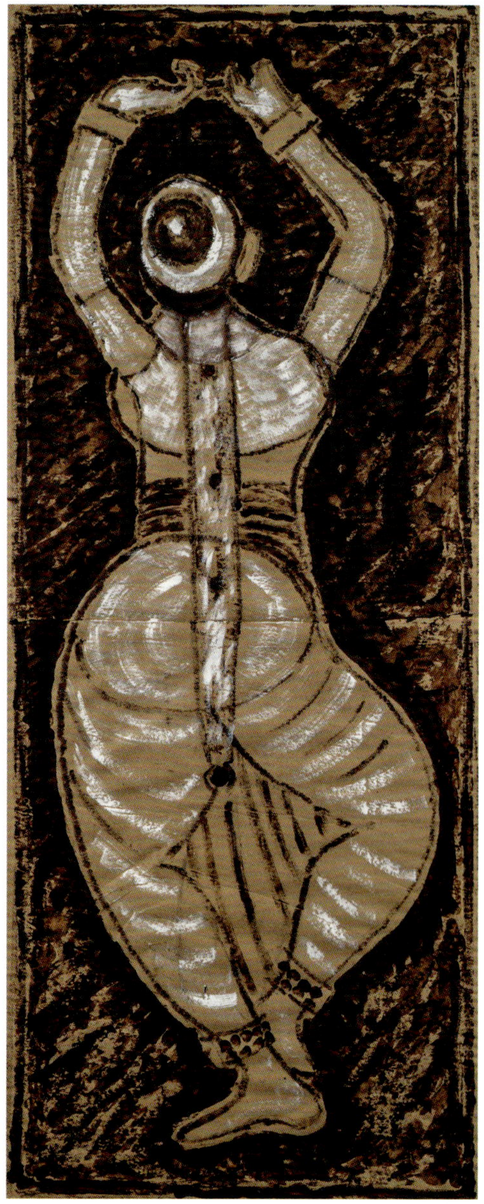

Untitled, oil on packing paper, 15.5 x 40 inches, 1990s, APF (17_4_10)

The Female Form, and the Lingam

Finally, an important theme that runs through many of his paintings was an interest in the sensual and the erotic, and in particular, the female form. Here is Prakash's declamation on the nude:

> I find that passion and sensuality are [an] integral part of art. It is not just for curiosity of form that an artist studies or wants to study NUDES. It is also for a sensual experience. I was told by a well-known artist that when he studied nudes his breath flow became fast and loud. I know that when I draw certain curves in whatever painting I am making, the pleasure of sensuality can be felt. Many a time the sensation is as if the real form is being experienced. When the Assembly building of Chandigarh was being built, Corbusier, on seeing the smooth finish of the concrete

Untitled, ink and acrylic on paper, 19 x 14.5 inches, 2000s, APF {16 (66)}

Untitled, acrylic paper, 23.5 x 41.5 inches, 2000s, APF {11.12_(7)}

> columns as they emerged from the shuttering is said to have remarked: "They are like the smooth thighs of a woman." This happens also while composing poetry, and I should think, while dancing or singing.[21]

There are two types of female forms in Prakash's paintings. One is a dancing figure, derived from classical Indian dance poses; and the other is a seated one. Most are classic nudes, or semi-nudes, but then quite a few are clothed, mostly in recognizable formal dancing dresses. The latter seem to be based on images of historical Indic sculpture and paintings.

Most of the dancing female forms belong to the register of formal investigations, searching out the beautiful via the substrate of the Modulor.

Untitled, acrylic on canvas, 21 x 28 inches, 2000s, APF {16_(36)}

Untitled, acrylic on canvas, 23 x 26.5 inches, 1990s, APF (17_4_11)

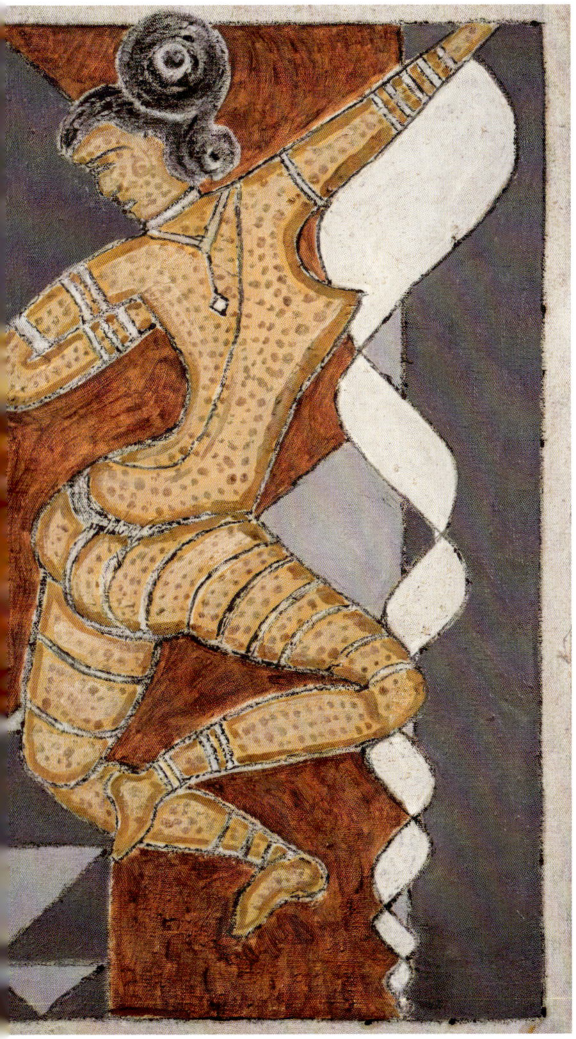

Untitled, acrylic on canvas mounted on board, 10.25 x 18.25 inches, 1990s, APF {2_(39)}

Untitled, acrylic on 0.5 mm ply, 18 x 24 inches, 2000s, APF {16_(15)}

Untitled, acrylic on canvas, 32.5 x 32.5 inches, 2000s, APF (17_5_30)

Prakash made several pairs of interpretive paintings, in which he would paint a particular figure both as replicated from a drawing, and as an abstracted figure integrated with the Modulor. Subtle differences in the posture of the body resulted. The abstracted figures tended to get more twisted and elongated as they tried to fit across their Modulor frames.

The seated figures play with the more normative expectations of the female nude. Some of them are significantly abstracted, composed from circles and free-form ovals, stretched along the axes of the Modulor. Others are more figural, more invested in the female body. One of these, based on sculpture found in *Marg*, was done in two iterations.[22] The first is a small canvas in earthy reds, yellows, and browns, and depicts a full-bodied female figure holding a flower, with especially wide hips, an exceptionally thin waist, and large, upright breasts. She sits on a throne and wears a crown. One can easily recognize her as a Hindu divine figure. While the "original" is only 12 inches tall, the abstracted version is 3 feet by 3 feet. In the latter, her limbs become muscular and supple, her breasts enlarge and dominate the frame, while her head completely disappears. Instead of the studied background of Modulor frames, large, generous, free curves swirl through the painting in a defiant gesture of freedom.

There is another large yellow and brown canvas with crimson accents, of a big-bodied woman, that hung in the studio until his death. A seated woman with large, pendulous

Untitled, acrylic on canvas, 34 x 34 inches, 2000s, APF (17_5_21)

breasts sits across the base of her Modulor frame, looking straight back at her spectator, her eyelids half-shut in the classic pose of an enlightened Indic figure, while her diaphanous dress is clearly designed to reveal. In the long annals of the female nude, strong female figures that look back at the "camera," well assured of their sexuality, are few and far between. Manet's 1863 depiction of a prostitute as *Olympia* is one. Prakash's *Woman in Yellow, Brown and Crimson* another.

In general, however, Prakash worked with a fairly normative division of the gendered body. The female body was to be explored and valourized, while the male figure was to be abstracted and coded symbolically. Most of the male figures in his paintings are carefully framed, stationary ascetics. They sit in standard yogic poses of meditation and penance, presumably lost in deep thought. The paintings seek to simply frame their equipoise, heedful of their need to not be disturbed.[23]

The Hindu sign of the male principle, the giver of form, is the symbolic form of Shiva, the *lingam-yoni*, or the phallus encircled by a womb. A person raised within a Western sensibility, still residually schooled in the Victorian sense of morality, could easily be forgiven for being shocked by the preponderance of the *lingam-yoni* that can be found anywhere in the Indian landscape, from small souvenirs sitting on a car's dashboard to the massive black phallic forms found in the cores of many of the grand Shiva temples of the South, such as the one in Thanjavur.

The Shiva *lingam*, with and without its *yoni*, abounds in Prakash's paintings as well. It is always plain, undisguised, minimally abstracted, and unmistakable. If Le Corbusier's autobiographical sign was the bull (along with the crow and the donkey), then perhaps Prakash's might be identified as the *lingam*.

If much of his art is distinctly phallic, the *lingam* can also be parsed as part of his broader interest in the curve. In this respect, it is the counter curve to the dominant form of the upward-turning arc of the bird in flight, open to the sky. If the upward-turning arc opened itself to the sky, Prakash's *lingam* arch always presented itself as firmly anchored to the ground, like a *stupa*. In many paintings the two arcs can be found together, balancing each other, but also in competition with each other.

As autobiographical signs, the two curves could be interpreted as Oedipally-inflected competing orientations to the world, one turned outward and more speculative, and the other focused inwards, more meditational and anchored to the exigencies of the real.

Untitled, acrylic on canvas, 23 x 27 inches, 2000s, APF {16_(24)}

Untitled, acrylic on
packing paper,
27 x 38 inches, 2000s,
APF (17_6_1)

Untitled, acrylic on
packing paper,
40 x 26.5 inches, 2000s,
APF (17_6_21)

Untitled, acrylic and poster paint on packing paper, 28 x 38 inches, 2000s, APF {6(3)}

The New Millennium

In 1999, Chandigarh Administration held a massive conference to celebrate the fiftieth anniversary of the city's inauguration, led by Charles Correa and featuring a list of celebrity architects and architectural academics, almost all of them from the West. Prakash was invited to play a small role, but mostly his voice was side-lined.[24] Of the many great ideas floated, the only one that seemed to actually stick was the call to preserve Chandigarh. Faced with the uncertainties of globalization, the architectural community's dominant response was not to plan for growth, but to rally around the cause of preservation—a worthy mission, but not one attuned to Prakash's sustainable urban planning interests.

Nothing, however, stopped Prakash from painting. In the Archives today, there are over 600 drawings and about 150 full-sized canvases. This does not include the innumerable drawings and paintings he regularly gave away and sold in exhibitions, a tally difficult to estimate but certainly in the hundreds.

Around 2003, he stopped signing his paintings, arguing that the creative act was not an act of individual will, but a spontaneous force acting through the human body. The cosmos, he believed, acted on its own, and human agency was only instrumental. A signature as a sign of ownership seemed presumptuous. In the Louis Kahn-like syntax of asking the brick "what it wants to be," Prakash noted:

> For the last one year or so, I had the resurgence of the desire to paint or do something with art on a regular basis. This inner drive sent me to my studio every early morning before breakfast to spend at least a couple of hours there. That is where the 'painting' began to communicate to me: 'No, this is not done yet. You have to put more life into it. You are overdoing it. You have spoiled it. Your colours should have more texture, more body. Your lines should vibrate sing and dance'—such were the utterances from my works. I began to start several paintings at the same time. When I entered the studio one of the paintings would say: 'You have to work on me today.' In a sense the paintings asked me to paint in them the way "they" wanted to be painted.
>
> ...We do not create. Something within us seeks creation. We are only a medium for that creativity. It is our opportunity to discover or to recognize that creative moment within us and let it be expressed—born. The more I can rid myself of the myth of being a creator, the better from me. If I can just "be" and let things happen, then only the expressions which are ingrained in my being shall have a chance to come out. Otherwise they will die with me and then wait till "they" get the next opportunity

Untitled, acrylic and poster paint on packing paper, 26 x 40 inches, 2000s, APF {6_(1)}

Untitled, acrylic on packing paper, 28.5 x 40.5 inches, 2000s, APF (17_6_18)

> for expression in the next life...whenever I "try" to create I cannot create. The creativity in painting "happens." The more I can release myself from the "efforts" of creativity, the better are the results. Thus I am not the "creator." I was then asked, 'Why do I then sign my paintings?' Actually I don't sign my paintings. Most of the time I am required to. In fact, most of the paintings in this exhibition are unsigned...[25]

His last works were a series of 24 inch by 36 inch abstract paintings made with acrylic on packing paper. Packing paper was one of the first things he had painted on in Ludhiana. Sometimes dated, but always unsigned, these were some of his finest works. Though still carefully framed and composed, with some familiar themes like wriggling snakes and upward/downward-turning curves, there is an unfamiliar sense of relaxation and even abandonment to their compositions. Lines move around the sheet as if they are in search of new margins, figural compositions threaten to burst into life, and colours are deployed with an uncustomary lack of caution. There is a carnivalesque sense to some of them; one a mirthful portrait of a clown.

An interesting comparison can be made between one of the oldest available Prakash compositions, a sculpture from the mid-1960s, and one of his last paintings, dated 17 January 2007. They are remarkably similar; both formal

Prakash at the Chandigarh Lalit Kala Akademi workshop, APF

Untitled, charcoal on paper, 21 x 28 inches, 2000s, APF {16_(21)}

investigations into the spatial and volumetric possibilities of the free-form curve. Both of them are dedicated to the search for balance, and imply centres and axes of rotation (single vertical in the sculpture, multiple and diagonal in the painting). The painting has a "navel," an orange and red centre of gravity; while the sculpture has several holes, each the implied focus of its own curved-zone. If there is a difference it is that the painting seeks to break free of repose and containment, brushing aggressively against its edges, while the sculpture, even though it is a free-standing object in space, works resolutely within its cylindrical confines.

An important part of Prakash's life in his last years, still continuing from the role he was assigned by Mulk Raj Anand, was participating in and conducting the affairs of the Chandigarh Lalit Kala Akademi (CLKA), of which he served as secretary and president for several terms. His approach to the Lalit Kala Akademi was "counter-celebrity"—opposed to inviting well-known artists and critics—and instead invested in encouraging the "the common

Untitled, acrylic
on packing paper,
29 x 42 inches, 2000s,
APF {11.12(13)}

Untitled, acrylic
on packing paper,
29 x 42 inches, 2000s,
APF {11.12(8)}

man" to cultivate a taste and appreciation for art by trying his/her hand at it. He always insisted on organizing artists' workshops not in isolated enclaves but in the middle of everyday communities such as schools and colleges, and once even in the foyer of a cinema hall.[26] Some of Prakash's best work, painted with a sense of freedom precipitated by the time-bound public situation, were done in the context of such workshops.

The very last painting he exhibited was at the 2008 annual exhibition of the CLKA—a stand-alone monochromatic figure of Rama in grey with acrylic, annotated with the text मर्यादापुरुषोत्तम राम (*Ideal of Manliness*), which is the honorific title usually connected with Lord Rama identifying his exemplary conduct and character. The Secretary of the CLKA who curated the show noted that Prakash insisted that this particular painting be exhibited, a tell-tale sign of his significant turn to spirituality, even though most of the work that he was doing at this time was multi-coloured and abstract.

Our Get-Together

An important anchor in his last years was also the monthly meeting of his group of intellectual friends. In 1972, Prakash had revived his old "Modern Architects Group" concept, but this time he did not restrict it to architects. He christened this new interdisciplinary group, dedicated to freewheeling discussion, as simply "Our Get-Together." People from all disciplines were invited to join. Most of the members were retired academics, civil servants, doctors, and other professionals.

After Prakash's retirement, "Our Get-Together" really took off, with never a monthly meeting missed. Each get-together was held in a different member's home. After a few minutes of socialization and snacks, a member would present on a pre-announced topic for about 30 minutes, followed by open, animated discussion and debate. Attendance was strictly maintained to weed out members who stopped participating actively.

No topic was off-limits. A personal investment in the discussion of the day was encouraged. Issues discussed in 1999 included: "Theory of Everything," "Modern Urdu Poetry," "Women and Men," "My Favourite Poet," "Madness and Creativity," "First Fifty Years of Film Music," "Postmodernism Ideology," "Bureaucracy, Past and Future," "Kargil," "Remembering Kabir," "The Future of Chandigarh," "Elections," "Political Trends," "Why Democracy," and "The Internet."[27]

The core membership of the group had forged their careers, in one form or another, in the context of the Nehruvian nation-state. Besides architects, the group included senior doctors, engineers, academics, judges, IAS officers, police officers, and poets, most of whom in one capacity or another had served in state institutions. Their conversations embodied the Nehruvian-age ethos, when it was thought that intellectual leadership could steer the nation through decolonization into prosperity, and many of the concerns of the group can be seen as late-stage critiques of the Nehruvian legacy.

"Our Get-Together" acquired canonical status in the intellectual life of Chandigarh. Starting out entirely with men, the group moved to actively recruit women into its fold during later years. This was not a group armoured in a governmental or non-governmental institution format, or supported fiscally or otherwise by an external body. Like Abhinet, it was an "amateur" group of professionals and thinkers who met and discussed current issues of their own cognizance and impetus, studiously avoiding anything like a publication or a souvenir to document their deliberations. It was a group of organic intellectuals, very much in the Gramscian mould.

In 1997, reflecting on 25 years of the group's discussions, Prakash wrote:

> [T]his GET TOGETHER keeps going on its own momentum. There is no driving force behind it, no president, no secretary, no rules, and no subscription. That is its strength. That is perhaps its purpose. It derives its strength from WITHIN.[28]

For each meeting of "Our Get-Together," Prakash would send postcards to every member, reminding them of the next meeting, each adorned individually with a handmade sketch.[29] These postcards were collected by many members, while others studiously returned them as if they were valued works of art. Today these postcards have acquired the status of collectors' items.

"Our Get-Together" met steadfastly once a month right until Prakash's death in 2008, and continued after it too.

Zindagi Retire Nahin Hoti

In 2006, Prakash was approached by a local street-theatre company to participate in a workshop for retired people that they were organizing. Mixing the young with the old, their aspiration was to workshop a synthetic work that spoke across generations. Prakash participated willingly, but immediately took umbrage to the idea that he had retired. "I have retired from my official job, but not from life," he hollered at them. Immediately, this became the theme of the theatre workshop which produced a spontaneous play titled *Zindagi Retire Nahin Hoti* (*Life Does Not Retire*), with Prakash in the starring role.

Although meant for a one-time performance, *Zindagi Retire Nahin Hoti* became a theatre festival hit, and was performed dozens of times all over India. The play's theme and contention hit a chord, and audiences responded. Many performances were held in Prakash's Tagore Theatre. But in 2007, the governor of Chandigarh decided to "renovate" the theatre and hired a local architectural firm for the job. The principal architect decided to gut the entire interior and reorganized the plan to accommodate more seats. In the process, acoustics, and all the original design principles, were sacrificed for capacity. But since the exterior wall—the wrapper—was retained, the architect dubiously argued her work was a "preservation" job.[30] Prakash was visibly heartbroken by the destruction of Tagore Theatre.

On 11 August 2008, Prakash took a second-class seat on a train with the theatre group to perform *Zindagi*... yet another time in Mumbai. Surrounded by the happy troupe of troubadours, in the early hours of 12 August, he died in his sleep on the train at Ratlam railway station. "Our Get-Together" met as scheduled at Prakash's home the following Monday.

Scan image with the **BooksPlus** app

Aditya Prakash's studio, 2008

NOTES

1 See for instance: "Growing Problems of Cities," Review of *The Politics of Urban Redevelopment: A Study of Old Delhi* by Ajay K. Mehra, *The Tribune* June 1, 1991. (*APFA_D12*); "Housing as consumer commodity," Review of *Housing and Urbanisation: A Study of India* by Cedric Pugh, *The Tribune* Feb 2, 1991 (*APFA_D12*); "The Other Crisis of Delhi," Book review of *Delhi: The Deepening Urban Crisis*, edited by Patwant Singh and Ram Dhamija (*APFA_D16*)

2 This book was eventually published as: Prakash, A., Prakash, Vikramaditya, & Saxena, Navneet. (1999). *Chandigarh: The City Beautiful* (1st ed.). Chandigarh, India: Abhishek Publications.

3 See for instance "Building a New Capital," in Letters, *Indian Express*, 7th Sept 1985; "A New Capital for Haryana," The Tribune, 31st July 1985; "What Haryana's capital should be like" *The Statesman* (Delhi), 8 October 1985; "Haryana's New Capital: Beyond Corbusier" APFA D16.

4 See for instance his report on the Jharia Coal Fields, *APFA D403*.

5 "Chandigarh in the Melting Pot" *APFA D68*.

6 This event was funded by the Graham Foundation for Advanced Studies in the Fine Arts and the Office of the Dean, College of Art, Architecture and Planning, Cornell University.

7 For reasons that are not clear to me, the water tank located at the highest point of a house is often made into a dramatic sculptural object in many houses in the Punjabi countryside. Mostly they take the form of giant footballs, or eagles.

8 Some of the people who worked at Arcon were Sunil Sehgal (1986–1987), Sandeep Virmani (1986—1989), Paramjit Singh (1991–1992) and Tarvinder Kaur (1986—1987). Sunil Sehgal worked on the Jharia Coal Fields Township Competition Project, which won third prize.

9 "Artist Statement for 1994 show at Chandigarh's Alliance Française Le Corbusier"*APFA D3b*.

10 As a consequence, Prakash's paintings are held in private collections worldwide today. Several are also in museums, in particular the Chandigarh Museum.

11 See "*Art* Appreciation" *APFA D10_12*

12 In the Western academic context, in which I teach, it is sometimes difficult to convey the love and affection one can have for animals, other than as pets. Prakash always insisted on identifying animals as "productive" which can of course be interpreted as a kind of objectification of animals, but on the other, given his well-documented love for animals, as an attempt to re-cast human-animals relations in a mould other than that of the binary—pet versus meat. I am indebted to an email conversation with Mark M. Jarzombek for this insight.

13 "Art—As I see it" *APFA D12_1*, p7.

14 *The Hindustan Times*, Chandigarh City Edition, Thursday 2 Feb 2006.

15 A disciple of the Bengal School of painting under Abanindranath Tagore, Jamini Roy cultivated the folk painting traditions of Bengal and sought to modernize them in his own language. He liked to think of himself as a "patua" or a painter of "*pat*s," the scroll paintings that singing storytellers would carry around with them as they moved from village to village reciting epic poems.

16 This discussion is based on an essay by Michelle Rostami's unpublished essay titled "Aditya Prakash: Painting and Space Making" presented as part of the work of the Chandigarh Urban Lab 2014.

17 APFA D3b

18 Here it is relevant to note that Prakash designed at least a couple of temples for the Arya Samaj community, including one in Sector 7, Chandigarh.

19 One of the notepads in the Archives has a series of short quotations in Prakash's hand, which seem to be copied from an article (unsourced in the notepad), that support some of these ideas. Here is a selection:

"Indian sculpture in all temples is a statement of faith, an act of prayer. They are complete—fulfilled acts—in themselves. They are not objects on display."

"I went into churches because they were built from the heart...hearts so full of longing that the stones still cry out with their ecstasy."

"The music is in the eyes of the *tabla* player as he presses the skin to generate that sensual note from the depth of the drum. The drum reverberates beneath his fingers repeatedly and insistently responding to this desire."

See "Religious Sayings—Artistic Expressions" *APFA D12_2* The quotation about the churches seems to be from Elizabeth Bishop.

20 The majority of these seem to be concentrated on one particular *Marg* issue subtitled *In Praise of Bharata Natyam*, guest edited by Sunil Kothari, vol. 32, Number 3, December 1979. This issue was picked apart by Prakash, and lines drawn onto many of its images. Numerous paintings are derived from images from this issue.

21 "Art—As I see it" *APFA D12_1*, p. 8. See also "Passion and Art" *APFA D3a_3*.

22 The original image was from the *Marg* issue subtitled *In Praise of Bharata Natyam*, guest edited by Sunil Kothari, vol. 32, Number 3, December 1979.

23 Indian art from the very beginning has been abstract art in its very concept. At Mahabalipuram School of Architecture, when I asked whether they had any "models" for sketching, I was told, "It is forbidden." I have a feeling that making anything from any model has been forbidden from the very beginning in Indian tradition, whereas it is the very basis of study in Western tradition." ("Art—As I see it" D12_1, p. 9)

24 "The Chandigarh Conference," *APFA D18* The proceedings of the conference were edited and published as Takhar, Jaspreet & Babbar, Vandana. (2002). *Celebrating Chandigarh*. Chandigarh: Chandigarh Perspectives in association with Mapin Publishing.

25 APFA D6a.

26 It is difficult assess the success of these activities. The Archives of the Chandigarh Lalit Kala Akademi were not available to me at the time of this writing. Some of the people he developed friendships with in this process were the artist Prem Singh and the photographer Yog Joy.

27 Extensive records of the meetings of "Our Get-Together" are available in the Archives, mostly in *APFA_D101, D118 and D132*.

28 "Our Get-Together" *APFA D118*.

29 In a newspaper story published in *The Tribune* by Parbina Rashid, Prakash noted, "Each month I sketch 26 to 30 postcards...In the beginning I used to use my brain and drew lots of peacocks and other motifs, but later I realized there are books available which provide more sophisticated ideas. Ever since then I stopped using my brain...It takes about 15 minutes if it is my own design, but takes longer if I am copying from one of those books. Copying something definitely take more concentration." APFA_D5.

30 As one might expect, Tagore Theatre "renovation" destroyed Prakash. My critique of Tagore Theatre renovation can be found here: Vikramaditya Prakash, "Not 'Tagore Theatre,' Please", *The Hindustan Times* (newspaper),Chandigarh, India (September 2008) The architect's rationale can be found here: https://www.worldbuildingsdirectory.com/content/tagore-theatre-chandigarh?t=Tagore, accessed Wednesday, 21 March 2018.

Scan image with the **BooksPlus** app

CONCLUSION: GLOBAL MODERNISM

In March 1987, in a short unpublished piece titled "Let Your Deeds Match Your Ideas," Prakash pondered his role models in life, the kind of figures who could "bring thoughts to a standstill."[1] He quickly identified Mahatma Gandhi as such a figure, "the bare body, the bare head, the ungainly form, yet commanding an attention which surpasses all reason." From here, he posed the question: what would it take to lead the life of a genuine Gandhian acolyte? Casting doubt, he wondered if there ever "could be another such man, or near enough?" The best example that he could think of was that of one Dr. V. N. Vasantharajan, of whom he heard about at an Environment Society function.[2] He described Vasantharajan as a man who "refused to provide himself with an automobile" (which Prakash had), who "proved that…artificial fertilizers are going to produce premature moratorium of the soil where they are used" (while Prakash had been an integral part of the pesticide-based "Green Revolution"), who "chose his areas of research with purpose, but without care as to the rewards" (certainly Prakash's own self-image), and who "was so dedicated to his work that he almost lived in his laboratory." Finally, with understated candour, he noted that Vasantharajan "died practically unknown, unsung, un-martyred, that too in the prime of his life, at only 45 years of age." His final assessment of Vasantharajan? He was an "eccentric," but only when compared to "a world full of mediocrity, compromise, and opportunism in all walks of life."

Speaking in 1986 on the 25th anniversary celebrations of the Chandigarh College of Architecture, he summarized his thoughts on architectural education—what can be taught and not—and in the midst, tried to articulate his feelings about the measure of his own life, indexed against the "greats" that he had worked with.[3] He cast it as a measure of "creativity":

> Creativity is God's personal gift of every individual. It is there somewhere in the seed. It may take a few generations of maturing, and also, the "chance" of appropriate circumstances for the "gift" to find expression. Let no one [feel] that God has been unkind to him because he finds that he is not a "Corbusier." Life is continuous from generation to generation. Sometime in some generation the moment of that extra "Creativity" comes which sets a person above the rest. But in making a "Corbusier" several generations have ~~contributed~~ [*sic*] to contribute.

Via the strikethrough, done by pen, Prakash was clearly distinguishing between his own life's work—"contributed"—and the life's work prospectus faced by the students of architecture that he was addressing—"to contribute." "Great" work by "star" architects was only possible if it was supplemented by "generations" of work

Prakash at one of the bicycle stands designed by him in the 1960s, c. 2007, photograph by the author

by others who go unrecognized.[4] But, how exactly the supplementary contribution was to **be** parsed was not quite clear, or rather not quite apprehensible, to Prakash:

> What am I trying to say? I cannot fully fathom it myself. But, it is to give expression to a feeling of "Hope" in that one should not feel frustrated if one has not done something very great in his lifetime—because the life does not end with one's death. It goes on. I feel that having retired from the principalship of the college, I am not finished. I must have left something (if I had something in me) which will find fruition through someone—a teacher, a student, a passer-by. What is true of me should be true of everybody.[5]

By his own assessment, thus, Prakash's work, like that of the above mentioned Vasantharajan, was not finished, but would find "fruition through someone" else. It was possible for a life's work to be recognized in one's own lifetime. But more likely, if done diligently and with perseverance and patience, it was likely to reach fruition through the diffracted process of a life's entanglements with the lives of others—teachers, students, passers-by.

The many, many lives that were touched by, that influenced and were influenced by Prakash's are of course too many to ever be accounted for within the folds of a single book. A life's entanglement with that of others is by nature diffracted and ongoing. It is thus in this sense that this book, and the Archives that are organized around it, can be seen as part of the ongoing Prakash oeuvre, finding fruition through someone. And then there is my voice as author, not only as Prakash's son, but also as a product of Chandigarh, the Chandigarh College of Architecture, and the city's modernist milieu, that can also be accounted for in the registers of the Prakash legacy. On that authority, I would like to offer the following readings of Prakash's "legacy", not as summations of his most "impactful" achievements, but as strings of thoughts, the tangled mesh of ideas and inferences, that has spun around me as I have compiled this book. *At 55 years old, ten years after my father's death, my confrontation of the question of his legacy is motivated as much by the impulse to know my inheritance as it is to know where it fits in the world today, and the one to come. In writing this book I have watched myself, as if via an out-of-body experience, trying to adhere "strictly to the facts" and failing repeatedly, skidding off the rails and slipping almost into eulogy. Dispassionate critique would have required a sterner constitution, but all said and done, who really would want to read such a dry account? Nathaniel Kahn taught me that when he made his amazing discovery film about his own famous, lost, father.*

In my mind's eye, the "real" audiences of this book have been my wife, who is an Italian-Wichita American, and my children, who, being doubly-so hyphenated, will have to search for their place and purpose in "Amerika," and in the world. This book is as much about their future as it is about their past.

But then, there are so many other registers, so many other communities and discourses that I as an academic feel I must also address and speak to. One of the early readers of this manuscript categorically thought I had to provide an authoritative "reading" of Prakash's work to verify my scholarly credentials. I have taken this injunction as license, here in the end, to speak as an expatriate scholar of colour who practises out of the United States and champions global history and postcolonial theory. So, it is for my academic audiences that the following interpretive readings are offered.

Others may well choose to just stop reading right here.

Nehruvian Modernist

Prakash's oeuvre can be firmly indexed to the history of the "magnetic"[6] Nehruvian nation-state. The late colonial moment, just before Independence in 1947, with the flag of nationalism flying high, set up his life. With a father focused on a colonial Hindu reformist ideology, the Arya Samaj, as the path to advancement, and a home life by contrast sustained almost entirely by women-managed homecraft and animal husbandry, some of the core conflicts of Prakash's life were written into the script of his childhood. Written in also was a deeply internalized sense of being helpless and abandoned, inculcated by the absence of a mother, and externalized by the drive to rely only on himself for his advancement.

In England, like Nehru, Gandhi and many nationalist and expat upper-class Indians of the Empire, Prakash both drank deeply from the intellectual and cultural milieu of English liberalism, and, in the face of the implicit and explicit racism he faced every day, resolved to deploy the same package of liberal thinking for nationalist purposes at home. A whole generation of Indian architects, like B. V. Doshi, Achyut Kanvinde, Charles Correa, M. M. Rana, U. E. Chowdhury, returned to Nehruvian India with the "best" international training under their belts, chafing from the slights of colonialism and eager to help build the nation.

As part of the Chandigarh Capital Project team, Prakash found himself in the "rookie" position of being the junior-most officer in a strictly hierarchic set-up dominated by European "masters" and British Civil Service-trained Indian administrators and engineers. He had to struggle to establish himself. He had to unlearn his British architectural training. He had to imbibe the modernist way of thinking. He had to prove himself.

Prakash's formation of the "Modern Architects Group" as one of the first things he did after joining the Chandigarh Capital Project team can be recognized as an attempt at self-empowerment, the struggle to take over the Chandigarh torch in young Indian hands, quite like the struggle of the new nation's effort to activate its own voice and agency. With their unique form, uncompromising aesthetics and acoustics, Tagore and KC theatres can be recognized as the apotheoses of these debutante days. It is perhaps precisely because of their singularity that both Tagore and KC have been put to the sword in the recent past.

Prakash's early attempts to build with mud and to introduce the cow into Chandigarh met with failure, but succeeded in planting a seed of doubt in his mind about the modernist vision. The spectre of famine, one of the earliest indictments of the Nehruvian state, took him to Ludhiana in the early 1960s and although his brief was to replicate Chandigarh, Prakash used the opportunity to rethink the architectural and urban principles upon which he had been raised. In Ludhiana Prakash learnt new techniques of agriculture and renewed his engagement with animals, albeit in the form of scientific animal husbandry. A new set of foreign "experts" were installed in Ludhiana, but this time they were scientists, not architects, and Americans, who, with their new technologies and brash attitudes, also brought with them a sense of friendship and openness that contrasted with the deference expected in Chandigarh. Empowered by his newly acquired American cameras and tape-recorders, Prakash wandered into the old cities and villages of India, looking for ways to rethink the Indian city. Ludhiana was also where he began to paint, sculpt, and write academic papers.

Kairon's assassination, Indira Gandhi's unexpected rise to power, the partition of Punjab, the deaths of Nehru, Le Corbusier, and Jeanneret and finally the OPEC-originated energy crisis set the stage for what should have been the most productive period of Prakash's career—his return to Chandigarh as Principal of the College of Architecture in 1967. Seeking to capitalize on the rampant inflation that was unleashed by the energy crisis, Prakash made the case for a massive state-sponsored renewal of architecture and urban planning under the banner of building "self-sustaining" settlements. His city foregrounded the interests of the poor, privileged manual labour and the dignity of the beast of burden, and made farming and animal husbandry the rural-inspired centre of his neighbourhoods. The Chandigarh College of Architecture, with its Research Cells, was the fount of this urban restatement—that fell mostly on deaf ears.

By the late 1970s, postmodernism's interest lay in establishing a historicist Indian aesthetic with an accompanying retrospective cultural vision. Architectural education moved from studies of 'model' cities and villages to establishing structuralist morphologies of the old Indian city, the Indian *haveli* and such. Prakash's urban concepts, which now in the 21st century are finally beginning to be normalized under banners such an urban farming, food security, and inter-species relations, were considered ultra-Le Corbusian and overly hippie in their time and were met both with derision and apprehension.

In the 1980s, amidst the chaos of terrorism in Punjab and the assassinations of Indira Gandhi, Sant Longowal, and then Rajiv Gandhi (1991), the Indian nation-state found itself adrift in the neo-conservative world of Reagan and Thatcher, widely castigated for its anaemic "Hindu rate of growth." As China instituted economic reforms under Deng Xiaoping, India tried to assert its presence on the international stage via a series of postmodern "Festivals of India." Modern architecture died in India in the 1980s with the Festivals. In 1992, once India sought to follow China by joining the post-Cold War world of economic globalization by restructuring its economy, whatever remained of the Nehruvian state was effectively put out to pasture.

Prakash's retirement in 1982, though painful at the time, eventually proved to be a blessing in disguise, giving him several decades of active work to reimagine his life. This took the form of art, theatre, and public critique, with a new-found interest in the spiritual re-surfacing to preoccupy him in the 1990s and 2000s. In terms of art, this was the most prolific period of his life, as his aesthetic slow-morphed from the gestural to the studied. His turn to the spiritual may have been as much a technique to turn away from the tribulations of the neo-liberal Indian state as it was a growing awareness of his own mortality. In the end, his insistence on not signing any of his paintings, and his belief that work and creativity were simply things that happened by themselves using his body as an intermediate agency, summarized his life's lesson.

Prakash's devotion to the "masters" was symptomatic of the neocolonial construction of the Nehruvian nation-state. But the necessary job of critique, and in particular of self-critique, exampled courageously by Nehru in the form of his international Non-Aligned Movement, was a challenge that few in the Capital Project team took up like Prakash did. The modernist project for him was not a settled thing; it was about constant critique, experimentation and re-assessment.

Thus, Prakash's career trajectory, like that of many other Nehruvian Indian modernists, such as Achyut Kanvinde, Habib Rahman, Joseph

Allen Stein, C. S. Jhabvala, Durga Bajpai, and Piloo Mody, was that of a struggle, with and against the forces of the omniscient state, with and against the ethics and aesthetics of the modernist project. But, what made Prakash's work distinctive was its richly multi-disciplinary character. The painter, sculptor, photographer, theatre person, academic, architect, planner, and arm-chair philosopher that Prakash evolved into, put his cross-disciplinary interrogation of modern life on the same path as that of some of the best modernists of the 20th century. And in the firmament of Indian modernists, the diversity of the Prakash oeuvre was unique.

But it wasn't just a question of wide-ranging interests. Prakash delved into a variety of media and disciplines in search of the continuity across their lines, in search of the threads that wove them together. His active mind was always at play. He used his cameras, his paintings, his attention to the rural, his get-togethers, and his Indian Modulor as apparatuses to gauge, know and embrace the patterns of life, and the patterns of beauty that already existed in the world as a way to propose a future life, and a future beauty.[7]

Prakash's life-work was also defined by a set of abiding contradictions. The first of these was between his very materialist, project-oriented focus on the pragmatics of the built work—from the scale of furniture to that of the whole city—and his equally passionate dedication to the very formal and ethereal in art. Although there is virtually no mention of Marx, or any presence of Marxist literature in Prakash's library or papers, there can be little doubt that his work was enjoined to the Leftist cause. Materialism, the dedicated investment in trying to bring about tangible material transformation in the life of the "common man," can be defined as the mission of his life's work. From his designs for the *rehri* to the linear city, his entire urban vision was dedicated to this cause.

On the other hand, the sheer volume of his aesthetic output testifies to his lifelong passion for the non-materialist, for art and the search for the beautiful. Unlike the glaringly public stage on which he proselytized his urban schemes, art was a strictly personal and private search. This schism between the material and aesthetic can be understood as a consequence of his life's story by which he as a gendered male in Indian culture—a role he never questioned—was expected to bear the responsibility of an earning professional, while his personal desire was to become a painter. Trying to reconcile these two interests can be said to be the unstated desire of his life's work; a desire that was probably always impossible and remained unresolved.

Onto this schism must be layered the (post) colonial burden of having entered the world of professional knowledge and architectural thinking through the epistemologies of the colonial West (first in London and then in Chandigarh), and then struggling to reconcile those with his lived memories of having grown up in rural India. The conflict here was Prakash's persistent faith in the Euro-colonial project of Enlightenment-based modernism—which was verified by the Nehruvian nation-state—and his own sense of some vital insights into life and its micro-grained possibilities gained from his own life experiences, particularly as a child. Prakash organized this conflict around the well-worn figures of Nehru and Gandhi, and spent the latter half of his career trying to reconcile the two. First postmodernism and then neoliberalism buried the Gandhian project with the Nehruvian. Only in the NGO sectors of postcolonial India, such as in the work of Sandeep Virmani's Hunnarshala Foundation, did Prakash find expression of his urban ideas in his lifetime.[8]

Part of this schism was Prakash's deeply ingrained (post)colonial belief in the inherently benevolent mission of the nation-state that was to be actualized via its officers as the responsible agents of civil society, and the ever-increasing failure of the Indian state, both in the Nehruvian period and after, to deliver on its expectation. Prakash felt that if the trained architect—who was expected to study things from an allegedly unbiased professional perspective—did not speak up for the cause of the rural poor, the unrepresented, then who would? In this sense, his work and stance can firmly be yoked to the ethics of a subaltern practice. And yet, as a dyed-in-the-wool modernist and a dedicated foot-soldier who believed in the developmentalist vision of the benign state, Prakash's professional agency was undeniably "top down." Until the end, Prakash believed that the state had to be the primary responsible agent of civil society and never spoke of, or advanced, any of the kinds of participative design and planning modalities that are considered essential to subaltern practices.

Diffractive Modernism

The question of Prakash's relationship with the "masters"—Le Corbusier, Pierre Jeanneret/Drew/Fuller/Nehru/Gandhi—and his sense of his own identity as an orbital agent poses the question of postcolonial agency and its persistent longing for recognition. Given that Prakash's work is closely self-identified as belonging to the modernist canon—even if in dispute with it at times—it is impossible to conduct an assessment of its legacy without locating it within the normative hierarchies of modernism, with its deep investment in "masters" and their ateliers of excellence, all of which are located in the West.

In postcolonial theory this is identified as the metropolitan modelling of the world, a legacy of colonialism, by which the West, with its heroes of "original" thinkers, is constructed as the mythologized centre of an international discourse whose margins are constituted by the rest based on models of influence and derivation. In architectural theory, we can recognize this in discourses such as "critical regionalism" or "tropical modernism" by which a set of supposedly "universal" principles, inevitably originated in the metropolitan West, are centralized and verified precisely by the ways in which they are regionalized/localized/particularized in the peripheries of the world.

Critics of this centre-periphery discourse reimagine it in a more de-centred form, in the shape of a differential global network of inter-connected, inter-constitutive agencies acting relationally. These reimaginings, variously coded under different monikers such as "trans-nationalism," "global cosmopolitanism," "trans-localism," "global history," and such, offer a way to rethink the work of architects such as Aditya Prakash, and architectural and urban events such as Chandigarh in something other than a centre-periphery model.

In service of this kind of re-imagining, I would like to offer a proactive, against-the-grain reading of one specific moment in the Prakash oeuvre. This is the translation of Le Corbusier's design for the School of Art, on which Prakash was the apprentice junior architect, into the design of the College of Architecture that was executed solely by Prakash, albeit as a "faithful" reproduction. Significantly, while the School of Art has been included in Le Corbusier's oeuvre for the World Heritage Nomination, the College of Architecture, though a near-identical building, has not. I am not privy to the nominating committee's exact logics for making this distinction, but I assume it has something to do with Prakash's translation (or transposition) of the School of Art design into that of the College of Architecture.

Here are the "facts" of our case study.

In a previous essay, "The Chandigarh Capital Project", in this volume, I have described how Prakash remembered the process of designing the School of Art with Le Corbusier, which he later reproduced in an essay done for the Indian design journal *Architecture + Design*, as "Learning from the Master." In this article, which clearly establishes the master-disciple hierarchy of the relationship, Prakash described the way in which the "master" came to Prakash's office, sat on stool, and had him draw on the blackboard a grid, by dictating precise dimensions drawn from the Modulor. A brick-pier dimension having been established, Le Corbusier then dictated the section, again by dimensions alone, which together formed the design code of the building: an expressive north-light admitting section, with an alternating rhythm of larger and smaller bays set up to furnish spaces for various sizes. From here, the specific task of partitioning the spaces to make the rooms and the studios—the work of the "free plan"—Le Corbusier left to Prakash.

That the genetic DNA of a building, what we nowadays call its "design thinking," was its rhythm of piers and its section, and that this DNA could be so precisely communicated via the use of the Modulor, had a profound effect on Prakash.

In 1959, soon after the experience of working on the School of Art, the design of the College of Architecture was entrusted to Prakash, who, eschewing the opportunity to think of a new design of his own, decided and persuaded the administration that Le Corbusier's design of the School of Art should be re-used for the College of Architecture. Prakash's thinking, one assumes, was that in fundamentals, an institution of architectural education was not different from that of art education (or "audio visual training" as Le Corbusier called it) and thus the same design DNA applied. And then perhaps, we might suspect, for Prakash a college of architecture in Chandigarh *had* to have the Le Corbusian stamp, the old master's own disenchantment with academic architectural education notwithstanding.

There was a small problem, however. Not with the re-use of the design, for which apparently both Jeanneret and Le Corbusier gave their approval, but in the budget available for the College of Architecture, which was less, as a percentage per square foot, than that of the School of Art.[9] Forced to work with this abridged budget, Prakash's choices were either to stage the building, i.e. construct as much as he could with the available budget, and hope for more in the future to complete the structure, which would have truncated the start of the college; or, to simply shrink the building by the percentage required, which would also have met the budgetary requirements since materials, rather than labour, constituted the vast majority of the cost of construction at the time.

Prakash chose the latter. There was precedent for this, as Le Corbusier himself had shrunk the design of his Governor's Palace when it was found to be too large for the budget that was available. The key was that the building could not simply be scaled down—as in a photocopier—but had to be stepped down, using the prescribed dimensions of the Modulor.[10]

This became Prakash's opportunity to learn the Modulor, which he did with dedication and diligence. The Archives are replete with Prakash's drawings outlining the various possibilities and logics of the Modulor with the red and the blue series, the double squares, the shifting centres, the radial transpositions, and of course the six-foot man, all faithfully reproduced in various formats. Along the way, however, Prakash introduced a few "modifications" into the mix. Based as it was on abstract mathematical contentions such as the Fibonacci series, Le

Corbusier's Modulor defined very specific dimensions, which when translated into feet and inches, often resulted in cumbersome fractions such as 9 x 8½ inches, 3 x 8½ inches, 10½ inches, and so on. When building with concrete, such dimensions can be poured (or at least approximated), but when building with the Indian brick, these dimensions become unwieldly. The standard Indian brick—3 x 4.5½ x 9 inches—works in factors of 3, and so constructing in-between half dimensions is very difficult, making it cost-prohibitive. And so, as an act of pragmatic realism, Prakash introduced approximations into the Modulor dimensions, based on whole multiples of the Indian brick. Thus, 9 x 9 ½ became 9 x 9, 3 x 8.5½ became 3 x 9, 2 x 3.5½ became 2 x 3, 4 became 4.5½ inches, and so on.

By ½ inch approximations, thus, Prakash modified the Modulor, making it workable in India.[11] And then, while he was at it, Prakash also introduced into this working Modulor some new, additional dimensions, that are not deducible from the geometries at all. These new dimensions Prakash described invoking again the logics of pragmatism, as being simply useful: "Some dimensions which do not find place in either series may usefully be included as variations." These were: 8 x 3 inches as Ceiling Height, 6 x 9 inches as Door Height, 5 x 3 inches as Eye Level, 3 x 6 inches as Counter Height. These "variations" in fact constituted the significant bulk of the dimensions that Prakash used in his own architecture.

This sets up the question: is the Prakash Modulor, the Modulor? Are buildings based on these new Modulor dimensions legitimate Modulor buildings, properly ascribable as originating in the Le Corbusian oeuvre as was the original intent of Prakash's study of the Modulor? Was the Modulor properly imported by Prakash? Or, more generally, what are the mechanics of the porting of architectural thinking? How was the *idiom* of modern architecture literally ported to, and re-ported by, and among the members an architectural team, with all its attendant hierarchies, such as that of the Chandigarh Capital Project?

How exactly, or rather, *when* exactly, does a work slip out of becoming an original? When is, and when isn't, an attempted reproduction not just a copy, but a creation? Restated, our question at hand concerns the mechanics of translation, of the transportation and the very transportability of architectural ideas, of the corruptions that (necessarily) ensue in the process, and with that the attendant problem of maintaining authenticity/originality; or inversely, of ensuring or measuring authentic/original interpretations.

In postcolonial terms, this can be politicized as the problematic of the master-slave dialectic, i.e. how to build a local modernism that is based on European models, or colonial models—the "signs of the masters"—as one's own. Its more global framing, as I articulated earlier, is the problem of metropolitanism or regionalism, i.e. the dialectic of derivative regionalism, critical or otherwise, and its struggle to identify a local identity and aesthetic that is distinct from, and yet based on, the idioms and ideologies of the metropoles. This is a global problem.

What can the ½ inch shift teach us about this problem?

In *practical* terms, the dimensional shift is inconsequential, effectively imperceptible, a smart fuzz to achieve significant economy of means. This can be considered the argument of pragmatic realism or pragmatic regionalism, an aesthetic culture of tolerance and accommodation that pays little heed to questions of originality and authenticity.[12] Appropriation as necessary, sometimes characterized as the "*jugaad*" mentality, is its operative logic. The entire informal sector, a major area of research for Prakash, operates by this logic. Chandigarh, from its infamous furniture to its master plan, can be argued to be a product of such thinking, born as it was in the impoverished conditions of a bootstrapping India recently independent from two centuries of colonial exploitation. Like India's blatant disregard of intellectual property in pharmaceutical products, postcolonial nations, particularly in their infancy, have had little concern for the niceties of authenticity and originality.

Opposed to the appropriative, is the fetishist investment in the original. In terms of authorship, when considered from the standpoint of the Western secular humanist model, the authentic kernel of an aesthetic work lies in the "spirit" or the "idea". Here the "spirit" or the "idea" is indelibly (and legally via the institution of the copyright law) indexed to the innate personhood, or "soul," of the author, that is considered to be unproblematically singular, identifiable, and the seat of intentionality. Though its focus, its centre, is the human subject, the idea of an autonomous subject ultimately relies on the secularization of an Abrahamic, theological sense of "soul" as the local residence of a transcendental "God." An author, especially in his or her manifestation as a signature artist—an "auteur"—creates the work recognizable for its originality.

Given Le Corbusier's obsession with his signature (indeed, he is said to have ensured that he religiously signed and dated every single scrap of drawing that he touched), and the corresponding veneration with which people like Prakash worked to inculcate and preserve the "master's" voice, the modern elision between authority and authorship is hard to sideline. The ½ inch shift, in this register, can only be registered as a blurring of the edges, a little "corruption" that is inevitable, and even welcome, but which as such only serves to reinforce, to bring into focus, the centrality of the centre.[13] This, in its various forms, is the argument of influence or derivation that measures corruptions or interpretations for their fidelity to the original. Regionalisms and localizations are versions of this argument.

But, binary epistemologies, such as originality versus corruptions, invariably trap all arguments, whatever their variations, between their poles, leaving critical agency stranded somewhere in mid-space trying to straddle the two ends. This is what sets up "hybrid" agential practices, such as critical regionalism or local-global, as optimistic optimizations, symptoms of the underlying desire to escape the stranglehold of the binary. From a postcolonial perspective, forever trapped in the peripheral orbits of metropolitan centres, such binaries are ultimately and inevitably disempowering.

Non-binary ways of thinking and being in the world tend to be prospective and future oriented. The search for such alternate models and epistemologies are not of course confined to postcolonial theories. They are paralleled and intersected by other agencies and identities that similarly struggle with hegemonic binaries. Some of these that I have been reading of late are situated in areas such as transgender studies, inter-species relatedness, thing theory and psychedelic research. All of these can broadly be described as being post-humanist in character and scope, wherein post-humanist implies some kind of search for epistemologies and agencies that are not centred on the "normal" human experience.

One post-humanist world view is offered by Karen Barad in her book, *Meeting the Universe Halfway: Quantum Physics and the Entanglement of Matter and Meaning*.[14] Trained as a theoretical physicist, Barad works as a queer-feminist critical theorist, with a focus on aligning the contentions of quantum mechanics with those of post-structuralism. Based on the implications of her reading of quantum theory as outlined by Niels Bohr, Barad argues that human subjectivity (the realm of ideas and knowing) and objective reality (the real world as studied by sciences such as physics) are in fact not immune to each other, as argued and required by traditional (including Einsteinian) physics, but constitute each other intra-actively. Knowing, in other words, is a constitutive property of being, just as much as being is an intrinsic aspect of knowing. This reading of quantum physics leads her to theorize the notion of a post-humanist subjectivity wherein the knowing human subject—the seat of the putatively abstract realm of ideas—can in no way be separated from the very material world it seeks to know. Matter and meaning have a "diffractive" relationship, each constituting the other purposefully, and matter, in Barad's provocative words, "feels, converses, suffers, desires, yearns, and remembers."[15]

With the knowing subject no longer the autonomous agent of authorship as the source of creativity and ideas, concepts such as the Modulor can no longer unproblematically be ascribed to authorship, such as to a certain Le Corbusier, free from their particular incarnation in the world. The Modulor as a concept, in other words, exists *only* as constituted or realized, in its various resultant iterations, momentary resultants of diffractive events. The Modulor as an idea only exists as iterated and not as an a priori concept. What this suggests is that the Modulor as "corrupted" and "variated" by Prakash *is* the only way in which the Modulor can exist, i.e. as an instantiation or an iteration. There is no "original" Modulor that is transformed; there are only iterations, continually diffracting into each other, producing new iterations.

Iterability over originality offers a new post-humanist way of beginning to constitute subjectivity in situations such as that of the workings of the Chandigarh Capital Project team. For Barad, things interact with each other diffractively, like two waves that transform each other via their interaction: "Diffraction as method, as methodology, is a matter of reading insights through rather than against each other in an effort to make evident the always, already entanglement of specific ideas and their materiality." Diffraction, thus, is a key term here, in that it offers a way to describe the way two entities—ideas and their manifestations—do not interact with each other causally, i.e. ideas causing forms, but intra-actively, i.e. they constitute each other via their interaction. In the same way, architects engage each other not via the normative modes of "collision" or "collaboration," but rather as mutually constitutive onto-subjectivities.[16] There wasn't a known Aditya Prakash that interacted with a certain Le Corbusier and a Pierre Jeanneret on the plains of Chandigarh and transformed as a consequence. Rather, the only Prakash and Jeanneret and Le Corbusier that we know, and can know, are the ones that were produced and continued to be produced by their diffraction in the process of working in the Capital Project Office on projects such as the School of Art and concepts such as the Modulor.

In a diffractive post-humanist model, global modernism is not a source of ideas that spread out from the West to the rest of the world, but a diffractive concatenation of practices around the world that intra-acted, and continue to intra-act, with each other as they bounce around the architectural contours of the discursive and material world. This is the key image to hold in the mind as a reference to think about Prakash's work in Chandigarh and Ludhiana, and its interactivity with that of those like Pierre

Jeanneret, Le Corbusier, B. P. Mathur and others. It is also the image, as a process, to begin to think about the story of modern architecture in the world as a historical-cultural happening, connected to and like all other historical-cultural processes. This is not to deny hierarchies and the play of power in such processes; indeed, they are replete with them, and in some ways structured by them. Rather, this is a way to think about the aesthetic agency of actors like Prakash in a global register in something other than an origin and influence model.

An archival photograph of the Capital Project team constitutes its team strictly hierarchically, with Le Corbusier, Jeanneret, Fry, and Drew in the centre, and the rest arrayed around them as per the expanding bureaucratic hierarchy. In 2009, Glen Barfield, my collaborator on a study abroad programme to Chandigarh, beautifully superimposed many of Prakash's Modulor drawings in an effort to capture their harmonic qualities. Barfield's collage, when superimposed on the archival photograph of the Capital Project team, fortuitously opens a way to generate a visual understanding of the diffractive processes that in fact constituted the workings of that team.

Finally, by way of conclusion, I would like to offer a post-humanist reading of two of Prakash's aesthetic obsessions—the swirling curve and the figure of the animal—as counter-intuitive speculations.[17]

The swirling curve of his paintings, while palpably inspired by the Modulor drawing, can also be connected to Prakash's passion for the acoustic curve, found in his theatres, and so many of his late buildings. What connects the swirl to the continuous line, to the acoustic, to the sensuous? I would argue there is a sense in which the curve, as the acoustic curve, asks to be heard, to be comprehended and remembered as something other than a visual event. It has a visceral quality. Diffraction is a propagative process, particular to waves, that is not available to an eye/I-centric universe of the visual. In other words, it belongs and strains to give voice to the domus of the ear, that is always struggling to be heard, over the empire of the Eye. Sight vs hearing. To hear well, it is often useful to close one's eyes. Acoustic spaces in this sense are "blind." It is as if Prakash's acoustic buildings and paintings sought to "connect" to each other, an alternative community to the Cartesian visual.[18]

An Arendtian notion of democratic space requires self-conscious individuals sitting across the table seeing eye-to-eye, speaking their mind clearly.[19] Chandigarh, we remember, was designed as the architecture of democracy. Perhaps, as alternative to that, diffractive acoustic spaces respond more to alliances that

Scan image with the **BooksPlus** app

Capital Modulor overlay, APF

are lodged in the unconscious; as tied together by music, emotion, arousal; an architecture of desire.[20] What might such acoustic spaces "say," not as articulations of particular subjectivities, but as themselves, as events in the world?

Architectural work as that of the listening ear. Prakash's work was always shot through with the desire, successful or not, to give voice to the "common man," to provide an articulation for the inaudible.[21] The cause of the common man was for him aligned with the cause of the animal. Of all the voices in current tumult around sustainability and ecological living, none is perhaps more silenced than that of the animal. While we have developed elaborate plans for energy saving and solar harvesting, the food-security movement steadily turns a blind eye to the question of meat and non-pet animals as part of the city. Animals, and the possibility of inter-species relationships (beyond pets), are still considered pariahs in modern Western civilization, on the left and the right. Even in India now, urban animals are considered to be either a pest or a "sacred" cow.[22]

Prakash's love for the cow extended beyond the question of the productive use. It asked for an openness to imagining the urban, and urban sustainability, as something other than the anthropocentric, perhaps something more animist, even shamanistic. Prakash's cow was not intended to make the modernist city culturally "Indian". Rather, the animal, and the animist/shamanistic access to the world that came with it, can be read as his offering, his loving critique of the idea of the modern. It offers a world-opening way to re-know modernism, a way to access the animist and even the shamanistic within the modernist project—if one is curious, nuanced, expansive and brave enough.[23]

NOTES

1 "Let Your Deeds Match Your Ideas" *APFA D16*

2 I have been unable to conclusively identify who Prakash is referring to here. I presume it is to Dr. V. N. Vasantharajan, who was a Professor in the Microbiology and Pharmacology Laboratory of the Indian Institute of Science, Bangalore in the late 1960s and through the 1970s. Numerous references to him are found in the *Journal of the Indian Institute of Science*, Indian Institute of Science, Bangalore.

3 "Random Thoughts on Architectural Education" *APFA D6b*.

4 Prakash uses the "Star" architect term in the preceding section of this address. "Random Thoughts on Architectural Education" *APFA D6b*.

5 "Random Thoughts on Architectural Education" *APFA D6b*.

6 As described by Prakash in "Chandigarh — In Retrospect", *APFA D17, p.17*.

7 I am indebted to Thorey Munro for this insight.

8 Hunnarshala was founded by Sandeep Virmani, who worked with Prakash. See hunnarshala.org

9 I have unfortunately not been able to determine what that exact differential was.

10 See Le Corbusier's annotation to this effect in *Oeuvre Complete*.

11 I am not sure if Prakash was the sole "author" of this move or if the Chandigarh Capital Planning office under Jeanneret (and possibly with Le Corbusier's consent) adopted this strategy in general in Chandigarh, at least for all the brick buildings, which were the vast majority. In any event, even if it was an office-wide decision, Prakash was certainly the local 'authority' on the Modulor, which would place the implicit authorization of this idea around his authorship.

12 There is reason to believe that Le Corbusier himself would have ascribed to this principle. Prakash orally on several occasions narrated to me an incident that suggests this attitude. While the School of Art was being constructed, Prakash in the course of a site visit discovered that the grid had been surveyed on site three degrees off true North as was required. When Prakash rushed to report this error, Le Corbusier was reported to have said, "We are architects, not astronomers. Don't worry."

13 In a phenomenological reading, altered by ½ inch, the veracity or the truth of the work could be considered to have been altered, and thereby its poetics brought into question. It seems quite clear to me that was never an idea in contention either for Le Corbusier or Prakash.

14 Barad, K. (2007). *Meeting the Universe Halfway: Quantum physics and the entanglement of matter and meaning* Durham [N.C.]: Duke University Press.

15 Barad, K., Dolphijn, R. and Van der Tuin, I. (2012). "Matter feels, converses, suffers, desires, yearns and remembers". Interview with Karen Barad. In *New Materialism: Interviews & Cartographies*. Ann Arbor, MI: Open Humanities Press, pp. 48–70

16 See also Gayatri Spivak's conception of "subjectitity," as a corrective of (inter) subjectivity, to characterize similarly socially constitutive processes in Gayatri Chakravorty Spivak "City, Country, Agency" in Prakash, V. (1997). *Theatres of decolonization: (architecture), agency, (urbanism): Proceedings: The second "Other Connections" Conference: Chandigarh, India, January 6–10, 1995*. Seattle, Wash.: Office of the Dean, College of Architecture and Urban Planning, University of Washington.

17 I am indebted to my friend and collaborator Mark Jarzombek for this discussion.

18 The acoustic curve as a way of talking, and listening, and in that sense building an acoustic community finds echoes in contemporary critical theory (what is often called "post-structuralism"), and of course Le Corbusier's conception of acoustic space and ineffable space, particularly in his descriptions of Ronchamp, its curves and their relationship to the landscape. Here we can also think of the various radio antenna, and the various VLAs aimed at the sky, trying to listen to the heavens (versus looking at the sky, and the look across space, as with the eye, as preferred by the Renaissance and modernist senses of democratic spaces).

19 Arendt, H. (1958). *The Human Condition*. (Charles R. Walgreen Foundation lectures). Chicago]: University of Chicago Press.

20 And here one can also think of Nehru's stirring "At the stroke of the midnight hour..." speech and remember that it was an acoustic event, transmitted across the airways in the pre-television age.

21 Like the subaltern who "cannot speak," as articulated by Gayatri Spivak.

22 On the topic of animal studies, the postcolonial and the environment, particularly the notion of "interspecies kinship between human and non-human animals" see Govindrajan, R. (2018) *Animal Intimacies: Interspecies Relatedness in India's Central Himalayas* Chicago: University of Chicago Press.

23 I am indebted to Thorey Munro for this injunction.

INDEX

A

Abhinav Publications 223

Abhinet 8, 188, 189, 190, 191, 221, 264

A&B News and Architects' Journal 45

Acciavatti, Anthony 219

acoustics 46, 86, 90, 265, 274

Advance (magazine / journal) 31, 138, 147

Aggarwal, Prahlad 188

Agricultural Engineering College 114, 117, 124, 138

agricultural revolution 146, 147, 149

Ahmad, Jameel 221

Alliance Française 268

Amritsar 139, 154, 218, 223

Anand, Chetan 11, 26, 92, 132, 139, 147, 185, 186, 187, 219, 262

Anand, Mulk Raj 11, 26, 92, 132, 139, 147, 185, 186, 187, 219, 262

animals 37, 116, 142, 172, 175, 235, 236, 238, 239, 241, 248, 268, 274, 285, 287

ArchitectureTalk 11

Arcon Architects 8, 226, 231, 232

Arendt, Hannah 286

Argus 7, 118, 119

ARIBA 42, 43, 46, 47, 49, 60, 86

Arora, Atul Vir 188

Arya Samaj 33, 34, 246, 268, 273

Assembly building 68, 104, 151, 221, 250

Athens Charter 15

Atlantic Ocean 41

Avermaete, Tom 12, 146

B

Babri Masjid 240

Bachchan, Amitabh 221

Bajaj Art Gallery 234

Bakaya 51

Bansal, Mukul 218

Barad, Karen 282, 283, 286

Barcelona 104

Barfield, Glen 13, 284

Basu, Robin Kumar 51

Bedford Square 45

Bengal school 39

Bergamo 15

Bharatiya Janata Party 240

Bhatia, Harish 12, 188

Bhatti S.S. 12, 147, 151, 153

Bhatti, Surindera Singh 151

Bhushan Steel 194

Bierig, Aleksandr 219

Bijapur 218

Birla Cotton Spinning and Weaving Mills 34, 35

Birla (Family) 33, 40, 50

Blackfriars Underground Station 42

Bohr, Niels 282

Book of Birds, Arthur Singer 207, 221

Bose R. 102

Bose, Subhash Chandra 33, 102

Boys' Hostel 4, 109, 114, 116, 126, 127, 227

boys' hostel, Ludhiana campus 85

Bridge House 42

Bridgwater 15

Brown, R. 221

Brussels Pavilion 104

Buckminster Fuller 26, 164, 216

C

Canadian Centre for Architecture 11, 25, 29, 52, 53, 55, 58, 62, 146

Capital Project Office 66, 86, 97, 103, 283

Casciato, Maristella 11, 15, 102, 146, 147

Casson, Hugh 45

Chandigarh 4, 7, 8, 11, 12, 13, 15, 16, 17, 18, 25, 26, 28, 29, 30, 31, 34, 40, 47, 48, 49, 52, 53, 54, 55, 56, 59, 60, 62, 63, 64, 65, 66, 67, 69, 70, 71, 72, 73, 75, 76, 77, 78, 79, 85, 92, 94, 95, 97, 98, 99, 102, 103, 104, 107, 111, 114, 116, 118, 120, 132, 133, 138, 139, 146, 147, 148, 149, 150, 151, 152, 154, 156, 158, 163, 164, 165, 169, 173, 175, 176, 181, 184, 185, 186, 187, 188, 189, 190, 191, 192, 193, 194, 197, 201, 207, 211, 216, 217, 218, 219, 220, 221, 223, 224, 225, 226, 227, 229, 234, 235, 236, 238, 241, 250, 259, 262, 264, 265, 268, 269, 271, 272, 273, 274, 277, 278, 279, 280, 281, 283, 284, 286

Chandigarh Architects Forum 28

Chandigarh Capital Project team 29, 56, 139, 176, 273, 274, 283

Chandigarh College of Architecture 4, 8, 12, 13, 18, 29, 64, 78, 85, 102, 103, 114, 149, 152, 201, 211, 217, 218, 219, 221, 223, 271, 272, 274

Chandigarh Lalit Kala Akademi 223, 262, 269

Chandigarh style 66, 77, 92, 102, 114, 151, 191, 192, 216, 226

Chaura Bazaar 154, 155, 156, 157, 168

Chhapgar, A. F. 104

Ching, Francis D. K. 220

Chowdhury, U. E. 62, 148, 165, 219, 273

Churchill, Winston 41

Chuttani P. N. 158

CIAM 15, 17, 49, 102

Cole, Henry 38

colonial India 26, 34, 38, 40, 208

Corbu House 85

Correa, Charles 26, 114, 152, 259, 273

Corrigall, Duncan 219

Cunard Line 40, 41

Curtis, William J. R. 152

D

Das, RamChander 33

Decca LPs 49

Deewar 221

Delhi Polytechnic 37, 38, 39, 40, 41, 45, 50, 54, 241

Department of Science and Art, London 38

Desai, Madhavi 102

Dhamija, Ram 268

District Courts 66, 67

Dolphijn, R. 286

Dome of Discovery 45

Donaldson, James 79

Doshi, Balkrishna 15, 39, 50, 218, 221, 273

Doxiadis, Constantions 26, 163

D'Oyly Carte Opera Company 45

Dr. Edwards (Victoria, BC) 142, 146

Drew, Jane 16, 48, 49, 51, 54, 59, 60, 62, 63, 64, 94, 102, 147, 186, 192, 277, 284

Dr. Sutton (Ohio SU) 111, 116

Dutta, Arindam 50

E

Edinburgh 51, 163, 218

Edwards, Donald 12, 142, 146
Egypt 41, 48, 210
Ekistics 163, 219, 220
Emergency 215
Empire State Building 120
England 15, 26, 45, 49, 273
Evans, Robin 104
Evenson, Norma 185, 220

F

Facebook 217
Faiz 210
Farooqi 50
Festival of Britain 15, 45, 138
Festivals of India 221, 275
Forster E. M. 185
France 47
Franconia 7, 40, 41, 51
Fry, Maxwell 15, 16, 17, 48, 49, 51, 54, 59, 60, 62, 63, 64, 67, 94, 102, 147, 186, 192, 284
furniture 25, 28, 30, 98, 104, 276, 281

G

Gandhi, Indira 149, 164, 214, 215, 216
Gandhi, Rajiv 223, 224, 225, 275
Ganesh 248
Ganges 102, 219, 246
Gargi, Balwant 92, 188, 220, 221
Gautherot, Marcel 120
Geneva 149
Gerrard (multi-disk changer) 49
Ghalib 210
Gilbert and Sullivan 45
Gill, J. S. 95
Glasgow Empire Exhibition 47
Glasgow School of Art 47, 48, 134, 135
global modernism 8, 29, 283
Golden Temple 223
Goswamy, B. N. 140, 147, 201
Government Museum 72
Govindrajan, R 287
Green Revolution 29, 107, 111, 116, 146, 156, 158, 271
Gropius, Walter 152
Gupta, Atreyee 146, 147
Gupta, Savitri 53

H

Haryana 149, 153, 181, 220, 223, 224, 268
Hervé, Lucin 147, 236
Hill Road 48
Himachal Pradesh 149
Hine, Lewis 120
Hissar 107, 146, 177, 228, 229, 230
Hoddesdon, England 15
Holland, Jessica 51
Hungerford Rail Bridge 42
Huxley, Aldous 31

I

IGNOU 220
Indian Air Force 169
Indian Institute of Architects 217
Indo-Swiss Training Centre 94, 95, 97, 104, 114
Industrial Training Institute 95
Iran 153
Italy 15, 47
ITDC 217
Iyer 104

J

Jackson, I. 51
Jagat Theatre 67
Jalandhar 226, 228
Janata Party 215
Janj Ghar 97
Jarzombek, Mark M. 11, 13, 268, 286
Jawaharlal Nehru University 217
Jeanneret, Jacqueline 25, 29, 52, 53, 55, 58, 62
Jeanneret, Pierre 16, 25, 26, 29, 48, 49, 52, 53, 55, 58, 62, 63, 64, 65, 73, 94, 102, 111, 133, 147, 148, 149, 175, 229, 277, 283, 284
Jinnah, M. A. 33
J&K Academy 192, 193, 194, 197, 198
John's High School 207
Joshi, K 12, 102
Joy, Yog 269

K

Kairon, Pratap Singh 94, 149, 218, 223, 274
Kala Wati 34
Kalka Mail 54
Kanvinde, Achyut P. 26, 152, 273, 275
Kapoor, Prithiraj 26, 92
Karol Bagh 53
Katyal K.K. 191
Kaur, Surinderpal 220
Kaur, Tarvinder 268
KC Theatre 30, 69, 71, 103, 104
Kerala 153
Kharar, Uttar Pradesh 35, 37
Khorakiwala, Ateya 146
Kiran Theatre 67
Kishangarh 158, 160, 161, 162, 218
Kolkata 175
Kothari, Sunil 269
Krauss W.E. 146
Krishnaswamy, Lakshmi 11, 220
Kurukshetra 228

L

Lado Rani 34
Lake Club 78
Lambretta 154
Le Corbusier 4, 15, 16, 17, 25, 26, 29, 31, 34, 39, 45, 47, 48, 49, 51, 54, 59, 60, 62, 63, 64, 65, 67, 68, 72, 73, 75, 76, 78, 79, 86, 94, 97, 98, 102, 103, 104, 118, 139, 146, 147, 149, 151, 152, 154, 165, 186, 187, 190, 210, 211, 214, 216, 218, 219, 220, 221, 225, 229, 236, 238, 240, 257, 268, 274, 277, 278, 279, 281, 283, 284, 286
Lefaivre, Liane 103
Lenzlinger 94, 95
Lions Brewery 45
Little Titchfield Street 45
London 7, 15, 16, 18, 38, 40, 41, 42, 45, 47, 49, 50, 51, 59, 60, 64, 68, 72, 102, 103, 104, 138, 163, 231, 277
London County Council 47
London Transport 47
Ludhiana 4, 16, 18, 26, 29, 95, 107, 109, 111, 112, 114, 117, 118, 120, 125, 130, 132, 133, 137, 138, 140, 142, 146, 147, 149, 150, 154, 155, 156, 157, 164, 165, 168, 175, 177, 211, 218, 226, 227, 231, 261, 274, 283

Luthra, P.L. 12, 102
Lutyens 37
Lyallpur 146
Lynch, Kevin 77

M

Mahatma Gandhi 26, 33, 35, 48, 50, 172, 271
Malhotra, Goldy 11, 52, 58, 146, 147, 148, 186, 188
Malhotra, Jeet 11, 52, 58, 146, 147, 148, 186, 188
Malik 221
Malta conference 41
Manet, Édouard 257
Mangatrai, Champa 188
Mann, Michael 50
Marg magazine 139, 244, 248
MARS group 15, 102
Martin, Sir Leslie 45
Mathur, B.P. 12, 50, 54, 85, 114, 148, 177, 220, 284
Matthew, Sir Robert 45, 48, 163, 218
Mauritius 218
Mayer, Albert 48
McGill University, Montreal 146
Meerut 228, 229, 231
Mehndiratta, Virendra 12, 188
Mehra, Ajay K. 268
Metcalf, Thomas 50
Mitter, Parth 50
Modern Architects Club 28, 63, 64, 66, 102, 149
Modulor 7, 29, 60, 73, 76, 77, 78, 79, 81, 84, 103, 152, 210, 211, 214, 220, 221, 235, 236, 241, 242, 247, 248, 251, 255, 257, 276, 278, 279, 280, 283, 284, 285, 286
Moiret and Wood 41, 42, 47
Moiret, Peter 41, 42, 47, 51
Moiret, Rita 51
Moore, Henry 134
Moro, Peter 45
Moscow 221
Ms. Dutta 50
Mughal 208
Mukherjee, Pallav 158, 218
Mumbai 39, 102, 103, 147, 175, 234, 265
Mumford, Lewis 48
Munro, Thorey 4, 11, 286, 287
Munshi Ram 35
Museum of Knowledge 72, 104
Muzaffar, M. Ijlal 219
Muzaffarnagar 7, 15, 18, 33, 37, 175

N

Nalanda 218
National Dairy Development Board (NDDB) 226
National Thermal Power Corporation (NTPC) 224
Neelam Theatre 66
Nehru, Jawaharlal 16, 25, 33, 48, 52, 58, 59, 60, 97, 107, 114, 149, 164, 217, 219, 223, 273, 274, 275, 277, 286
Nehruvian 8, 25, 26, 29, 30, 53, 116, 139, 149, 154, 163, 186, 188, 214, 215, 216, 219, 223, 240, 264, 273, 274, 275, 277
Nek Chand 147
New Delhi 4, 12, 18, 29, 33, 37, 50, 53, 54, 102, 103, 149, 152, 163, 175, 187, 188, 191, 217, 218, 219, 220
Nilokheri 92, 104
Nimmo 92
Nowicki, Matthew 48

O

Offenbach, Jacques 45
Ohio State University 107, 111, 146
Olpadwala, Porus 225
Open Hand Monument 102
Our Get-Together 8, 28, 264, 265, 269

P

Pakistan 40, 146
Palampur 107, 146
Pancholy, Dr. M. 90, 104
Panipat 37, 50
Paris 16, 51, 72, 98, 103, 221
Parker, Dr. Frank 146
Partition of India 40
Patel, Sardar Vallabhbhai 33
Patiala 192, 228
Perriand, Charlotte 98
petrol pumps [of Chandigarh] 71
Planners Group 221
postcolonial [India] 26, 29, 31, 34, 48, 50, 75, 103, 116, 154, 172, 188, 219, 273, 277, 280, 281, 282, 287
Prabhawalkar, A.R. 52, 64, 102, 148, 149, 150, 151, 218
Prakash, Brij Nandan 187
Prakash, Vikramaditya 3, 4, 50, 268, 269
Progressive Artists' Movement 139
Public Works Departments (PWD) 37, 38
Pugh, Cedric 268
Punjab 15, 31, 62, 92, 102, 107, 111, 114, 116, 117, 139, 146, 147, 149, 153, 219, 223, 228, 274, 275
Punjab Agricultural University 31, 107, 111, 114, 117, 146, 147, 228
Punjabi Suba 149
Punjab Lalit Kala Akademi 139
Puri, Amar 158, 218
Purnami, Chetna 13, 226

Q

Qadri, Sohan 147
Queen Elizabeth 41

R

Rajasthan 54, 153
Rajvansh, Priya 92
Rama 240, 248, 263
Ramgoolam, Seewoosagur 218
Rana, M.M. 273
Randhawa, M.S. 146, 147, 148, 150
Rao, P. V. Narasimha 224
Rashid, Parbina 269
Ratlam 265
Regent Street Polytechnic 45
rehri 158, 218, 220, 276
Research Cells 8, 151, 154, 274
Rimbaud, Arthur 186
Rock Garden 147
Rogers, E.N. 15
Rohe, Mies van de 104
Rohtak 220
Rolleiflex (camera) 7, 118, 119, 120, 127,

137
Rossellini, Anna 104
Ross, Launcelot Hugh 47, 48
Rostami, Michelle 221, 268
Royal Albert Hall, London 45, 46
Roy, Jamini 39, 86, 140, 241, 268
Rue de Sevres 72
Rummel, Dean 146
Ruskin, John 33

S

Sanchi 218
Sandhu Residence, Sector 27 226
Santiniketan 86, 140
Sarin, Madhu 185, 220
School of Art (Sector 10, Chandigarh) 39, 47, 48, 73, 75, 78, 134, 135, 278, 279, 283, 286
School of Planning and Architecture, New Delhi (Delhi Polytechnic) 37
Schumacher, E.F. 26, 220
Scriver, Peter 50
Secretariat, Chandigarh 60, 76, 78, 221
Sehgal, Nayantara 59
Sehgal, Sunil 268
Sert, J.L. 15
Seychelles 153
Shakespeare, William 33
Shamli, Uttar Pradesh 37
Sharma, M.N. 12, 102, 111, 146, 148, 149, 150, 221
Sharma, Rakesh 158
Sharma, Saumya 220
Sharma, Shivdatt 12, 102, 107, 146
Shingh, Prem 269
Shiva-Parvati 248
Shoshkes, Ellen 218
Shot Tower 45
Siegel, Amie 104
Sikri 218
Silva, Minnette de 15
Singh, Davinder 104
Singh, Giani Rattan 88
Singh, Giani Zail 76
Singh, Manmohan 224
Singh, Nonika 241
Singh, Paramjit 268
Singh, Patwant 268
Singh, Shiv 147
Sir JJ School of Art, Mumbai 39
Skylon 45
South Asia 15, 50, 208, 210, 221
Spivak, Gayatri Chakravorty 103, 286, 287
Srivastava, Amit 50
Stein, Joseph Allen 26, 152, 276
Subzi Mandi 34
Suez Canal 41
Sukhna Lake 65, 102, 148, 193, 202
Sukhna Lake lights 202

T

Tagore, Rabindranath 86, 92
Tait, Thomas 47
Taj Art Gallery 234
Tales of Hoffman 45
Team X 79
Textbook Press 95
Thakur, N.C. 188
Thames 42, 44, 138, 168
Thapar, P.N. 111, 114, 116, 146, 149, 150, 186, 228, 230
The Mikado 45
The Miracle Box 47
Thoreau, Henry David 33
Tolstoy, Leo 33
Transeau, E.N. 146
Tropical Modernism 49
Tuin, I. van der 286
Tyrwhitt, Jacqueline 15, 163, 218
Tzonis, Alexander 103

U

UNESCO World Heritage list 28
Unité d'Habitation 45
Urdu 208, 210, 211, 221, 264
Uttar Pradesh 15, 37

V

Varma 59, 97, 102, 186
Vasantharajan V.N. 26, 271, 272, 286
Vellani, Zul 26, 92, 104, 219
Victoria, BC 142, 146
Virmani, Sandeep 11, 164, 168, 170, 171, 177, 179, 180, 219, 220, 268, 277, 286

W

Washington DC 221
Wattas, Rajnish 218
Watt, C. 50
Weber, N. 102
West Africa 48
Wood 41, 42, 47, 50, 51
Wood, Leslie 41
W. W. Wood and Sons and Partners 50

X

Xenakis, Iannis 104

Y

Yoder, Bob 146

Z

Zafar 210
Zurich 94